IDA RUBINSTEIN

IDA RUBINSTEIN

judith chazin-bennahum

*revolutionary dancer,
actress, and impresario*

Cover Art: Ida Rubinstein as Salomé, 1912. Costume and drawing by Léon Bakst. SOURCE: THE TRETYAKOV GALLERY, MOSCOW.

Frontispiece: Ida Rubinstein portrait, 1910. Photo by Manuel Frères. SOURCE: JEROME ROBBINS DANCE DIVISION, THE NEW YORK PUBLIC LIBRARY FOR THE PERFORMING ARTS, ASTOR, LENOX, AND TILDEN FOUNDATIONS.

Published by State University of New York Press, Albany

© 2022 State University of New York Press

All rights reserved

Printed in the United States of America

No part of this book may be used or reproduced in any manner whatsoever without written permission. No part of this book may be stored in a retrieval system or transmitted in any form or by any means including electronic, electrostatic, magnetic tape, mechanical, photocopying, recording, or otherwise without the prior permission in writing of the publisher.

For information, contact State University of New York Press, Albany, NY
www.sunypress.edu

Library of Congress Cataloging-in-Publication Data

Names: Chazin-Bennahum, Judith, author.
Title: Ida Rubinstein : revolutionary dancer, actress, and impresario / Judith Chazin Bennahum.
Description: Albany : State University of New York Press, [2022] | Includes bibliographical references and index.
Identifiers: LCCN 2021035658 | ISBN 9781438487977 (hardcover) | ISBN 9781438487991 (ebook) | ISBN 9781438487984 (paperback)
Subjects: LCSH: Rubinstein, Ida, 1883-1960 | Women dancers—Russia (Federation)—Biography. | Women dancers—France—Paris—Biography. | Choreographers—France—Paris—Biography.
Classification: LCC GV1785.R83 C43 2022 | DDC 792.8092 [B]—dc23
LC record available at https://lccn.loc.gov/2021035658

I dedicate this book to my husband David
and for all the gifts we've shared.

CONTENTS

acknowledgments - ix

preface - xi

1 russian beginnings. an early taste for the stage - 1

2 on the way to paris, far from her home, and stardom - 39

3 the war and benevolence - 83

4 between the wars. fame, some shame, and pain from losses - 97

5 war again and the menace of anti-semitism - 137

epilogue. why remember ida rubinstein? - 151

appendix. productions by ida rubinstein - 153

notes - 167

bibliography - 183

index - 191

ACKNOWLEDGMENTS

WHAT A JOY TO BE WITH DAVID on this long journey into Rubinstein's fascinating life. We traveled to Paris many times and to St. Petersburg, New York, and Washington, DC, seeking the sources of this mystery woman. And he keenly read through many drafts of my manuscript. Lynn Garafola inspired me to dig into the exotic and occasionally puzzling career of Rubinstein and warmly gave me valuable advice. I thank my daughter Ninotchka for her insight and cheer in the course of our many conversations about Rubinstein. Our children Rachel and Aaron and grandchildren, Hannah, Max, Jacob, Mariana, and Jonah deserve a hug and a bravo for seeing me through another long research project. I am deeply grateful to my most trusted friend, Kathy Milazzo, who read through the text a number of times and helped me to critique and shape the narrative in its different forms. She beautifully sliced and augmented it when necessary.

Assisting me with the Russian translations were Tamara Tomasson and Eric Newton. Tamara carefully decoded articles, while all along Eric shared the ways the Russians characterized Rubinstein, and he directed me to the fascinating digital film of her dancing. Sarah Williams Gonzales immediately offered her capable services in seeking the sources of various photos of Rubinstein. Since the beginning of my writing career, Nancy Zeckendorf has encouraged me to tread the sometimes difficult trails that one must pursue when doing research. Another dear friend, Beth Aldrich, led me to rich and promising materials held at the Library of Congress, while Judith Brin Ingber gracefully supplied her encyclopedic knowledge of Jewish dancers and choreographers. She and Dawn Lille, comrades in every sense, dancers and writers, were always there for me. Early on in the course of working on this project, Tomi Kushner introduced me to a book on the life of Gabriele d'Annunzio, a major figure in Rubinstein's career. Jim Tuller generously and judiciously scanned the dance collection at the New York Public Library for photos of Rubinstein and relayed them to me; Walter Putnam's expertise on Paul Valéry enhanced my work on the *livrets* Valéry wrote for Rubinstein. Howard Sayette, my Metropolitan Opera Ballet partner who worked with Irina Nijinska, kindly sent me a version of Bronislava's *Boléro;* Mary Anne Newhall, a dear colleague, sought out books and articles that were of great value in the course of writing this book. Liora Bing-Heidecker also informed me of new sources germane to this project. I am deeply indebted to Bruce Robertson, former director of the University of California, Santa Barbara Art, Design & Architecture Museum, who graciously helped me to attain permissions for artwork. I must also gratefully thank Richard Sorensen from the Smithsonian Museum for his patience and kindness in helping me with the Romaine Brooks paintings.

The many hours of research in libraries here and abroad were aided and abetted by some of the most selfless people—the librarians and their staff. I am profoundly grateful to Daisy Pommer, Andrea Felder, and Arlene Yu, the Collections manager at the New York Public Library for the Performing Arts, who pointed me to the photos I needed and really supported me in that endeavor. Linda Murray, curator for the New York Public Library Jerome Robbins Dance Division, deserves kudos for her passionate delight in helping those working on all aspects of dance research. It is a pleasure to note my indebtedness to SUNY's Jenn Bennett-Genthner for her gracious help with copyediting. I must also recognize the many librarians in Paris, who patiently directed me to the relevant files I needed, especially those at the Bibliothèque de l'Opéra, the Arts du spectacle, and the Jacques Doucet collections.

Finally, I'd like to offer a boisterous shout out and thank you to Richard Carlin for being a steadfast and loyal believer in my work and my terrific editor for several of my books, including this one.

PREFACE

IT HAS BEEN YEARS SINCE I began chasing the phantom of the exotic Ida Rubinstein (1883-1960), an actress, a dancer, a savvy producer of sumptuous productions, a philanthropist, and a brilliant woman. Her name appeared in the newspapers and gossip columns in Paris for nearly half a century from 1909 to 1949. Audiences flocked to see her perform. Critics and writers of the time, and those who followed, were predominantly male and often decried and dismissed her both for her sex and her religious origins. Sadly, she has faded into oblivion, barely remembered by dance or theater scholars. Was it because she was Jewish? Was it because she was a woman and a foreigner? Anti-Semitism, misogyny, and xenophobia penetrated the core beliefs of French society, as will be seen in the course of this narrative.

Rubinstein became a friend and disciple of Sarah Bernhardt, but lost her luster after World War II. Her exotic hunting expeditions, her long and beautiful body clothed in the most expensive fashions of the day, and her love life—she had both male and female lovers, one of whom, Walter Guinness, the famous Lord Moyne, helped support her opulent theater pieces: all these qualities grabbed the attention of "Tout Paris" critics and journalists. And she

Ida Rubinstein, portrait painted by Romaine Brooks, 1917.
SOURCE: AMERICAN ART SMITHSONIAN MUSEUM.

was a fascinating personality onstage. I had been intrigued by Rubinstein's complex attributes and contradictory abilities, and wanting to know more about her, I began by exploring the archives for articles about her, reviews of her pieces, and commentaries on her contributions to the theater and to society in general.

In recent history, Rubinstein as a startling performer has not been entirely forgotten. A Russian pair, sister-and-brother ballet dancers Ilse and Andris Liepa, decided to tour their version of the Ballets Russes's *Cléopâtre* to Paris. At the Théâtre des Champs-Elysées in late June 2009, Les Ballets des Saisons Russes gave the premiere of "Cléopâtre—Rubinstein." "The idea of bringing Rubinstein back to life on a Paris stage first occurred to Andris Liepa, the guiding spirit of this latter-day Ballets Russes, when he saw his sister, Ilse, dressed for the filming of his restoration of Fokine's *Schéhérazade*."[1]

In addition, I wanted to put in a personal word and speak about my own experience with one of Rubinstein's productions, although somewhat distant. When I was a dancer in the Metropolitan Opera Ballet Company, we spent summers at the Santa Fe Opera, and in 1961 I danced in Rubinstein's beguiling creation, Stravinsky's *Perséphone*. We had gorgeous scene and costume designs (designed by Vera Stravinsky), choruses and Gide's poetry that dazzled the ears, and the marvelous score conducted by Stravinsky. The lovely choreography by Thomas Andrew probably had little to do with Kurt Jooss's original version. Rubinstein's role as Perséphone was superbly performed by Vera Zorina. More recently, a London production of Ida Rubinstein's life, *Final Act*, will be launched, possibly in 2021. Starring an American Ballet Theatre ballerina, Naomi Sorkin, the solo play will evoke Rubinstein's celebratory performances and important life passages.

Some years ago, while writing a biography of René Blum, the director of the Ballets Russes, I came across Rubinstein's name and company performing in his theater in Monte Carlo, and when my good friend, the American dance historian Lynn Garafola, offered me important correspondence that she had collected from Rubinstein's Russian youth, as well as some from her early years in Paris, I was delighted and dove right into reading and figuring out what kind of a young woman she was destined to become.

For a number of years, Lynn Garafola presented papers and published articles on the enigmatic and barely known diva. She laid the groundwork in scholarly circles in the US for subsequent writings on Rubinstein. Her lively discussions about Rubinstein's productions, especially her 1994 article on *Le Martyre de Saint Sébastien* (Circles of Meaning: The Cultural Contexts of Ida

preface xiii

Rubinstein's Le Martyre de San Sébastien) and other Paris performances, reveal and vivify in detail how a particular work appeared and appealed to audiences.

Another inspiring writer and early proponent of Rubinstein, Charles Mayer, wrote an essay titled *Ida Rubinstein: A Twentieth-Century Cleopatra* (1989), as well as encyclopedia articles that include extensive bibliographies. Also, I spent quite a bit of time in the Paris libraries, at the Opéra, at the Richelieu in the Arts du Spectacle, and in the Jacques Doucet and Music divisions. The New York Public Library for the Performing Arts contains documents of interest, and especially the Library of Congress in Washington, DC, where John Wayne, a curator, devoted an important inventory to her life and career, having acquired many materials from her secretary, Mme Ollivier. (Elizabeth Aldrich, dance historian and curator at Library of Congress kindly led me to the LOC collection.) It was surprising that having assembled all this information about her that Wayne had not published her biography, although he had plans to do so, prior to death.

It is also a wonder that there is a dearth of reliable information on Rubinstein's life, especially in English. Vicki Woolf, the author of *Dancing in the Vortex: The Story of Ida Rubinstein* (2000), brings forth vivid details of Rubinstein's childhood and the milieu in which she grew up. Unfortunately, this work contains no footnotes or bibliography, so one wonders from where Woolf's information came. Michael de Cossart explored Rubinstein's profession and rivalry with Diaghilev in an article and in his book *Ida Rubinstein (1885-1960): A Theatrical Life* (1987). More information has come to light since these early studies. Nathalie Stronhina wrote a very revealing chapter, "Les racines russes d'Ida Rubinstein" in Lécroart's 2008 French publication *Une utopie de la synthèse des arts á l'épreuve de la scene,* but her essay and this anthology have not been translated into English.

Probably the most detailed and well-researched book about Rubinstein is also in French and is written by the French scholar, Jacques DePaulis. *Ida Rubinstein, Une Inconue Jadis célèbre* (1995), covers many aspects of Rubinstein's life and performances and is a valuable bibliographic account of events occurring with and around Rubinstein. What I found missing in DePaulis's work and discovered in Garafola's articles and letters was a new tactic to understanding Rubinstein, an approach that addresses her as a whole woman. My methodology utilizes a psychological analysis coupled with a corporeal reading of her performances. Rubinstein was incredibly well educated, yet this fact has not been made clear. She was able to hold her own with the most revered artists of her time and to entice them to work for her and her companies. She was both charismatic in conversation and sensually captivating onstage.

In these pages I have not written a comprehensive analysis of all the productions that Rubinstein produced or performed in. Rather, I have highlighted some of her performances, as well as her letters and writings that featured her aspirations to grandeur and her aesthetic beliefs. Since I was a dancer and approach performance from the point of view of embodiment, I comment on her physical presence and bodily movement in developing her characters onstage. Finally, I try to uncover the devastating effect of her having been born a Jew and how this affected her critics and audiences. Her disappearance could be linked to the fact that her Judaism drove some of the critics to maddeningly stupid and racist reviews.

Therefore, this manuscript seeks to redress the lack of contemporary published works on Rubinstein's significance in the worlds of dance, theater, art, and religion and to restore her legacy to the annals of history. Her life spanned a crucial time period in the first half of the twentieth century, when anti-Semitism led to the Holocaust of the Jewish people throughout Europe. Rubinstein had a complicated relationship with her religion and culture, eventually deciding, near the end of her life, to convert to Catholicism. The media, colleagues, and the public always seemed to pigeonhole her and find fault where it was not merited. For dancers and actors, Rubinstein's choices illuminated the ways women in performance negotiated their roles and their aesthetic philosophies. Here I seek to reveal how Rubinstein served as the zeitgeist of her era, changing the way the whole body was used and the mind engaged to fulfill her vision of an aesthetic totality of theater.

CHAPTER ONE

Russian Beginnings
an early taste for the stage

IDA LVOVNA RUBINSTEIN was born in Kharkov in the Ukraine. Unsure of the exact date of her birth, Garafola looked for her birth certificate and found it in Kharkov, in the Grand Choral Synagogue, written in both Russian and Hebrew, stating that she was born in September in 1883. Her parents were highly respected in upper-class Jewish circles with great riches both in banking and in the grain trade. They were considered among the wealthiest families in Russia, and despite the family's Jewish background, were privy to most of the same advantages that the aristocracy enjoyed. Rubinstein lost both her parents at an early age—her mother when she was five and her father at the age of eight, either from cholera, or typhus.

Rubinstein was taken from Kharkov in the Ukraine to live with her wealthy Aunt Horwitz in St. Petersburg, the Russian capitol founded by Peter the Great. It is a resplendent city surrounded and penetrated by waterways, like Stockholm and Amsterdam, and, scattered throughout the horizon are a series of Baroque structures, magisterial and lyrical palaces filled with art and the highest sense of Italian and French decorative styles. These opulent buildings represented the dying czardom and withering aristocracy soon to be thrown

Ida Rubinstein's Russian home, 2 Angliskaya, St. Petersburg.
SOURCE: AUTHOR'S COLLECTION.

into oblivion in 1917. Although Russia, during the autocratic regime of Czar Nicolas II, ruling from 1894 to 1917, was dangerously arrogant, it was still a Russia full of hope for the future, with its wondrous nineteenth-century inventions such as the train, the telephone, the Belle Époque's fashion and style, the economic and modern industrial advances, the welcome freedom for the serfs, and a rich cultural environment with writers, composers, and artists inspired by European initiatives creating new ways and visions.

But it also presaged continuing and monstrous acts endangering all Jews. Rubinstein's family, as rich as they were, certainly took account of the anti-Semitic outbursts in 1881 and 1882, as well as the profoundly hostile and frightening Kishinev pogrom in 1903 when forty-nine Jews were killed and 1,500 homes were destroyed. The Rubinstein family wealth, however, was known to be philanthropic, and they endeavored to place themselves in a modern industrial world. Rubinstein would never deny her Jewishness, but her quest for aesthetic perfection strove to supersede religious boundaries.

Contrastingly, Kenneth B. Moss, a distinguished scholar of Russian history, offers an illuminating comment to introduce a study of Ida Rubinstein:

"We should think about late imperial Russian Jewry not only as more Russian and more imperial than previously thought, but also as enthusiastic participants in the life of a modern society that afforded them the possibility of a 'vibrant cultural life.'"[1]

The photos of Rubinstein in various libraries depict an enthusiastic woman of extraordinary character and, depending on the photo, multiple sensibilities and qualities—frail and imperial, sad and triumphant, seductive and aloof. When Rubinstein was growing up, the fashion for nude bathing and freeing the body of corsets and clothes was spreading across Western Europe.[2] Being influenced by such views, she would not shy away from celebrating her body in her future productions. Her tendency to disrobe will be explored in later chapters.

Vicki Woolf, the author of *Dancing in the Vortex: The Story of Ida Rubinstein,* also comments on the disappearance of outward signs of Judaism in the Rubinstein/Horwitz family[3] and that they were driven by their desire to be accepted by the elite of Russian society. Woolf, on her first pages, brings up the horrors of the pogroms that plagued Jews in their confined villages outside of the rich urban centers. Jews "were disliked by landowners and peasants alike, a hatred based upon Medieval Christian tradition; inevitably they became scapegoats when times were hard."[4] Woolf imagines the luxurious surroundings that Rubinstein enjoyed as a youngster, even the kinds of vodka and caviar and rich borscht that were served in her opulent apartment at 2 Angliskaya.[5] Waiters in red-blue-and-gold-dressed suits acceded to their every need. One wonders where Woolf uncovered these details. She speculates that the rooms were filled with paintings and objects admired during that time and with a huge library of thousands of books. "In this haven of sophistication, she was formally educated to a level of high achievement."[6] Though why Rubinstein did not attend university, with her inquiring mind, does cause some puzzlement. Perhaps it was because she always wanted to be in the theater. Woolf explores the idea that Mme Horwitz encouraged her niece to attend opera and ballet performances, especially since the court played a vital role in the activities of the imperial ballet and getting close to the court was the essence of upper-bourgeois aspirations. Horwitz and her niece were regular participants at the Maryinsky Theatre. But it became apparent to her family, when Rubinstein turned twenty-one, that she had no business attaching her hopes and dreams to a life in the theater. Rubinstein disagreed.

Not surprisingly, events in Rubinstein's life, although studied by very few writers, caused many scandals and much gossip. In an effort to uncover information and stories about her early years growing up in St. Petersburg, I sifted through comments from a number of authoritative sources. Details about Rubinstein's family fortune are few and often differ. For example, I found a 2015 Ukrainian article on Rubinstein online in the *Jewish Observer* titled "Mystery Woman," a Russian-language text that speaks about her resistance to questions asked about her past. What it does say is that "she was born to the parents, the father an honorable citizen of Kharkov, Lian or Leon Romanovitch Rubinstein and the mother, Ernestina Isaacovna. Rubinstein came from one of the most prosperous families in Ukraine and Russia. Her grandfather founded the banking firm, Roman Rubinstein and Sons. The family owned sugar factories, a brewery named New Bavaria, warehouses and stores."[7] According to the *Jewish Observer*, they spent this formidable wealth on charitable causes and the cultural development of Kharkov. The Ukranian publication notes that Ida Rubinstein inherited the "best qualities of the Rubinsteins: drive, energy and most importantly artistic inclinations and force of personality, pushing her way to success. When her parents died, she inherited an enormous fortune."[8]

Since Rubinstein was associated with a known and powerful family, as she was related to the Rothschilds and the Cahen d'Anvers. Rubinstein's aunts, Marie Kahn and Julia Cahen d'Anvers held glittering settings at their salons and were known as the "Jewesses of Art."[9] Rubinstein was sought out for her opinions and personal intentions. Many paintings of Rubinstein idealized her exquisite body and her gentle animal-like quality. Long legs, a thin body, and an aquiline nose, coupled with an innate elegance and grace enhanced her Venus-like aura. A French/Russian writer, Nathalie Stronhina, reflected that her growing up in Russia, until the age of twenty-six, was a threshold to her future fame. Having Russian connections not only to the rich and famous but also to very "prestigious names" such as Léon Bakst, Vsevolod Meyerhold, Michel Fokine, Alexander Glazunov, and Serge Diaghilev before she joined them in Paris, endowed her with immediate credibility as an artist and performer. These relationships, which began in Russia, led to her generative collaborations with remarkable artists such as d'Annunzio, Claude Debussy, Paul Valéry, and Robert de Montesquiou, who introduced her to Sarah Bernhardt.[10]

Stronhina makes the persuasive point that wealthy Russians, especially from Jewish families, became important figures (*mécénats*) in the cultural landscape, offering an inexhaustible number of rubles to the parks, gardens,

Ida Rubinstein, 1910. Portrait painted by Valentin Serov. SOURCE: UTCON COLLECTION/ ALAMY STOCK PHOTO.

libraries, hospitals, and the arts, including museums. Wealthy Jews lived on the level of the richest and aristocratic, "Marchands de premiere guilde." At the same time, if you were not among the gifted, there were strict prohibitions against Jews of a lower class, who were not allowed to live in the urban centers of Russia, but were relegated to the Ukraine, to the old boundaries of Poland, and Belorussia, and were treated on the same level as criminals. But privileges and permission to live away from the "Jewish Pale of Settlement" only came with large payments to the imperial treasury.

Rubinstein grew up without religion, or *"croyances"*—beliefs that, according to Stronhina, might have been detrimental and would have prevented her from developing into a freethinker and lover of all forms of art, literature, and languages. She opined that religion tended to restrict freethinking. Art became the spirituality that she sought all her life.[11]

Stronhina also reminds us that Rubinstein is still remembered in Russia, perhaps not so favorably, for a number of reasons. The famous Russian portrait painter Valentin Serov painted an unusual singular image of Rubinstein reclining, naked and looking quite beautiful and enigmatic (1910). Long famous in France, she was quickly forgotten after World War II, despite many portraits and photos that kept her image in the news while she was alive.

russian beginnings

Russians disliked her seductive persona, believing that she lured Serov into an illicit affair that destroyed his marriage. The portrait remains and so in Russia she is remembered.

DePaulis indicates that her mother Ernestine may have had gypsy origins (*d'origine tzigane*), and mentions that Rubinstein's father had a brother, Daniel, a wealthy businessman, who also lived in St. Petersburg. DePaulis affirms that Alexandre Benois wrote about Daniel as being an "exquisite person and a great friend of the Count Benckendorff,"[12] a protector of Bakst, and an important companion. However, Rubinstein never mentioned this uncle. DePaulis quoted Michael de Cossart, who claims that the great banking families of the time, particularly the Cahen d'Anvers, would have helped her to save the major part of her bountiful fortune in 1917, when revolutionaries were appropriating land and money. But by then she and probably her inheritance were safely in France.[13]

DePaulis, like her other biographers, stressed that she did not identify with Judaism, though her family came from a very orthodox background, but that they chose to forget their origins. It seems understandable in light of the atrocities waged against Jews.

It is strange that she did not hold her family in high esteem. DePaulis refers to a letter in the Paul Claudel Society archive about Rubinstein's elder sister, Mme Lewisohn, who was killed during the bombing of Paris in 1918.[14] Rubinstein had wrathful, angry feelings about this sister, who disapproved of Rubinstein's profession and her behavior onstage. In Rubinstein's will she left no one in her family any funds or gifts. DePaulis seems not to agree with Michael de Cossart about her inheritance after the Russian Revolution; he poses the question "What happened to the Rubinstein fortune after the Revolution?" and responds by bringing into the conversation the prosperous Lord Moyne, Walter Guinness, who was guiding Rubinstein financially. "In private Rubinstein had started an affair with the English sportsman and millionaire Walter Guinness who stood ready to indulge her every whim."[15]

Like Rubinstein, Guinness's life was surrounded by dramatic events. He had been considered one of the heroes of the British military, having performed bravely during World War I. The private nature of their relationship remains somewhat of a mystery, because Rubinstein was a fiercely private person and probably destroyed all his letters. What she wanted the public to know, she would reveal to the writers and critics who avidly followed her career. It is a supreme irony that Rubinstein and Guinness were very close friends for almost thirty-five years; they seemed so different from one another

Walter Guinness, First Baron Moyne, 1918. Photographer unknown. SOURCE: BASSANO LTD., PUBLIC DOMAIN.

Ida Rubinstein with pet tiger, 1912. SOURCE: THE CHRONICLE/ALAMY STOCK PHOTO.

and yet he cared for her until he died. He funded her performances, accompanied her on their grand safaris and hunts, and bought her the luxurious yacht *Istar* as a gift.[16]

A few words explaining Rubinstein's everlasting devotion to Guinness and his to her are helpful here. Apparently, they met in 1909,[17] and surreptitiously kept their intimate friendship alive as they pursued other relationships and experiences; all the while, she was able to receive large gifts of money from him, not only to fund her sumptuous productions, but also her nursing activities during both wars. (It seems that no financial or written documentation about the funds Guinness provided Rubinstein have been discovered.) However, there are numerous anecdotal stories that confirm his generosity toward Rubinstein's productions. For example, Jacques DePaulis writes in "Un Mécène atypique" or "A Rare Philanthropist," "What's important to remember here is that Walter Guinness has dedicated a great portion of his fortune to sustain without fail all of the performances of Rubinstein and her for the duration of 34 years."[18] So careful were they that we rarely hear of Rubinstein and Guinness as a couple, but Paul Claudel, the esteemed French poet, understood their relationship, as did Léon Bakst.

Guinness, born in 1880 in Dublin, was the third son of Edward Cecil Guinness, owner of the celebrated Irish breweries. He went to school at Eton and had a tremendous curiosity about a great variety of things in nature and culture. As a soldier he was awarded prizes for his heroism in South Africa and later in Turkey and Egypt. He married Evelyn Erskine in 1903, and had several children. When he retired as lieutenant colonel, he was awarded the Distinguished Service Order. Subsequently, he entered politics and worked closely with Winston Churchill's government. Ida and Walter seemed at first strange bedfellows, but their affair endured for a long time.

A good indication of the depth and longevity of their relationship appears in Paul Claudel's work. In his *Journal,* he refers to the date September 2, 1921, when the ship André Lebon left from Marseille with passengers Mme Saussine, Mme Lartique, Mme Rubinstein, Mme Guinness, Walter Guinness, and himself. Claudel quipped that the conversations on board were a "dialogue of the dead."[19] They all talked endlessly about the past. It was no secret that the Colonel Guinness and Rubinstein were on their way to Africa, to Djibouti to hunt for large animals. In a letter to a friend, Audrey Parr, confided on September 13, 1921, that Claudel disclosed he traveled to Djibouti with Rubinstein, "as always beautiful, and her lover, the Colonel Guinness who was son of a brewery owner. They are on their way to hunt antelope and lions in

Abyssinia. Rubinstein told me that next spring she was hoping to remount *Le Martyre de San Sébastien* at the Opéra," which she did in June 1922.[20]

Rubinstein also wrote a letter to Léon Bakst dated September 11, 1921, about this same hunting trip. She tells Bakst, "I am writing from the Red Sea. I cannot stress how hot it is here. I am going to send this letter from Djibouti where we arrive tomorrow and from where I am departing on horse to search for lions and their skins that I promised to bring you."[21] Rubinstein clearly treasured Guinness's support and friendship. Without him, she would probably not have been able to achieve many of her productions or to survive the two World Wars.

An interesting French novel about Rubinstein's life by Donald Flanell Friedman, *Rubinstein: Le Roman d'une vie d'artiste* (2011), writing in the first person, poetically evokes her youthful and romanticized thoughts and experiences, her dreams, and fears. There are no footnotes or references to his sources to ascertain where he attained his information, but it is clear he is an excellent researcher. He dedicates his book to the Brothers of the Abbaye de Citeaux and notes Rubinstein's attachment to the thirteenth-century Cistercian Abbey near Dijon, dedicating her last years to meditation and prayer in her quest for a transcendent belief.

Friedman suggests that the Rubinsteins were also related to other powerful Russian Jewish families, for example, the Poliakovs and the Raffaloviches who financed the construction of the TransSiberian railroads and founded huge commercial banks in St. Petersburg. He noted that, as a youngster, Rubinstein would often visit her uncle Daniel Poliakov, who lived in the ancient palace of the Strogonoffs that was reconstructed in all its opulence for his family. The palace is described in detail. In addition, Friedman recounts that the Rubinsteins were also connected to the Cahen d'Anvers and the Camondos, French bankers.[22] When Rubinstein paid an unfortunate visit to her sister in Paris, she also became acquainted with the sisters Warshawska, Loulou Cahen d'Anvers, and Marie Kann. There were also Elizabeth Cahen, connected to the famous Forceville family, and Louise Malpurgo, who inherited a fortune from ship-owning and insurance companies, from Trieste.

Friedman avows Rubinstein's early disenchantment with her stifling and narrow-minded family. This is interesting in light of the fact that she was given such an enormous advantage, with governesses and tutors in music; languages such as Latin, Greek, French, German, and Italian; salon soirees; and visits to many theaters and museums. But those benefits did not quiet her restless spirit. He quotes her statement in an edition of *L'Écho*, September

9, 1932, when she is forty-nine years old. Here she declares that "I lived the life that I wanted, and it was not won easily, born in Russia to a family who thought a theatrical life was a disgrace, I had to break away firmly from my milieu."[23] Friedman early on asserts that the epidemic that killed her parents was typhoid fever. Nobody whom I've read seems to agree. Typhoid fever is acquired after drinking infected water. Cholera is also carried in polluted water, but it is more likely her parents died of the latter.

Friedman and her other biographers underscored Rubinstein's love for Ancient Greece, and remind us that at the tender age of fifteen, she was permitted a trip there with her governess and tutor—a journey she never forgot, returning to its startling beauty and knowledge by performing the roles of its canonical tragedies. From the very beginning, she kept apart from other children, finding in books, concerts, and her tutors enough stimulation and excitement. She studied piano assiduously, sinking herself into the music she often heard in her aunt's home. She loved to recite poems and extracts from literature, easily learning long narratives by heart. Friedman thought that Rubinstein had been baptized into the Russian Orthodox Church[24] soon after her move to St. Petersburg; perhaps she forgot this event. After some time, her aunt allowed her to follow the acting lessons of Yuri Ozarovsky, the professor at the conservatory in St. Petersburg, and to become a close associate of Lydia Yavorskaya, a celebrated actress who ran her own theater.

RUSSIAN JEWISH HISTORY

So why did the Rubinstein family have conflicting views on being Jewish, causing them to both embrace and discount their heritage? Jews migrated to southern Russia and its regions several thousand years ago, as inscriptions, tombstones, and Greek sources inform us, then more substantial numbers of Eastern Jews arrived, fleeing from persecution by the church in Byzantium. By 700 CE, they comprised the largest single group in Crimea, or Tauris, as it was called. "In several centuries they rose to great power and prosperity and lived cooperatively and comfortably with Christians and Muslims."[25] Gradually there arose serious hostility, and by the seventeenth century, they were not allowed in Russia and the Ukraine. Later in the eighteenth century, Jews were permitted to move from Western and Central Europe, to Poland, Lithuania, and Russia.

The meeting between Russians and Jews began officially when St. Petersburg, under Catherine the Great, annexed eastern Poland at the end

russian beginnings

of the eighteenth century, and so the Romanovs acquired about 500,000 Jewish subjects on the western border of the Russian Empire. Jews lived quite independently among the Poles, the Ukrainians, the Belarusians, and Lithuanians.[26] In the Pale, the virtual absence of both a Jewish peasantry and a Jewish nobility left the majority of Jews as petty traders, small shop or tavern keepers, artisans, money lenders, or others who floated from one job to another.[27]

Many hardships afflicted the Jews who lived in the Pale, that is, the area of Lithuania (the provinces of Kovno, Vilno, Grodno, and Minsk), as well as the western provinces of Vohlyn and Podnol, White Russia (Vitebsk ad Mogilev), Little Russia (Chernigov and Pitava), New Russia (Kherson, Ekaterinoslav, Taurida, and Bessarabia), and the province of Kiev. Rural settlements were to be closed to newcomers.

When Russia lost the Crimean War (1853-1856) to multiple European countries (France, the UK, Sardinia, and the Ottoman Empire or Turkey), new reforms were instituted, especially under Alexander II, who was famous for having freed the serfs. Sometimes called the Emperor of Mercy, he accorded certain Jews the right of residence and government employ. There was some discussion about freeing the Jews, and there were attempts to stop the endemic anti-Semitism. Jews were taught to speak and read in Russian, thereby encouraging them to rise in a very hierarchical system. Leaving behind their ritualistic clothing and beliefs was thought to allow them to join Russian society. But civic equality was not ordained and various uprisings in 1863 were attributed to the Jews, so Jewish schools were closed. Reports in European presses in the 1880s spoke about the violent outbursts toward Jews, but also blamed the Jews for their "allegedly oppressive commercial practices." The Ukraine had the largest concentration of Jews in Russia and most of the pogroms and deaths occurred there. The word *pogrom,* Russian for thunder or storm, was not, however, utilized until the early twentieth century.[28] Nevertheless, the era of rampant pogroms presaging the horrors of World War II had begun. Jewish physicians and jurists seemed to have escaped the limited opportunities forced on their brethren. Interestingly, during the Russo-Turkish War of 1877-1878, many Jewish physicians achieved the citation of Imperial Favor for their achievement in checking the then-raging typhoid epidemic.[29]

The pogroms of the 1880s were some of the severest episodes of ethnic cruelty in the Russian empire during the nineteenth century. Violence triggered by Alexander II's assassination on March 13, 1881, began to subside in 1883, the year of Rubinstein's birth, when thousands of Jewish homes and businesses had been destroyed by roaming mobs, several dozen Jews were murdered, and unknown numbers assaulted and raped.[30] One of the most difficult problems that had to be dealt with was that the czarist government could not be persuaded to stop the attacks against the Jews or to permit them to emigrate from Russia. These pogroms took place over the entire Russian empire, and a "national response" was not initiated. Legislation against the Jews was restrictive,[31] and the mobs understood that those who ravage the Jews would not be punished. The wealthy and comfortable Jews in St. Petersburg were accused of doing nothing to support or help their brothers.

The Rubinstein family's rise to great financial stability occurred when the czar allowed those who marketed grain and created large liquor concessions to gain significant power. Many benefited from their conversion to Russian Orthodoxy, becoming certified members of the wealthy, especially in St. Petersburg, which was the center of the aristocracy. "During the last three decades of the nineteenth century, social and geographic mobility among significant portions of the Jewish population transformed the Jews' relationship to Russian society and the imperial state."[32] It was evident that Rubinstein's family was one of the beneficiaries of this transcendent project and the new industrial Russia.

YOUNG RUBINSTEIN: LETTERS TO
ELIZAVETA ALEKSANDROVNA IUVITSKAIIA

Rubinstein's fanatical belief in herself and her abilities were not so unusual in St. Petersburg. It was a time when women, especially Jewish women, felt capable of realizing their aspirations. For example, "By 1882 more than two hundred female physicians had been trained in Russia, more than in any other European state. By the 1880s Jewish women accounted for 16 percent of the students enrolled at the Kiev Higher Courses, and 34 percent at the Women's Medical Courses in St. Petersburg."[33] If Rubinstein chose to go to university, she would have succeeded in any profession she desired. But she decided at a very young age that she was a performer, an actress who needed to be on stage. Her personal letters to her dearest friends deeply express her passions and her sense of drama. The letters are a significant part of Garafola's collection.

In my initial reading of the letters, I found that they reflect Rubinstein's tempestuous and flamboyant personality and lifestyle, and was struck by her persistence and dedication to the creation of art as well as to her belief in her rightful place in the most respected halls of international theater. Born

russian beginnings

to wealth and privilege, and despite the early loss of her parents, she knew that she was extraordinary and her faith in her destiny never left her. Her privileged upbringing afforded her a classical education with an intimate knowledge of languages, especially Italian, German, English, and French. She traveled and read widely, including the French luminary authors of the nineteenth century, as well as about the theater of Greece and Rome. She became an astute intellectual.

At the age of twenty-one, beginning in 1904, her letters mirrored the intense, urgent moods that overtook her. Her writing was breathless and bossy. And it's important to realize that in those days the letters arrived and departed fast and furiously hour-by-hour and day-by-day, often by pneumatique. She constantly swears to the truth of her promises and to her dedication to a new role, to a new endeavor, to a new trip somewhere, to learning a new language, and to the sincerity of her affection for her friends. She commands with imperative phrases and exhausts her reader with exclamations. She loved being onstage and studied acting and dancing with *acharnement* or fury.

Rubinstein possessed well-hewn manners in her early writing, thanking her friends and full of complimentary remarks about their warmth, kindness, and good intentions. Responding to a letter from a close associate who studied with her, Elizaveta Aleksandrovna Iuvitskaiia, she asks, "But when do rehearsals for your *Stepanida* begin? I still have not read it, but as soon as I return to Petersburg I will read it and then write to you; I always carry out your assignments to the letter."[34] One senses that Rubinstein has something uppermost in her mind, and that everything must attend to this desire.

In a Romantic vein, she often makes references in these missives to the weather, "so beautiful, quiet and warm. I spent almost the entire day outdoors, walking and riding, I'll return healthy. I kiss you, krepko." (*Krepko* in Russian is a term of endearment suggesting a firm or tight hug.) Also in December 1904, she writes to EAI, or Elizaveta Aleksandrovna Iuvitskaiia. "My dear Darling, You do not know how dear your love is to me. And I too have come to love you deeply and sincerely. As for pity on my part toward you, that is out of the question." She compliments Elizaveta on her being richly endowed, though her journey to her wished-for destiny may be difficult. Rubinstein's sympathy adds to her essential control of the relationship, a characteristic that emerges often in her letters. "I repeat, I have come to love you; often in my thoughts I am obsessed with you. So be wise, my girl." In French we say *sois sage*. "Be wise," but it really means stay out of trouble. "I kiss you, Goriacho!" (*Goriacho* in Russian is also a term of endearment meaning a fervent embrace.) Here we see that her breathless passion for her friend Elizaveta presages her future attraction and attachment to Romaine Brooks, the American painter in Paris just six years later. While it is difficult to determine if this letter provides evidence of Rubinstein's bisexuality, it certainly indicates she was passionate about more than just her work.

Art for Rubinstein was a prayer, a pilgrimage, a "journey," "My dearest girl, Today you set forth on the hard, but beautiful journey of service to art. Be strong and begin with faith, etc." The nature of belief and religion are not questioned as they imply love of art.

In a spring 1905 letter to Elizaveta she wrote, "Girl of my blood, 'sister?'" "Of late I have been in pain. Write me everything. You know my girl, that I love you deeply and am your friend and that whatever happens, you need not feel lonely. Begin to paint in color, work on Mar'ei, after all you'll soon be playing her. I am happy that you acted well in the last performance ... I believe unwaveringly, I believe that you can attain greatness. I kiss you krepko."

In April 1905, she wrote to Elizaveta: "My dearest girl: Be strong, my darling, be cheerful." She mentions Aleksandr Lenski, who taught in the drama department of the Moscow Theatrical School, and experimented and worked with a number of actors from the Maly Theater. Looking back at Rubinstein's dramatic training, Karina Dobrotvorskaya, a writer for the Russian publication, the *St. Petersburg Theater Journal*, suggests that Rubinstein fretted over which theatrical path, or method to follow, and that she eventually chose as her guiding mentor, Aleksandr Lenski. "In her acting roles she stunned her audiences with the luster of her diamonds, her playfulness with her scarves, her makeup painted in an exaggerated and severe manner, and topped off with ingenious hair designs. Lenski was a perfectionist and seemed to adore Rubinstein's remarkable gift for appearance, and even likened her to Sarah Bernhardt."[35] Rubinstein's passion for showing off and fashion was on display at the time that she auditioned for the Conservatory when, as Garafola notes, "she wore a sumptuous crimson dress with a kind of lace that seemed enchanting, a long train, costly brilliants, and elegant shoes."[36]

However, Rubinstein's health was not always perfect. She complains unabashedly to Elizaveta of her illness. "I simply cannot stop by, as I have completely fallen apart; I didn't even make it to rehearsal today. I have influenza and fever and fear that if I go out, I will become completely ill. And you dear girl, go to the doctor, this is essential. Under no circumstances go out! Rehearsal tomorrow evening. For now, I kiss you goriacho and ask you not to act foolishly." Rubinstein would always have a haunting fear of sickness.

russian beginnings

She often traveled to Europe for health reasons, to spas, as did so many of the upper classes at this time. On June 5, 1905, from Switzerland, she writes Elizaveta that it is, "difficult to read your letters, painful, for I am far from you and cannot warm you and cheer you up. But this time cannot last long." Is her friend depressed, seriously depressed? She asks about *The Tempest* that was being directed by Lenski in 1905. Elizaveta responds, "I am happy that Nelli has finished your dress. Do you like it? Lili sends you warm greetings, I kiss you, Rubinstein." Both women seem at odds with the world, with emotional ups and downs that afflict romantic souls, quick to be sad and quick to be happy.

In another letter in the fall of 1906, Rubinstein challenges Elizaveta, saying, "Do not be afraid for me; I did what was right. To reach a new goal one cannot fear a new path." This is typical, Rubinstein fears very little and has decided to embark on another trip to Greece; there, she will study the glories of the ancient past. She continues, "I still need to learn a great, great deal, which in Moscow would be impossible. As far as technique, that will come with practice which I can get from the school here." Here she means that she is shifting to study at the St. Petersburg Conservatory. She embellishes her thoughts about the meaning of life, "But the most important thing is to study, to explore all feelings, all thoughts, to experience everything, then to come to people with a full heart and an excited mind, to be mad for the truth and then to sing of this truth and to light all the world with my song." Could Rubinstein have read Walt Whitman or heard of his poems? "Either I do it, or I don't, one of the two. But I believe in miracles."[37]

In a fall 1906 letter to Elizaveta, Rubinstein writes that she has returned to school, having left the Moscow Conservatory. "I plunged into the new life about which I had dreamed, but I realized my complete mistake. It is impossible to combine life with the painstaking technical work that is essential to me in my art.... At last I have decided to dedicate the summer to the technical side of the affair. This is why I am flying off to Greece; there I will work until fall before I lose my senses, until that moment has come." Rubinstein thrives on these assertions and dreams of success and the completion of her goals. It is evident that Greece and its brilliant ancient theater tradition provide the culture and landscape for her pursuit of beauty and plans for creating a role in a Greek play.

In an undated letter to Elizaveta, she is still contemplating her trip to Greece, and writes that she has been in the hospital and had an operation: "Don't be angry with me; I lied out of love for you. Now I am out of danger, but all I do is lie here." Rubinstein plans her trip to Greece for a role she desires to play. "How we will work; maybe he, perhaps Sophocles, will give me something ancient? Tomorrow the gentleman who takes care of my affairs comes to see me; I will ask about money and write in the evening. Until then, I kiss you goriacho, Rubinstein."

Rubinstein's letters to Andreanova point to her hunger for attention both in the theater and in relationships. Such needs are not always negative indications of pathology, but, in Rubinstein's case, they reveal her strong desire for a rich, fulfilling life. These early letters signify that, even as a young woman, Rubinstein was highly motivated, educated, and well traveled. Her work would supercede such trifles as illness in the quest for her vision. Andreanova would not be the only recipient of Rubinstein's affections at this time, but they were probably the most innocent.

LETTERS TO AND FROM AKIM VOLYNSKY

Although we are not sure of the date, during this period, Rubinstein became enthralled by Akim Volynsky, a Russian literary critic, journalist, and art historian who became St. Petersburg's liveliest and most prolific ballet critic in the early part of the twentieth century. His book, the first English edition of his provocative and influential writings, *The Book of Exaltations,* offers a striking look at life inside the world of Russian ballet at a crucial era in its history. In 1906, Rubinstein's letters to Volynsky seem to suggest an emerging love affair with the celebrated ballet critic, Akim Volynsky (real name Chaim Flekser), who was born in 1865 in Zhitomir, the Ukraine, and who died in Leningrad in 1926; he was a generation older than Rubinstein.

Stanley J. Rabinowitz selected and translated forty of Volynsky's articles—vivid, eyewitness accounts that abound with details about the careers and personalities of such dance luminaries as Anna Pavlova, Mikhail Fokine, Tamara Karsavina, and George Balanchine, at that time a young dancer in the Maryinsky company, whose keen musical sense and creative interpretive power Volynsky was one of the first to recognize. His studies emphasize the spiritual and ethereal qualities of ballet.

As a young actress in Russia, Rubinstein's relationship with Akim Volynsky, predominantly in 1907 and 1908, shaped much of her thinking. Volynsky, an ardent ballet critic, considered himself a prophet of ballet, and viewed it as a means of spiritual renewal. He alleged that classical ballet provided symbols of a higher order of being. As a Grecophile, he asserted that Greek tragedy was one of the greatest art forms, with its singing poetry, gestural movement, and strong narrative. Euripides' *The Bacchae* represented the wellspring of his theories. Nietzsche and the Apollonian and Dionysian dialectic provided a path to the ecstasy of classical dance; as he stated, "A new sun will shine and with its brilliant rays illuminate all the summits of human engagement."[38]

Volynsky's opinions were often divisive, controversial, and always entirely his own. He discovered theater, and then ballet, late in his life, and his first ballet reviews only appeared in 1911, when he was fifty years old. Volynsky declaimed,

> In the art of ballet, the body rises like the phoenix from the ashes of the dark ages. Suddenly it is summoned to speak again and to rejoice—more accurately to participate in the general exaltation of life. We still have to give the legs freedom and ease of movement; ... The arms as well; they must be able to rise up like wings, to fly up and down, to form a circle over the head, and with a tender caress, to balance attitudes and poses. Every finger of the hand must be given meaning and stay alive. And do not forget the lightning that runs along the back, and the natural play of the head and shoulders. All of this body lives, sings and dances in a common choreographic exaltation.[39]

In one of her earliest letters to Akim, Rubinstein writes, "Many sincere thanks for your kindness. I will read your book with the deepest interest and would be happy if you would personally give me your impressions in Petersburg."[40] Rubinstein is nothing if not an opportunist—ready to befriend anyone who might push her career forward. But in Volynsky, Rubinstein senses a comrade in arms; he's Jewish, he's intellectually driven, especially by the essential and rich potential of art to change humanity, and certainly by the Symbolist movement and its idealistic approach to ballet, inspired by the great French poet Stéphane Mallarmé, who envisioned ballet as "an art capable of projection into the most absolute thought,"[41] exactly as Volynsky proposed and as Gabriele d'Annunzio presented in his plays. And for Rubinstein, theater and dance both aspired to the immaterial realm of poetry.

Volynsky's magnum opus, *The Book of Exaltations,* is an elaborate meditation on classical dance technique that is at once a primer and an ideological treatise. Throughout the book, Rabinowitz sets Volynsky's life and work against the backdrop of the principal intellectual currents of his time. Volynsky worked briefly as director of repertoire for the actress Vera Fedorova Komissarzhevskaya's important Petersburg company, the St. Petersburg Dramatic Theater.

Again in 1906, writing to Volynsky, Rubinstein seems torn about her education at the Moscow Theatrical School. "Lenski trains only the actress in me, but not the part of me that must subsequently realize my dream. He draws me away from our work. Something in me burns, and now I know no peace. I want to reveal my soul, to reveal all the beauty of the world...."[42] How prescient is her understanding of herself, her sense of importance to the world and to the future!

Despite these outbursts, her physical training at the Moscow Theatrical School prepared her to explore her body's expressive potential although she was by no means a stranger to using her body in creative ways. Lynn Garafola noted that when Rubinstein enrolled in the school, she studied "plastique," a movement system developed by Vasili Geltser. There, she also was taught plastic motion by Meyerhold, the famed theater director. It was called the movement system of "plastique."[43]

Did Rubinstein actually go to Greece in 1906? According to Stanley Rabinowitz, she accompanied Volynsky on one of her trips to Greece. He was contemplating a ballet scenario inspired by one of these trips. As a follower of Nietzsche and the Apollonian qualities of classical ballet, Volynsky imagined, the "Birth of Apollo," with his paramour Rubinstein playing the role of Leto, the mother of Apollo.

We begin to surmise that Akim Volynsky is sadly falling in love with her. In 1907 she writes, "Akim L'vovich, forgive me for hurting you, if you can." She seems ready to apologize at the drop of a hat, for shunning, or ignoring or turning away from people who've fallen in love with her. She goes on in a subsequent letter, "It pained me to read your letter, pained me that you were upset and miserable and that I had no words to soothe you."[44] What is going on here? Things don't seem to improve, as not long after, she writes, "I so often give you pain. Forgive me. There is something in me I cannot change. I am always glad to have your letters. I anxiously await the end. Now that spring is here, I want to leave. I think only of that. I do not even want to act. I close my eyes and see the sun and the sea, do not be melancholy." The coquette reigns, she asks him to come and visit her, telling him, "You were so sad today. I want you to be happy again."

In these brief text messages, probably sent by pneumatic, we envision her radical changes of moods like the changes of weather and try to understand what the "big picture" might be. Does Rubinstein have a grasp of where she wants her career to go? Or is she spontaneously seizing opportunities of the moment?

russian beginnings

In 1907 she wrote to Volynsky, "I will be at the Hermitage tomorrow. If you wish, come." Then she writes, "Tomorrow come to our box at the Maly Theater on the mezzanine right side," Again she tempts him, "Tonight I will go to see *The Daughter of the Sea*. (This may have been the Spanish play by Angel Guimerà.) I want to see the decorations. I will sit in the third row. But I think that it will bore you to see the poor acting."

Rubinstein will graduate from the St. Petersburg Conservatory and finds the time to invite Volynsky to her exams. She notes that she will be performing in *The Last Oxen* by Nemerovich-Danchenko on March 26; in *Sardanapal* on March 28; in *Richard III* (Anna) on March 30; in *A Winter's Tale* on April 1; in *Macbeth* on April 8; and in *Mary Stuart* on April 10. "I appear in one act of each play."

She sends a telegram to Volynsky: "Am delighted you will come to first performance Monday, greetings, Rubinstein."

A draft of a letter from Volynsky in 1907 to Rubinstein tells a grand story: Volynsky addresses Rubinstein, and confesses his ardor, "My Divine Rubinstein, I cannot live without you. We will not fear words or names . . . in ordinary life; in our life, all will be meaningful and beautiful. God has readied me for you, . . . allow me, Rubinstein, to call you my bride?"[45] And the letter continues with more grandiloquent admissions.

Does Rubinstein respond to these declarations? Perhaps the following letter (1907) from her was an acknowledgment of Volynsky's impassioned note? "I returned and found your note. Only you didn't have to write to me like that. Some time after perhaps, but not now. I was terrified that my gift was too great." Did Rubinstein sleep with him? Does he now expect too much from her? She continues, "Your letter is beautiful, but it does not speak about the miracle of which what you write is a harbinger, nor does it speak about the moment, which will wash away all your tortures and sufferings. And in this miracle I have to believe, otherwise it is impossible to live. I believe that sort of madness will come."

It is easy to speculate that his feelings were not reciprocated, and that she needs to wait before such profound outpourings will be shared. However, she continues to lure Volynsky on. In the planning of a trip to Greece, and perhaps to India with him, she writes about her "heart and mind" that are preoccupied with leaving.

On May 7, 1907, she discloses, "I believe boundless happiness awaits us ahead." When they both have begun their travels, she writes from Hotel Bessarabia in Pale Roial, in Kiev, saying that she is "delighted about our forthcoming meeting." Signing off as Rubinstein Gorvitz, her Aunt's name, derived from Horvitz or Horowitz. Why she signed off as Gorvitz is puzzling, but if one looks at her later passports from 1937 to 1947, she uses the name Lydia Gorvitz. And to complicate things more, Gorvitz became her married name as well.

The letters are moving quickly. She informs Volynsky that "We will be in Berlin on the tenth of May." Then "Serons Trieste lundi." We arrive in Trieste on Monday. We do not know who the "we" includes.

They do not seem to be living together on this trip, as she apologizes, "Forgive me for the evening in Venice. It was wrong. What I believe is that you are great. Will you help me in the affair that it is now time to begin?" What affair? What is she planning? Her next communication from the Isle of Wight in the English Channel refers back to their time in Corfu and contains a litany of regrets and complaints. "In four hours I leave again for South Hampton, but from there I myself don't know where, but it is impossible for me to remain here any longer.... It was so awful, so terrible, while we were in Corfu. The endless sea and sky and such stillness! And the stillness inside me." Rubinstein cannot live without mystery; she wraps herself constantly in a web of mystique as well as dismay and pessimism as she strives for her dreams.

The romance with Volynsky continues on a path of subterfuge and deception. On September 2 or 3, 1907, she returned to St. Petersburg where she sketches a note in Italian that she signs Lina Torelli. The letter states that she could not meet him at the Hermitage Museum and is sorry to have disturbed him, but asks if he might meet her tomorrow in the gallery of paintings that she will be "enchantée de la parcourir avec vous." She will be enchanted to walk through the gallery with him. "Waiting for your response etc." He returns his message in Italian saying that he is busy tomorrow and cannot meet at that time.

The next day, she writes again in Italian with her signature of Lina, saying that she will meet him the next day. And then, with the ensuing note, we realize what's going on. She sends a telegram on the September 4, 1907, saying that she is unable to meet him, as "My husband is arriving immediately, excuse the annoyance, do not lose hope in our meeting," and signs it Lina Torelli.[46] Now, it seems that Rubinstein has a husband, or is pretending to have one, that he arrived unexpectedly, and that she still hopes to see Volynsky in the near future.

The story of her marrying, as told by her biographers, offers more insight into Rubinstein and the tempestuous and autonomous qualities that seem

russian beginnings

to drive her one way or another. When she decided to marry her cousin, Vladimir Horwitz, or Gorvitz, it was for the facade of security and stability that would support whatever she decided to do onstage. It was a marriage of convenience. This is very telling since American women actresses and dancers were already able to perform and to tour without the benefit of marriage. Several of Rubinstein's biographers (Woolf, DePaulis, de Cossart, and Garafola) indicate that she married in 1908, but this letter from 1907 seems to contradict this assertion. Or, could it be that she was lying to him about her marriage?

A letter from Volynsky on September 5, 1907 sheds more light on this troubled relationship. He accuses her of lying to him, or of dissembling in such a way that he was befuddled. He says that he did not show up at the Hermitage, as he couldn't figure out what she was getting at, pretending to be Italian, and so on. Then, with "her new request to appear at the Hermitage," he refused so as to give her a chance "to retreat." But he continues with the Italian charade. "Brushing aside the tangles of this frivolous joke, I wrote to you openly in Russian," still addressing her as Lina Torelli and agreeing to meet her at the Hermitage around noon. Why did Rubinstein send someone else in her place to meet him? A certain Lidia Mikhailovna. She also wrote several messages, delivered to his doorman, to inform him of a change in the time when they would meet. Volynsky berates her: "Aren't you ashamed Rubinstein L'vovna? In my opinion, it's better for you to give up all this buffoonery. If you need something from me, I am at your disposal." He reassured her that their years of friendship were of value to him. But he was clearly offended and at his wit's end with her infantile games.

Soon after, on October 2, 1907, Rubinstein seems to be ill again. "I am so sad that I have to rest and cannot work.... But we will work if you want to.... Can one begin without faith? I shall not soar to the white light and intend to sit still for a whole six months." What is she talking about? Is the white light the spotlight on a stage? Is she so indisposed that she must be quiet for a while? Or is this some imaginative chatter?

In 1907, Rubinstein tells Volynsky that she will act the role of Elektra. "I will be her, must be her, otherwise life is not worth living.... I will perform our *Elektra* around the 27th." It is with Volynsky that she intends to create the play *Elektra*; she will discuss the project with him when they meet in the Rembrandt Room of the Hermitage Museum. She is convinced that this is her destiny, that with this role, "her soul is revealed."

In 1907, in this new endeavor she will once again work with the woman who gave her private acting lessons when she was a teen, Madame Ozarovsky, the rehearsal director of the Theatre Alexandra, equivalent to the Paris Comédie Française. Unfortunately, the *Elektra* production never occurred.

In 1907, in a moment of apotheosis, she dreams of "a radiant future coming closer," and wants to talk to Volynsky: "how I love and believe in that theater of the future. It will burn with a fire ever bright, so fearfully bright that it must kindle all the world."[47] Evidently, she sees herself as a kind of Joan of Arc, a heroine whose presence excites and inflames the universe. That passion, that sense of purpose and importance never abandoned her. Indeed, the last role she performed would be that of Joan of Arc in 1938.

In 1907, the final letter from Volynsky is a denunciation of their relationship. Although many of the words are illegible, the sense is clear. He is fed up, finished, demeaned, and insulted by her. I would "crucify myself," he insists, and finishes the sad note with "It came from that demon you were gaily making fun of. So allow me, dear Rubinstein L'vovna, to write my demon these last lines." He signed it A. Volynsky.

As far as we know, this was the end of their relationship, and her friendship with Elizaveta as well. There are no further letters from them in the libraries in Paris or here in America, though perhaps there are some in Russia. Many of the qualities that defined Rubinstein and drove her career with such fury reside in these letters; her single-minded passion for the next role, her egotism and self-involvement, her dreams of a theater that ennobles humanity, and her fear of failure.

But the story is not quite over. Recently, a friend discovered a new translation of Volynsky's meditations on his past life experiences and alerted me to the publication *And Then Came Dance: The Women Who Led Volynsky to Ballet's Magic Kingdom*. Volynsky wrote his "Retrospective" in 1923, just three years before he died, musing about some of the women he encountered as a young man about town. The book also contains many essays on Russian ballerinas whom he thought worthy of his attention, although he did devote several pages to Isadora Duncan. Volynsky enjoyed philosophizing and gossiping about the women he knew, trying to fit them into categories, such as neo-Aryan women and proto-Aryan women, and Druidesses and *amoureuses*. These odd streams of anthropological classifications rarely make sense in his discussions. He sees women as idealized spirits. "For Volynsky woman personifies the triumph of the poetic over the prosaic as she transforms reality

russian beginnings

into fantasy.... beneath Volynsky's concept of the feminine lives the perfect semblance of the Madonna."[48]

In his chapter on Russian Women he speaks about Jewish women, including Rubinstein, whom he "has known and valued more than others since childhood."[49] He quickly notes that she "has never been the object of my romantic admiration," which we know is untrue given the letters he wrote to her. Debunking any frivolous affair with a Jewish woman: "Any kind of European romanticism seems unworthy and unclean.... Love in a Jewish environment is a solemn, serious, and heavy duty affair."[50]

But his few pages reminiscing about Rubinstein are quite penetrating and somewhat disturbing. Volynsky seeks revenge on this woman who scorned him, by bringing her back to life in the essay, "Pandora's Box." He sees her as an ice queen, superficial, gorgeous, and stunning beyond description and oh so seductive in her fashionable attire that attracts everyone's gaze. As she is capable of holding deep conversations on all sorts of subjects, she immediately captured Volynsky's interest. "I am devoting a separate chapter to this woman who embodies in the highest degree a remarkable and self-willed type."[51]

He remembers meeting her "while she was studying drama at the Moscow Theatrical School and spent the summer months in St. Petersburg, where she created around her self-convulsive and fantastically sensational waves." In other words, she was not only a "knockout," but also a woman of enormous fascination. Volynsky seems hypnotized by her. "Her total essence, her whole being, her entire secret lies in her supreme decorative effect. Rubinstein is first and foremost plastique, ornament, beauty, the dream of fortune."[52]

But he goes on to destroy this astonishing picture by diminishing and attacking her abilities as an actress and a ballet dancer. "She's too emotionally dry for the stage, too rational, too lacking in impetuous spontaneity.... Nor is she appropriate for the ballet stage, with her imperfect long legs.... She is organically unsuited to the ballet because for ballet one needs the plastique not of costume but rather of a tender and harmonious body."[53] He concludes this short disquisition with a curious tribute to her fame, her notoriety, "which has cloaked her name and created from her on Russia's barren and gloomy soil such a luxuriant, luxurious magnificent and unforgettable flower."[54] Rubinstein's liaison with Volynsky, as fraught as it was, and as experimental as it seemed, may have influenced her subsequent dalliances with adventurers, poets, and dreamers, rather than with critics who were often her bêtes noires!

VSEVOLOD MEYERHOLD'S INFLUENCE ON RUBINSTEIN

Vsevolod Meyerhold, a Russian actor and director, a contemporary of Rubinstein, and an innovative and extremely brilliant theater maker, was to also have a lasting influence on the way Rubinstein's performances were sculpted. He first directed her in her notorious version of *Salomé* in 1908, and then again in *La Pisanelle* in 1913. Born of German parentage in Panza, Russia in 1874, Meyerhold suffered a terrible demise as he was imprisoned, tortured, and murdered on Stalin's orders in 1940. Early in his career he worked with the famed actress Vera Komissarzherskaya, as did Rubinstein, and became, for a while, a fervent Symbolist. The reigning current in the development of dramatic plots in Russia was Symbolism led by the "enigmatic Vyacheslav Ivanov."[55] Mysticism in the poetry and symbolism of the narrative would propel the story into supernatural situations. What the Symbolists experienced was an urge to get away from the "unnecessary truth" of the realistic stage established in Russia by Stanislavsky, whose attempts to reproduce real life they could not acknowledge as theater or even as art. When Rubinstein began performing, she was convinced, probably by her acting teachers, that the theater was a powerful weapon, as well as a place to engage one's beliefs in transformation and transcendence. Meyerhold's Symbolist theater was also fully in accord with the view that the theater was a form of worship.[56] One would have thought that Rubinstein would have been drawn to the groundbreaking theatrical ideas that Stanislavsky propagated, but, apparently, he was disregarded by her. Garafola noted that Stanislavsky believed that she "dismissed his Moscow Art Theatre as antiquated."[57]

Meyerhold cast his net very wide. To begin with, like Rubinstein, he also revered the Greeks. Writing in 1907, he observed that, "If it anticipates the revival of the dance and wishes to attract the active participation of the spectator in the performance, is not the stylized theatre leading to a revival of the Greek classical theatre?"[58] Meyerhold drew from many sources, including Asian theater, and looked to Gordon Craig's notions of puppet theater and mime, movement and rhythm. He was not interested in reproducing life and so-called authentic emotions. He was also cognizant of the transformative theories that François Delsarte (1811-1871) had posited some years before.

In the late nineteenth century, a very popular form of movement expression, the Delsarte System, became the way actors and would-be performers learned to train for their roles, either in salons reading poetry or acting in stage plays. Delsarte wanted to be a singer, studied at the Conservatoire in Paris, but became disillusioned by the fake posing and artificial gestures that were taught at the time. He developed a fascinating approach to bringing lifelike reactions for actors and singers. He accomplished this scientific mode by spending hours observing natural experiences, in parks, even visiting mine disasters to watch how people reacted with facial expressions and movement to such frightening events. Meyerhold did not reference Delsarte for his educational methods, but no doubt the spirit and energy of the effort affected him. Nor did Rubinstein discuss Delsarte's major contributions, but she also benefited from his work.

Surely Geltser and Meyerhold knew about the stunning discoveries of Jaques Emile Dalcroze, as well as Delsarte, toward the end of the nineteenth century and the early twentieth century. Dalcroze was a Swiss musician who created the musical form titled eurhythmics, a method of studying music through the use of expressive movement. He experimented with improvisational exercises that connected the body to the music, as Delsarte might have wished. When studying Dalcroze, children and adults move their bodies to feel the musical rhythms and forms, and realize the meaning of the music physically.

Geltser's "plastique," and Meyerhold's movement system absorbed Dalcroze's ideas. In Dalcroze, one walked, jumped, marched, skipped, clapped, breathed, beat time, and gestured. The voice was also used as a way to experience the music. An authority on the subject, Selma L. Odom elucidates this aesthetic breakthrough in her article in *Mime Journalm, Delsartean Traces in Dalcroze Eurythmics,* noting Meyerhold combines their emphasis on gesture, rhythm, and narrative in structured exercises that assist the actor in feeling his or her role.[59]

After Meyerhold left Komissarzherskaya, he was appointed chief producer at the Moscow Art Theatre and remained there, having an immense authority and voice for ten years from 1907 to 1917. Even though Rubinstein had moved to Paris, it is clear that his experimental approaches to theater were very much on her mind, and though she seemed to be wedded to her own needs for spectacular decors no matter what the subject of her work, she certainly knew about Meyerhold's experiments and the people who affected him. An ardent intellectual and aesthetician, Meyerhold wrote continuously about his evolving thoughts on producing and directing plays.

Most of all he was concerned with the techniques and styles used by actors in the realization of the play itself. As he continued to develop plays on the stage, he looked to interesting techniques of training. For example, he was intrigued by the work of the commedia del'arte performers, mostly because they improvised and worked predominantly with movement and gesture. Meyerhold found that the commedia del'arte inspired a philosophy of life that proposed, like Craig, that acting is movement and that movement is the most intriguing and most important theatrical element. This method also established a relationship with the audience that "acting" seemed to diminish. Soon after, he began to work with actor training and a system of biomechanics. He developed a series of Sixteen Études[60] and pantomimes, which he deduced from other theatrical practices. The classes or études included walking, stretching, and other bodily exercises that were keyed to a musical rhythm, but also contained moments of expression with a partner or a group. For example, "Shooting from the Bow" involved holding the imaginary bow in the left hand in front of the actor, running toward the prey with smooth, loping strides, and jumping with both feet to a stop when the prey is seen; then there is a sequence of forward steps while the actor draws an imaginary arrow from a case on his back, loads it in the bow string, draws back the string, fires, and leaps forward to land with both feet with a cry. The writer, Robert Leach observed that for Meyerhold, "Every part of the stage was keyed to a rhythmic element. Meyerhold was an accomplished musician and took immense trouble over the music."[61]

It was well known that many of his productions, certainly those with biomechanically trained actors, had a dance-like quality, and Meyerhold himself gained experience in dance when he played Pierrot in Mikhail Fokine's ballet, *Carnival* in 1910, with Vaslav Nijinsky as Florestan and Tamara Karsavina as Columbine. In an early work, Maeterlink's *Sister Beatrice* from 1906, "The group of nuns often spoke in whispers, carefully graduating and measuring pauses. It was through precise execution of the diverse pauses that Meyerhold created the rhythm of the production. It was by the pauses that the movements and gestures were cued."[62]

Most important was the rhythm of the motions, as well as the sense that the whole body is involved, and concentration on the centering of the body as it moves through space. The exercises were specific and focused, and were said to contain the fundamental expressive moments that actors generally encountered in their stage work. His goal was to teach the actor to respond creatively, but precisely, with movements that projected an emotion and had credibility. At the same time, Meyerhold held the belief that these activities needed to be structured according to certain rhythms. It was his directorial work on Wagner's *Tristan and Isolde* in 1909 that convinced him about the importance of rhythmic movement for the actor or singer. "Meyerhold used an externally imposed rhythm as the means of controlling the performance: it was essential to keep that rhythm all the time so as not to be seized by personal emotion."[63]

Rubinstein's theatrical narratives, as a dancer, as an avid piano student, and as an actress were closely aligned with the music she chose, or in her plays with an analogous hidden tempo to her gestures and actions onstage. There is no doubt that Meyerhold's sensitivity to rhythm and melody affected her early on and would influence her performances for the duration of her career. Furthermore, he would be her choice of director for perhaps one of her most renowned roles.

RUBINSTEIN'S RUSSIAN STAGE CAREER (1904-1908)

Rubinstein's birth as a young tragic actress in *Antigone* (1904) took place at Lydia Yavorskaia's New Theater in St. Petersburg. Ozarovsky, the director of the Theatre Alexandra, gave Rubinstein acting lessons when she was fourteen or fifteen. Preparing for the Antigone role, she traveled to Greece; she had invited Léon Bakst, to whom she had boldly introduced herself, to design the work. Since he had recently made the décor for Euripides' *Hippolytus* in 1902 and then in 1904, Sophocles' *Oedipus at Colonus*, he seemed the perfect partner. Meyerhold's influence on *Antigone* was readily apparent. The daring scenery, the beautiful, overflowing costume, and Rubinstein's interpretation, all created an atmosphere of terrifying emotion inspired by Rubinstein's determination to focus her production on ancient traditions, and Antigone's willingness to die for them.

The Russian Silver Age, an artistic period lasting from the late nineteenth century to the 1920s, affected Rubinstein's aesthetic preoccupations. It included avant-garde art, theater, cinema, photography, and sculpture, and also saw a strong upsurge in the exploration of the ancient world, including scholarly studies and literary translations by Mikhail Rostovtsev and Faddei Zelinsky.

> Zelinsky in particular may be regarded as the eminence grise behind Russia's dance revolution of the early twentieth century.... He supported Isadora Duncan and the offshoot companies inspired by her. He was especially interested in the link between the danse plastique and ancient Greece. Zelinsky even organized research trips to Tauride and Greece heralding the dancers to return to idealistic temples, satyrs and Pan.[64]

Ida Rubinstein as Antigone, 1904. Costume by Léon Bakst. SOURCE: HISTORIC COLLECTION/ALAMY STOCK PHOTO.

Rubinstein appeared in a one-act version of *Antigone* on April 16, 1904, a private evening performance, with costumes by Léon Bakst and directed by Yuri Ozarovsky, using the pseudonym Lvovska to hide her identity, though no one doubted who she was. She was a mere twenty-one years old, the age when she inherited a huge fortune that enabled her to begin to produce her own performances. In the course of her thirty-six-year stage career, Rubinstein danced or acted in at least ten productions inspired by Greek and Roman narratives. It was clear that she saw her destiny in the vicissitudes and heroics of mythological stories. She often identified herself as a divine being, cultivating the myth of her godlike figure, but a figure that hid a profound sorrow. She staged these tragedies in the grand fashion of the seventeenth-century French court, where all the arts converged in inspired perfection. We cannot forget that as a starry-eyed youth, she had marveled at the mythological power of female stage performers such as Isadora Duncan and Sarah Bernhardt.

In his biography of Bakst, André Levinson reached back in his memory of the occasion of Rubinstein's debut in *Antigone*.

> I clearly remember this unique production. And I see again the proud maiden as she is wrapped in the numerous and complicated folds of her black mourning robe. In working out this conception Bakst had drawn his inspiration from a tombstone or else had deciphered the clever pattern from the sides of a Greek vase. Later this young woman with her disconcerting and mysterious beauty, this mystical virgin, voluptuous yet frigidly cold, with a will of iron underneath a fragile frame, and possessed of a haughty and cold intelligence, who dressed in eccentric clothes, became one of the muses of our artist. Hers was the gift of driving his imagination to exasperation. Even after many years had elapsed she still held for him the all-powerful attraction of the strange, of the unreal, of the supernatural. His Muse—perhaps that is not the right term: rather, his Friendly Demon.[65]

John E. Bowlt in his essay, "Bold and Dazzling: Léon Bakst and Antiquity," suggested that Bakst sought his inspiration for Antigone's dress in the "graceful folds and the chiton thrown across the shoulder, and at the remnants of stylized patterns in the reliefs, columns, and stelae."[66]

Jacques DePaulis also pointed to Rubinstein's ravishing appearance, commenting that many critics found her figure astonishing, surprised by her Junoesque bearing, but also some reviews criticized her lack of experience, though talented, and wrote that her voice and diction needed work.[67]

Léon Bakst, 1912. Photographer unknown. SOURCE: ALPHA STOCK/ALAMY STOCK PHOTO.

That evening in 1904, the audience comprised a very chic group, of the literary elite of St. Petersburg, as well as some of the most sophisticated theatergoers in the city. Rubinstein's Antigone, magnificently draped in Greek-designed textiles, showed her to be both alluring and accomplished. Bakst was entranced! After this remarkable debut, Bakst went to see Diaghilev to tell him about this great talent.

In a 1913 Russian publication *Solntse Rossii* or *Sun of Russia*, Rubinstein recalls,

> I had my debut in St. Petersburg as Antigone.... What a brilliant idea it was to ask Léon Bakst to do the costumes! With his austere, peerless originality the great artist eschewed the conventions and traditions that overburdened and deformed classical figures. He conjured up from the depths of time the crude and naked spirit of those ages when Oedipus cried out and Antigone wept. He gave the human figure that acute sense of tragedy that emanates from the lines of the classics. Ever since then, Léon Bakst has never deserted me. I have an artistic compact with him that is very precious to me.[68]

Perhaps it was no accident that Rubinstein chose Antigone's heartbreaking story, given her sense of isolation as a child growing up without parents. Briefly, to remind the reader, Antigone, the daughter of the deceased Oedipus and Jocasta, returns to Thebes to bury her dead brother Polynices, whose body was left exposed and uncared for on the battlefield. He had fought for the throne of Thebes with her other brother, Eteocles, who received a proper burial as he sided with Creon, the current King. Antigone dies, as does her future husband Haemon, the son of Creon, both suicides. Haemon kills himself when he discovers that Antigone has hanged herself, having believed that Creon planned to bury her alive. The story reveals the tortured loneliness of a woman's single-minded sense of justice, not only as a beloved sister, but also as a citizen of Greece, who fears the anger of the gods.

While still in St. Petersburg in 1908, Rubinstein embarked on a crazy dream, the restaging of Oscar Wilde's *Salomé*, with none other than Vsevolod Meyerhold as director, and with her friend Bakst as scene and costume designer. She implored Michel Fokine to help her train so as to be able to execute his choreography believably in the dance of the seven veils. In Konstantin Rudnitsky's biography of Meyerhold, he quotes Fokine, who believed that "something unusual in the Beardsley style could be done with her. Slender, tall beautiful, she was interesting material from which I hoped to sculpt a special stage image."[69]

In the intriguing Garafola collection of Rubinstein's missives, some of the letters referred to Rubinstein's courageous decision to perform the role of Salomé. For example, Léon Bakst excitedly wrote Meyerhold that the costumes for *Salomé* were well on their way to being finished. He also had the models for the Jewish musical instruments and wanted to meet at Rubinstein's for a discussion about the play.

Rubinstein writes Vera Kommisarzhevskaia in August 1908,[70] apologizing for her late reply, explaining that she had just returned from Berlin. She is terribly excited that all is well and that work will begin in autumn on *Salomé*. Bakst will do the decors to be at the Mikhailovsky Theater for the "benefit of the Theatre Society." She expresses concern that Vera will not like the fact that Rubinstein is playing a benefit performance in costumes and scenery that will be used later for *Salomé*. She tells her, "I am infinitely happy to play Salomé for you. I so love her. Now I am studying dance in general, so that in the autumn, if need be, I can more easily work on this or some other dance."[71] We see once again Rubinstein's consummate ability to gracefully manipulate people to do exactly what she wants.

In another note to Meyerhold,[72] she asks him if he might write Samoilov to see if he would be interested in acting a role in the play. "It seems to me that a letter from you would have a stronger effect than if I were to write him." But she notes that he should do what he thinks best, and asks him, "Is there someone still in Petersburg who, in your opinion, could play Herod?"

To Meyerhold again[73] Rubinstein reveals that she is looking for Dal'skii's address and found out that he is in "hiding from the investigation and from the court," and that this person gave his word of honor to keep silent. But she says, we should proceed without him as he's "an unbearable fellow, they say." She is on her way again and wants to see him before her departure. We do not know Dal'skii or why he was hiding but he must have angered the Czar or his underlings.

Bakst writes to his wife that "Affairs in Paris will happen in autumn or spring, but now there is nothing fixed." He tells her, "La Belle Rubinstein will go to Sorrento to study with Fokine, while Fokine wants to go with Seriozha [Diaghilev] and me through Greece to the Crimea." Bakst says that he knows only one thing, and that is that he will travel with Nijinsky and Seriozha to Venice.[74]

Diaghilev's support for Rubinstein's fearless performance of Salomé certainly had its consequences in conservative Russian society, having been banned by the Holy Synod. Apparently, the scandal must also have

russian beginnings   33

reached the ears of Czar Nicolas II and challenged the futures of Fokine, Diaghilev, and Rubinstein. Several years earlier, there were consequences when Diaghilev sided with dancers in a conflict with their administrators. "Diaghilev's open support for the striking dancers in 1905 had also caused irritation. Homosexual entrepreneurs, blasphemous Jews, mutinous dancers—grounds enough to make Nicolas withdraw his support financially."[75] In a very real sense Diaghilev, Fokine, and Rubinstein had to find their futures outside of Russia.

In 1908, at the time that she was planning her performance of *Salomé* in Russia, Rubinstein paid a portentous visit to her sister in Paris. When she displayed Bakst's sketch of her skimpy costume to Dr. Lewisohn and his wife, Irene, her sister, they were astounded and abashed by what they believed was the indecency of Bakst's design for her; they thought she had lost her mind and subsequently had her admitted to a mental health clinic at Saint Cloud to recover her senses. Dr. Lewisohn, as a well-known professeur and doctor of psychiatry at the Sorbonne in Paris, evidently was infuriated by Rubinstein's brashness. After a short confinement at the hospital, she was released, and despite this incarceration she had no doubts about what she wanted to do and did it. She returned to St. Petersburg where she gave performances that put her on the path to an unparalleled career as an actress and a dancer. The shock of being treated so shabbily convinced her that she needed to avoid, even disdain, her family and marry in order to perform. The irony of marrying a person in her own family cannot be ignored. That decision would bring her the freedom to live as she wished. This horrific experience of being forced into a mental asylum where she received a course of sleep therapy permanently turned her against her family. Her first and only marriage to and divorce from Vladimir Horwitz, her cousin, remains a bit of a mystery. Unfortunately, I've been unable to retrieve any more facts about their arranged marriage. Rubinstein ardently protected her private life, especially any letters or documentation; her secretary intimated that Rubinstein burned all letters concerning her intimate relationships before she died.

The role of Salomé obsessed her. Soon after her unfortunate marriage to Vladimir Horwitz, she decided to dig into the atmosphere of the character by traveling to Palestine: "At twenty-two years old, having been married for a few days, she crossed the Syrian desert in order to reach her destination, Palestine.... There a Syrian Prince was so captivated by Rubinstein that he would offer the ultimate, he would give his gold watch and chain! The offer was graciously declined."[76]

Ida Rubinstein portrait, 1910. Photo by Manuel Frères. SOURCE: JEROME ROBBINS DANCE DIVISION, THE NEW YORK PUBLIC LIBRARY FOR THE PERFORMING ARTS, ASTOR, LENOX, AND TILDEN FOUNDATIONS.

In St. Petersburg, in 1908, when she acted and danced the role of Salomé from the drama by Oscar Wilde, it was a daring and unconventional choice, especially for a Jewish girl; despite the criticism and the censorship, she prevailed. The Russian Orthodox Church's Holy Governing Synod, which functioned as the state Censor, banned *Salomé* as sacrilegious. But Rubinstein was not deterred—she was able to pull strings, and though the actors were forbidden to recite Wilde's lines on stage, it was a sensation. Since Rubinstein was a first-rate mime, Bakst suggested that they do the whole production in mime. The plan went ahead and was a genuine triumph. Michael de Cossart describes the exotic and spectacular character of Rubinstein's performance.

> Never before had the St. Petersburg public been treated to the spectacle of a young society woman dancing voluptuously to insinuating oriental music, [c[omposed by Glazunov] discarding brilliantly coloured veils one by one until only a wisp of dark green chiffon remained knotted round her loins. (Although, as Alexandre Benois revealed, this "final and reprehensible moment of the dance was dissimulated by means of a lighting trick."

Sjeng Scheijen recounts how Rubinstein entreated Michel Fokine to teach her to dance in preparation for her Russian *Salomé*. She also implored Bakst to design costumes for the performances she staged. As a dancer she lacked classical skills, but her body language was unusually expressive. "On 20 December 1908, in the main auditorium of the conservatory, she performed the dance of the Seven Veils to music by Glazunov. Alexandre Benois was most impressed: 'To achieve her artistic aims she was prepared to test the limits of social tolerance and even decency—indeed to go so far as to bare herself in public.'"[77] Rubinstein would have no qualms about unveiling her body, having a deep sense of pride in the beauty of her arms and legs, perhaps inspired by the actress Maud Allan, who performed her *Vision of Salomé* practically nude in 1906. Dr. Davinia Caddy, music and dance lecturer, wrote of the presentations of *Salomé*,

> Barefoot and un-corseted, Salomé was a prime vehicle for self expression, associated with just the sensual movement and ambiguous, transformative power the dancers sought. Moreover, her Judean identity encouraged the connection between Orientalism and modern dance that would later influence not only the development of the style, but also fan-magazine and Hollywood iconography.[78]

Caddy also remarked on the singular importance of three different Salomés: "the American Loie Fuller, of silk drapes and flashing lights; the enterprising Rubinstein, a kind of fin-de-siècle Russian Cher; and the Canadian Maud Allan, supposed sex fiend."[79]

Ready to amaze her neighbors in St. Petersburg, "She celebrated the dance of the seven veils as a scene of disrobing described by contemporaries as highly risqué.... Rubinstein fanatically rehearsed with the greatest care every detail of her physical presentation as a femme fatale. The critics were impressed—some by her spectacular performance, some merely by her mysterious and erotic presence."[80] Mystery was part and parcel of an actress's sexual attraction.

With Bakst as the designer for sets and costumes, Meyerhold enacting stage directions, Fokine doing the choreography, and Alexander Glazunov who composed the music for the dance, all of St. Petersburg was poised to receive this remarkable production, and even more so after the Russian Orthodox's Saintly Synod banned its spoken performance. Finally, Rubinstein outfoxed them. As Bakst suggested, she performed the play without one word spoken, while the audience read the text in the program. Originally, the play was to be performed at the Theatre Mikhailovsky but was moved to the large room of the Conservatory on December 20, 1908. With all the changes, despite the questionably negative publicity, it was a resounding success. Oscar Wilde would have been disappointed that his prose was not intoned as he wrote the play in French for Sarah Bernhardt. "When Wilde asked Sarah how she would do the dance of the seven veils, she replied, with an enigmatic smile, 'Never you mind.'"[81] Salomé's dance took place but the famous plate with St. John's head was presented with nothing on it! People had to imagine that the head was there. Rubinstein's scintillating production of *Salomé* offers clues as to how the public chose to view the issues future critics would have with her Jewishness.

CHAPTER TWO

On the Way to Paris, Far from Her Home, and Stardom

AT THE SAME TIME AS PLANS FOR *Salomé* were stirring, larger aspirations gripped the team surrounding Diaghilev that would have profound implications for Rubinstein's next step in her career. A letter from Michel Fokine to Alexandre Benois engages in a discussion about composers for ballets planned for Paris. Benois was staying at the beautiful Italian resort Isola Bella, while Fokine rhapsodized about the village of Caux in Switzerland.[1]

Fokine expresses his joy visiting this little town, Caux, where he seems to revel in the relaxation and beauty of the place. He explains that he can't join Benois, as he's busy working with Rubinstein every day for her St. Petersburg production. Fokine goes on to criticize Benois's interest in the composer Nicolay Tcherepnin who was Benois's nephew by marriage. Tcherepnin eventually did conduct the first Paris season of the Ballets Russes. Fokine confesses, "I don't have a good feeling about him." And it is difficult to "fantasize, to get carried away where there is no trace of sympathy in the man."[2]

Tcherepnin was apparently disturbed by much of the libretto for *Pavillon d'Armide* and, "protested against our plans for the last scene, fought with us about the dramatic climax, wanted to change the whole fate of unhappy René de Beaugency, only because he was too lazy to write a few pages of music." René de Beaugency was a character danced by Michel Mordkin a year later in Fokine's *Pavillon d'Armide*. Not a very happy collaboration! Fokine retorts, "But maybe we can rouse even Glazunov, who would be first rate. Not long ago Glazunov wrote the music for Salomé's dance.... I am in ecstasy over it." Fokine ends the letter with a little admission, that "Here it is a little boring. There's nothing except three hotels, two of which stand empty, and only at ours is there any life."[3]

Fokine writes to Benois once again after he hears Benois's offer to organize with the help of Diaghilev, a season of Russian ballet in Paris.[4] A meeting took place during which Diaghilev, Fokine, and Benois were to discuss the 1909 season. Fokine assures Benois that he is fascinated by a Paris season but has to remain in Switzerland for a number of reasons, one of which is his dedication to Rubinstein, "who is living apart from her husband, to go away for three days and leave her without lessons is awkward."

Fokine also complains about not being able to gain weight and is on a strict regime that he hesitates to break if he left Caux. He asks Benois to have the meeting without him, if it is possible. Then he ponders the difficulty of producing a new season with new ballets, rehearsing old ballets and getting the "rowdy troupe decent," which of course he would be ready to embark on. He then explains how Diaghilev could get to Montreux Switzlerland, where Fokine might meet him, and once again tells him how much he'd love to see Benois, but he has no desire to travel.

IDA RUBINSTEIN IN PARIS

It comes as no surprise that Rubinstein jumped at the chance to move to Paris and work with Diaghilev and his colleagues in 1909. The political and economic situation in St. Petersburg and Russia had upended her world earlier, while she was studying acting at the Moscow Conservatory. In 1905 the country was reeling from revolution that began with a seething anger on the part of workers against Czar Nicolas II, as well as military mutinies. Following the loss of their war with Japan in 1905, and their shame when they lost one battle after another, something began to fracture within the fabric of Russian society. In St. Petersburg, "They had not forgotten Bloody Sunday, the nightmarish day of January 9, 1905, when guards, cavalry units, and police attacked a peaceful demonstration by Petersburg workers. That day almost 150,000 people had marched from various parts of the city to the Winter Palace."⁵ The Czar escaped to his country residence, but when the crowd approached the Winter Palace, the order came from the guards to fire on the people and perhaps as many as thousands died. Strikes paralyzed the city, factories closed, the stock exchange ceased, and schools and pharmacies shut down. It was a dress rehearsal, as Lenin stated, for the 1917 debacle. For Rubinstein and her family, the social disruption from the violence must have been devastating. Rubinstein was ready for the City of Light.

By the time that Rubinstein was invited to Paris, she had already constructed a fully developed strategy for the theater. In addition, she enriched her understanding of movement for the theater with Meyerhold and Fokine working assiduously on her stage and dance technique for her role in *Salomé*. Rubinstein's intellectual life was rich in its questioning and exploration of the meaning of performance, and especially her own place in the making of stage experiences. Though her letters tended to deal with practical aspects of her work, she gave interviews and lectures of surprising depth and insight. Even her youthful outbursts about the purposes of theatrical plays indicated a thoughtful and serious thinker. She loved talking to the young women in her audiences, and to ordinary people who knew that she was an amazing star. She lived very much in the swim of late nineteenth century writings on dance and theater, reflecting on the exhilarating tones of Nietzsche from his *Birth of Tragedy*, the *Gestamkunswerk*, or the total theater of Wagner, as well as the Symbolist, mystic beauty of essays on dance by Stéphane Mallarmé and Paul Valéry.

After *Salomé* the rather narrow world of St. Petersburg life opened up for her when Léon Bakst lured her to Paris and she never looked back. In the next years after her stormy affair with Volynsky, Rubinstein performed starring roles with Diaghilev's Ballets Russes, *Cléopâtre* in 1909, then Zobéide in *Schéhérazade* in 1910, both choreographed by Fokine. Fokine's marvelous sense of expressive movement for *Schéhérazade* drove the dramatic plot based on a story from the Arabian Nights. Nijinsky danced with "supple savagery"; while "Rubinstein as his haughty seductress moved with feline voluptuousness exquisitely carnal even by her standards."⁶

Rubinstein's experience attending the ballet at the Marynsky Theatre awakened her understanding and passion for the needed changes that the Ballets Russes fomented. The glorious classical ballets of Czarist Russia by Marius Petipa and Peter Tchaikovsky received a crushing blow when the Ballets Russes performed for the first time in Paris in 1909. Serge Diaghilev, the artistic director hired Léon Bakst to create the sets and costumes of extraordinary color and lush designs. A series of ballets created by Michel Fokine and Vaslav Nijinsky upended traditional attitudes toward formulaic ballet phrasing by filling movement with modernist gestures, angular and dissonant qualities. And these strategies were inspired by groundbreaking music composed by Igor Stravinsky, Claude Debussy, and Maurice Ravel. A riot ensued during the 1913 opening performance of Stravinsky's *Rite of Spring* and a tumult occurred after the curtain went down on Debussy's *Afternoon of the Faun* after Nijinsky last erotic movement. Rubinstein's brilliant movement and sensuality was seen as a timely contribution to the Ballets Russes's fame and fortune.

In the French journal, *Danser,* Marcel Schneider (1998) wrote pointedly about Rubinstein's remarkable opening performance as Cléopâtre on June 2, 1909, at the Théâtre du Châtelet; "Rubinstein fait sa gloire."

> So beautiful was she, suffocating in her beauty, strange, enigmatic, astonishing and costumed by Bakst with luxurious apparel and jewels with which Bakst adorned her. She was no longer a Queen of Egypt, a fairy-like "Orientale," a monster of cruelty and opulence, but rather an idea of woman, a stunning symbol of dream and poetry, An Eternal Eve, temptation incarnate.... But to become a star of the first rank or grandeur was another thing. Her thin body, her androgynous allure, her pointed nose, her limited talents for the classical technique, all prevented her from rivaling Pavlova or Karsavina.[7]

Others were also struck by the sensation she caused as Cléopâtre. For example, Jean Cocteau wrote, "On her head she wore a little blue wig with short golden braids on either side of her face, and so she stood with vacant eyes, pallid cheeks, and open mouth, before the spell-bound audience, penetratingly beautiful, like the pungent perfume of some exotic essence."[8] Even Marcel Proust remarked on her sublime legs, although he meant to be condescending.

From the moment she arrived in Paris in 1909, Rubinstein knew how to attract attention. In *Bloomsbury Ballerina,* Mackrell characterizes her showiness: "An electrifying beauty, Rubinstein possessed an infallible instinct for publicity, and that summer was to be seen drinking champagne out of lilies and parading through the city with a panther on a lead."[9]

During her tantalizing performances as Cléopâtre at Théâtre du Châtelet June 2, 1909, Rubinstein's "dazzling beauty and exotic personality" rivaled

Ida Rubinstein as Cleopatra, 1909. Costume and drawing by Léon Bakst.
SOURCE: ARTEPICS/ALAMY STOCK PHOTO.

that of any cinema star, as Arnold Haskell remarked. Haskell and Nouvel tell the story about the ballet *Cléopâtre*.

> Bakst hit upon the idea that caused a great sensation in Paris—namely, her entrance in a palanquin, swathed like a mummy, and then the gradual unfolding of those veils to reveal the perfect figure. Another dramatic effect had to be devised to show the consummation of Cleopatra's passion without causing offence, and Benois conceived the now famous scene where the corps de ballet dances round the lovers with veils, making a living tent, while other dancers throw roses at them.[10]

Cléopâtre's passion surged toward her slave, Amoun, played by Fokine, whose destiny was to die after consummating his love for Cléopâtre.

Bakst landed on his idea for the designs of *Cléopâtre* that were reminiscent of his work with Rubinstein and Meyerhold on *Salomé* in St. Petersburg at the Mikhailovsky Theatre in 1908. Bowlt suggested that "*Cléopâtre* was perhaps the most harmonious of the many collaborations between Bakst and Rubinstein, the exotic dancer and whimsical impresario who, for all her caprices, never doubted the "incomparable originality" of her designer."[11]

In another fascinating description of Rubinstein's ardent performance as Cléopâtre, the writer, Vincent Cronin, emphasizes how she slowly and tantalizingly uncovers herself: "She made her entrance carried in a glistening coffer against a setting of giant figures hewn from tawny rock. Four slaves, Cocteau recalled, 'unwound no less than eleven veils from her swathed figure. The twelfth, dark blue veil Cleopatra undid herself, letting it fall with a sweeping circular gesture ... to reveal her face set off by a small blue wig from which on each side hung short golden braids.'"[12] In Nijinska's *Early Memoirs,* she recalls the stunning vision of Rubinstein as Cléopâtre: "She was slim and the etched lines of her limbs gave her an astonishing and unique individuality. With the individuality of her gestures, adaptable only to the structure of her body, one could say that she had created a Rubinstein style of gesture."[13]

It was not Rubinstein alone who transfixed Paris audiences, as Anna Pavlova, Tamara Karsavina, Michel Fokine, and Vaslav Nijinsky also appeared triumphantly in the first season of Diaghilev's Ballets Russes. But success usually also generates barbed chatter.

Benois, in a letter to V. N. Argutinsky-Dologorukov in July of 1909, voiced several complaints: "Naturally that beast Seriozha (Diaghilev) did not even bother to have (Modest Aleksandrovich) Durnov or Valichka (V. F. Nouvel) tell me his next move. Naturally he did not bother to see Kessler." Harry Kessler

Michel Fokine and Ida Rubinstein, 1920. Drawing by unknown artist. SOURCE: JEROME ROBBINS DANCE DIVISION, THE NEW YORK PUBLIC LIBRARY FOR THE PERFORMING ARTS, ASTOR, LENOX, AND TILDEN FOUNDATIONS.

kept valuable diaries, a German aristocrat and art lover who traveled widely and knew the crème de la crème of society. Benois also criticizes Diaghilev for mixing things up, commissioning a ballet in ancient style from Ravel, when he should have commissioned it from Debussy. "Where is Seriozha? Did he settle accounts? Where did the inventory end up? Here the wildest rumors are flying, the whole New Times clique, also Viktor Grigorovich Val'ter. This latest swine wrote such an odious column about the season (Vladimir Dmitrievich) Nabokov did not consider it possible to publish."[14]

Alexandre Benois was also fairly critical of the Russian writers who reviewed Diaghilev's company in 1909 and *Cléopâtre*. Benois complained as follows:

> In this column, God knows what was said about Seriozha, about Nijinsky, about the ballet, about the distortions of the operas.... This fellow orally told everybody that Rubenstein [sic] had paid Seriozha 30,000 francs for every stage entrance, etc. Then, he says the most extraordinary thing, he lambastes his own country. You cannot imagine with what envy and swinishness the motherland has greeted our triumphs. Seriozha's stock hasn't gone up at all.[15]

Then, Benois finishes with another angry quip: "In a day the *Petersburgskaia Gazeta* adds to the dirty tricks...." Rubinstein, of course, paid nothing to appear with the company, and garnered glowing accolades.

Rubinstein not only captured the attention of the Parisian public, but her subsequent role, Zobéide, with Diaghilev's company caught more admirers and chatterers, in spite of the defamatory Russian opinions that would continue throughout her life. On the September 4, 1909, there is an excerpt from the *Journal of the Abbé Arthur Musnier (1879-1939)* that includes a revealing piece of gossip. The letter describes how the poet and gallant Robert de Montesquiou became entranced with Rubinstein and became her lifelong friend. De Montesquiou was at the top of the list of "le Tout Paris," famous for his playful power and aristocratic pretentions. He became the model for fictional characters, Marcel Proust's Baron de Charlus, a licentious gay man, and Joris-Karl Huysmans's Des Esseintes, an eccentric, reclusive, aesthete.

The letter begins, "Robert de Montesquiou left my home. He told me that he was preparing to move and asked that I perform a Mass every month on the 12th for his friend Gabriel Yturri. [Yturri was his longtime secretary and lover.] He led me to Versailles and a beautiful tomb that Robert consecrated. Bees have made their honey between the wings of an angel. He wrote an article that was published in *Gil Blas* about the dance." The Abbé goes on to write that he lunched with the important salonière Mme de Caillavet and the author Anatole France.[16]

Another critic, Pierre Rantz, wrote in *Comoedia* about Rubinstein's Cléopâtre: "She gave a stunning performance with a brilliant technique. One might say that she suddenly came to life as an Egyptian goddess, with pure and aristocratic lines, a strange and harmonious beauty; she is a total poem of antique and languorous grace."[17]

There was no question but that de Montesquiou fell in love with Rubinstein as an object of beauty and a woman of great mystery and talent. He took it upon himself to coach her, to guide her every move in Paris, as he understood the role of a Parisian aristocrat and how to show her off without tarnishing her reputation. He thought it dangerous for her to continue doing "mime" roles, as he considered them unworthy of her.[18] After her performance as Zobéide in *Schéhérazade,* she realized that she could never be a true ballerina and reach the status of the Ballets Russes's great dancers. She did not need de Montesquiou's opinion about her lack of ballet training that would hinder her all her performance life. Rubinstein was truly and always more of an actress. And certainly that is why she would soon turn to acting and later start her own company. She soon had options, as some have suggested that her departure from Diaghilev was due to her new relationship and infatuation with d'Annunzio, who represented the promise of a great acting career.

DePaulis recounted the enormous effort Diaghilev expended to find funds to cover losses from his first spectacular show at the Châtelet, and to provide for the next season's new productions at the Paris Opéra on June 4, 1910 of *Schéhérazade* and on June 25th Stravinsky's *L'Oiseau de feu.*[19] In 1910, Rubinstein revived her role as Cléopâtre in Berlin before the Paris opening of the Ballets Russes. It seemed that Rubinstein had also signed a contract to perform *Cléopâtre* and *Schéhérazade* at La Scala in Milan in January and February 1911, the two ballets that made her famous. Fokine also signed a contract with La Scala as dancer and Maître de Ballet for the performances there.

A sad but interesting sidelight to the story of *Schéhérazade* concerns an unfortunate breach between Diaghilev and Benois. It was known that the scenario was probably conceived by Benois, but Diaghilev, for whatever reason, put Léon Bakst's name in the program as the librettist.[20] Could that have been because Bakst created extraordinary sets and costumes for the ballet? Garafola reminds us that Bakst was promoted to be the company's artistic director over Benois in 1910.[21]

Ida Rubinstein in a group, 1910s. Michel Fokine is in a striped suit, next to him is Léon Bakst, and next to Bakst is Olga Preobrajenska. Photographer unknown. SOURCE: JEROME ROBBINS DANCE DIVISION, THE NEW YORK PUBLIC LIBRARY FOR THE PERFORMING ARTS, ASTOR, LENOX, AND TILDEN FOUNDATIONS.

The ballet *Schéhérazade* was certainly not a lighthearted fairy tale, with its violence and eroticism. It told the story of a great Sultan Shahryar, who goes hunting and leaves his "Favorite," the beloved and beautiful Zobéide in charge of the harem, unaware that she would permit an extraordinary love fest with the women in her harem and her black slaves. Passionately in love with one of the men played by Nijinsky, the Golden Slave, she is shocked by the sudden appearance of the Sultan. He, incensed by the bacchanal taking place, brutally orders the murder of all the women and the men, as well as his precious Zobéide who dies without a scream, dignified and majestic. It is impossible not to feel the incipient racism of this scenario, which might explain why the ballet is not re-created very often. Lynn Garafola characterized it as "the height of ballet camp." She exclaimed, "With Zobéide in the arms of her Golden Slave, scimitars flash and the curtain falls on a stage full of corpses.... The Golden Slave ravished rather than courted his mistress; flaunted rather than concealed his body; loosed rather than bridled his physical prowess. Sex incarnate, Fokine's erotic primitive did onstage what respectable men could only do in fantasy."[22] At the time, perhaps because of its transgressive spectacle of sex onstage, it was a great success. Bakst surpassed himself with striking decors in brash colors. They created an atmosphere of violence and eroticism that the Paris Opéra was not in the habit of experiencing.

As for Rubinstein's role of Zobéide, Fokine established that her calm and gravitas were accomplished "with a minimum of means."[23] He summarizes her gestural strategy, "Everything was expressed with one sole pause, one sole movement, a turn of the head.... The departure of her husband displeased her and she indicated her displeasure by turning her head away when he came to embrace her.... Then she remained seated perfectly immobile while the carnage took place all around her. Death approached but not the horror or her fear. She remained immobile. What a powerful expression in the absence of movement!"[24]

Ida Rubinstein in the role of Zobéide in *Schéhérazade*, 1910. Photo by Drouet. SOURCE: JEROME ROBBINS DANCE DIVISION, THE NEW YORK PUBLIC LIBRARY FOR THE PERFORMING ARTS, ASTOR, LENOX, AND TILDEN FOUNDATIONS.

As Fokine explained, Rubinstein's talents were more a question of mime than dancing, and there was her brilliance. The French writer, Fernand Nozière observed that,

> It was impossible to imagine what Rubinstein would do when she entered the stage. By her style and her nature, she represented without any effort the inheritor of all the Oriental culture. In her clear gaze passed a secret joy when she bid her husband adieu and became the mistress of the palace. Her lips entertained a secret and perfidious smile; already her hands were impatient to seize the next pleasure.... She placed her exquisite body lying against the door that separated herself from her lover.[25]

Having attended the performance Diaghilev's assistant, Boris Kochno, spoke emotionally about the work. "Between the green partitions and the red ground, a hothouse of passion, the confused atmosphere unleashed a startling cruelty, along with heated desire and lust, even if Nijinsky weren't there, ensconced in the cushions, or agitated by the sudden leaps of a captive beast."[26]

Rubinstein's performance charisma was at its height in 1910, after her stardom in both *Cléopâtre* and *Schéhérazade*. Diaghilev realized her potential as a stage personality and invited her for the next season to consider a role in Nijinsky's *L'Après midi d'un faune* with designs by Bakst. It was well known that Nijinsky was experimenting with a remarkable movement style at odds with the classical technique, and Rubinstein was offended by what she saw at the rehearsal.

Her reaction to Diaghilev was negative, as life for Rubinstein was becoming very intense and convoluted. Lydia Nelidova, Nijinsky's lead Nymph, wrote: "Rubinstein had agreed with Vaslav (Nijinsky) and Diaghilev to perform the role of the nymph, and Vaslav had mounted his ballet with her in mind, the tallest among her nymphs and, more important, taller than he as the faun."[27] Apparently Fokine had been slighted for the jobs of dancer and choreographer for *L'Après midi d'un faune,* and this might also have influenced Rubinstein, who was loyal to Fokine and was saddened by this rejection. When she went to a rehearsal to see Nijinsky's piece, her response was as follows:

> In my part there was not a single natural movement, not one single comfortable step on stage. Everything was topsy-turvy; if the head and feet were turned towards the right, then the body was turned towards the left. Nijinsky wanted the impossible. If I had submitted to his direction I would have distorted my body and would have been transformed into a maimed marionette.[28]

Ida Rubinstein as Zobéide in *Schéhérazade*, 1910. Photographer unknown. SOURCE: JEROME ROBBINS DANCE DIVISION, THE NEW YORK PUBLIC LIBRARY FOR THE PERFORMING ARTS, ASTOR, LENOX, AND TILDEN FOUNDATIONS.

A laughable, but disturbing contretemps occurred when Diaghilev paid a visit to Rubinstein's apartment to discuss possible plans with her. The incident with her pet panther encapsulated some of the future problems they faced together. It is described in detail in Sjeng Scheijen's biography of Diaghilev.

> [Diaghilev] was wearing a large frock-coat, to which the panther, waking up from a nap, took an instant dislike. It bounded in Diaghilev's direction and he promptly leapt up on to a table with a cry of terror. This, in turn, frightened the young animal. It took refuge in a corner where it crouched, howling and snorting, its whiskers bristling. Ida thought that she would die of laughter as she picked the panther up by the scruff of the neck and threw it into the next room. Diaghilev was saved.[29]

Diaghilev never forgave her. And certainly her rejection of Nijinsky's invitation irked him as well, as it symbolized her self-assurance and independence that served her well all her career.

Rubinstein may not have appreciated Nijinsky's breaking classical rules but she too at times had her own substantively different approach to dance. Susan Jones in her intriguing *Literature, Modernism and Dance* found Rubinstein's approach to performance quite alluring and original, not only in its concentration on exceptionally interesting narratives, but also in her choice of choreographers and their original ideas for movement. "As Fokine and Nijinsky found movement far outside of the traditional ballet technique, so Rubinstein commissioned choreography that extended and expanded the classical formulas, such as *Bolero* and other Nijinska works."[30]

Jones takes the stance that dance and literature have an abiding relationship inherent in the current of modernism and she emphasizes the fact that Diaghilev's Ballets Russes affected writers deeply and used well-known authors such as Jean Cocteau. At the end of the nineteenth century, Symbolist aesthetics and writers such as Yeats and Nietzsche were valuable and influential for dancers such as Loïe Fuller, Isadora Duncan, and Rubinstein. Jones's point is absolutely on the mark, as Rubinstein felt a tremendous sympathy with Émile Verhaeran, Paul Valéry, Stéphane Mallarmé, and Friedrich Nietzsche: she would enlist Verhaeran for her *Hélène of Sparta,* and Valéry for her *Amphion (*Poetic drama/ballet) and *Sémiramis.*

AFTER DIAGHILEV: MARTYRS AND FEMMES FATALES

Rubinstein's dramatic exit from the Ballets Russes mirrored a moment of changes in the European cultural landscape that augured the advent of modernism. There was cubism, "experimentalism, objectivism, classicism (new in that it was a reaction to romanticism) as well as influences as diverse as primitivism, exoticism and folk and ancient cultures—began to permeate all the art forms."[31] No doubt that Diaghilev's project promulgated many aspects of this new ethos. He hired many modernists including Stravinsky and Picasso. Rubinstein's sensibility and affinities advocated Symbolism in its theatrical expression. Perhaps that veering away from what the future would destine was her attempt to hold onto outmoded ideas. But she was to some extent in synchrony with her audiences, who also adored the poetry of d'Annunzio, soon to become her poet laureate.

Robert de Montesquiou, the beautiful gay aristocrat who frequented everybody of any cultural status, knew exactly what he was doing when he introduced the Italian poet, Gabriele d'Annunzio to Rubinstein. It became a lifelong friendship, not a romance; but they were totally in sympathy with each other. Several descriptions of their first meeting, one that is slightly absurd and apocryphal, was d'Annunzio going backstage after watching her perform and falling on his knees and kissing her feet, and then progressing all the way up to her thighs.[32]

The truth is that de Montesquiou brought them together, knowing that Rubinstein could serve as a fascinating muse for d'Annunzio, and that d'Annunzio would become enamored of her. De Montesquiou met d'Annunzio when he invited d'Annunzio to the "Palais Rose" outside Paris in Vesinet, where the most fashionable and outrageous Parisians gathered to dine. D'Annunzio was not truly in love with Rubinstein, rather he observed in her demeanor qualities that brought to mind his haunted memories of the early Christian martyr, Saint Sebastian, a theme that had long fascinated him. D'Annunzio's affairs were legend; at the time, he was running away from Nathalie de Goloubeff, a beautiful actress and woman about town. Paris was awash in illicit relationships; sexual freedoms abounded and the prospect of Rubinstein playing the alluring role of a male Saint piqued the interest of both men and women.

At this key moment in Rubinstein's life, she also consorted with and befriended some very unusual women. The beginning of the twentieth century witnessed an amazing event, the emergence of "Paris-Lesbos," a hidden and mysterious subculture, many of whom came from the highest echelons of society. This extraordinary group of Left Bank lesbian artists and writers included Liane de Pougy, Élisabeth de Gramont, Radclyffe Hall, Una Trubridge, and, of course, the lynchpin of the group, Natalie Barney, with whom Romaine Brooks had an enduring affair. Rubinstein also fell under the spell of Romaine Brooks.

Beatrice Romaine Brooks, born in Rome in 1874, came from a wealthy American family. Her mother, Ella Waterman, inherited a huge fortune in mines and land, while her father, Henry Goddard, a major in the army, disappeared quickly from her life and died of alcoholism. Romaine suffered long periods of an existential loneliness and deep sadness. Abandoned by her beautiful, unstable mother, and morbidly sick brother, St. Mar, she was left to fend for herself practically all her solitary youth. Apparently, Ella, who revealed a perversity unknown to many a mother, also had leanings toward theosophy and unhinged magical beliefs. She rarely stayed in one hotel or country for very long. It is a nightmare fairy tale. At the age of six, Romaine's mother Ella was living in a New York hotel, planning to travel across the Atlantic, and deliberately left her daughter in the city without leaving her a forwarding address. The family washerwoman, Mrs. Hickey, took Romaine into her life in New York, though she lived in very slumlike circumstances. The child Romaine may have gone to bed hungry, but she was given pencil and paper to while away the time and find solace, preparing for her lifelong career as artist. Her mother never looked back for Romaine and viciously controlled Romaine's finances as she grew into a teen. Sent to boarding schools and ignored by her mother, she found herself in a rigidly run convent at the age of fourteen, where she tried to commit suicide; but painting remained her heartfelt saving grace. A realignment with Ella took place gradually, along with a substantial inheritance.

These early experiences shaped her distant and troubled relationships, moving often from one to another, including Ida Rubinstein. However, Brooks learned from her lesbian friends that as long as you kept up appearances, you would not be disdained by society.

> That society would tolerate unconventional behavior as long as its outward forms were adhered to.... So she took a mansion on the fashionable Avenue du Trocadéro when she moved to Paris in 1905. She employed a butler and a chef, had first a carriage and then a chauffeured car, went to the right parties, painted the right people and was presented to an English monarch.[33]

Romaine Brooks, self-portrait, 1923. Smithsonian Museum. SOURCE: AUTHOR'S COLLECTION.

These were some strategies that Rubinstein also utilized.

Soon, Romaine began an irregular calendar of lovers, notably with Winnaretta Singer, the daughter of the Singer Sewing Machine mogul, Isaac Singer. Winnaretta had been "married" to the Prince Edmond de Polignac, a gay aristocrat with whom she had no conjugal relationship. Having inherited a vast amount of wealth, Winnaretta held musicales, salons with contemporary composers such as Darius Milhaud and Virgil Thomson, playing their music and also courting the so-called beautiful people in Paris. Though music seemed to be her favorite enterprise, she was a dedicated supporter of the Ballets Russes. Brooks, intrigued by Singer who was ten years older, attended her salons, occasionally making inappropriate remarks. That was because Brooks held the opinions of the rich classes in Europe and America and did not hide her anti-Semitism. During one of these salons, she called the Jewish playwright Henri Bernstein, "un sale juif," a dirty Jew.[34] Romaine was left embarrassed and somewhat outraged, as Winnaretta was part Jewish; the event became an item of awkward gossip. Brooks painted an interesting portrait of Winnaretta despite these contretemps, and Winnaretta's lack of appeal. Singer and Brooks stayed together until their fling ceased when Rubinstein entered the picture.

In 1910, Robert de Montesquiou, ever the engaging cupid, brought Romaine to witness the erotic attraction of Rubinstein in her sensational debut as Zobéide in *Schéhérazade*. When they met backstage it was instant beguilement. Like Ida, Romaine had married for the conventional protection of their unusual life choices, but both Ida's and Romaine's marriages failed quickly. Ida became Romaine's muse, and their lives inextricably linked.

Ida Rubinstein, *Le Trajet*, or *The Crossing*, 1911. Painting by Romaine Brooks.
SOURCE: AMERICAN ART, SMITHSONIAN MUSEUM.

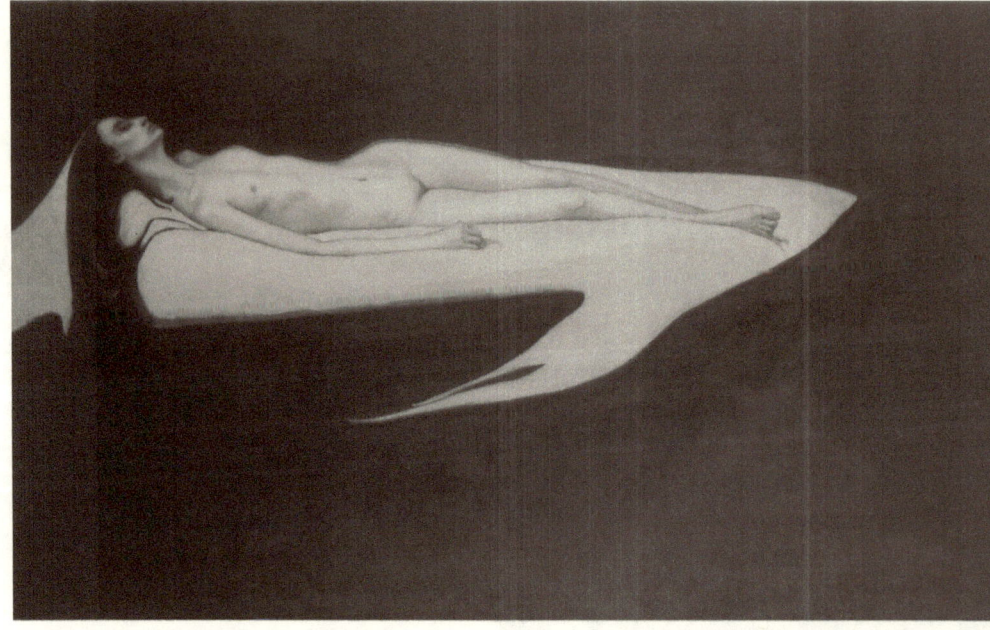

Ida Rubinstein, *Venus Triste,* or *Weeping Venus,* 1916–1919. Portrait painted by Romaine Brooks. SOURCE: MUSÉE DE POITIERS, FRANCE.

Several portraits that Romaine painted of Rubinstein have captivated spectators for many years. In the painting *Le Trajet,* or *the Crossing,* she captured Rubinstein lying on a white wing, "flying through darkness, dead or asleep. In the *Weeping Venus* too, she was dead or sleeping, incorporeal and deathly white."[35] Above all the comments on Brooks's nude depictions of Ida Rubinstein, the word *sensuality* reigns supreme: "The discreet balance between faithful representation and refined artfulness is coupled with an abundant sensuality, one enhanced by her sexual possession of Ida's body."[36] Rubinstein hated posing for her portrait; she could not hold still and found the task unworthy. The only way Romaine could carefully render the body and expressions of Rubinstein was to take photographs of her. "One can see from the photographs that Romaine took,... what intuitive grace gave such authority to Ida's slightest gesture and why all of Paris was in awe of her."[37] "For Brooks Rubinstein represented an ideal of woman, thin, slightly androgyne, with a cool appearance and a mysterious expression."[38]

While Rubinstein was working on and rehearsing for the role of Sebastian in d'Annunzio's *Le Martyre de Saint Sébastien,* Romaine became enchanted with the poet and womanizer, d'Annunzio, shifting her affections to him as long as he paid attention to her, which he did, although not for long.

on the way to paris, far from her home, and stardom

The ménage à trois with d'Annunzio, Rubinstein, and Brooks was a tangled and sometimes fraught scene. Rubinstein was enamored of Romaine, while Romaine began to pull toward d'Annunzio until he rejected her. Everything halted when the war broke out. But it was another opportunity for Romaine to paint Rubinstein.

Perhaps what startled and attracted people as World War I raged was Romaine's painting that immortalized Rubinstein as a glorified nurse in black with a white head wrap; titled *The Cross of France*; it was eventually sold to raise money for the Red Cross. Rubinstein looked sturdy and determined as she gazed beyond the town of Ypres burning in the distance; it came to be a symbol of the triumph of resistance to the brutality of the Germans. Unfortunately, Romaine's fascination with Rubinstein abated as she watched Rubinstein deepen her interest in caring for the wounded and her continuing self-absorption. Their affair waned after the outbreak of World War I.

Eventually d'Annunzio gave up his infatuation with Brooks which left Brooks free to commence an affair with Natalie Barney, the talented American poet whose Temple of Friendship at the 20 rue Jacob "was the scene of readings of works by poets killed during the war [WWI] accompanied by sweet and sad music."[39] Her salons took place from October 1909, each Friday from 4:00 p.m. to 8:00 p.m. Barney's aura of "being beautiful and a fearless millionaire from Ohio,"[40] attracted diverse and fascinating invitees. There, women could hold hands and embrace. Barney was called "Moonbeam," as her hair was silvery blonde. She possessed a summerhouse in her garden flanked by Doric columns, called the Temple of Love, which became the seat of one of the great literary salons and perhaps the most open bastion of lesbianism of the epoch. Barney welcomed Paul Valéry, Ernest Hemingway, Max Jacob, F. Scott Fitzgerald, André Gide, Gertrude Stein, Colette, and Ezra Pound. Over a thirty-year period, her long list of lovers included Colette, Romaine Brooks, Renée Vivien, Liane de Pougy, and Élisabeth de Clermont-Tonnerre. Barney was known as the "Amazone of Letters"—*amazon* in French means both an equestrienne and a lover of women; her memoir was titled *Pensées d'une Amazone*.[41] When Colette, the enormously popular woman writer, lived with Barney, she spent many hours dancing for Barney, as she prepared her music hall career. Colette also acted with Paul Poiret, the Parisian couturier for the rich and famous, in Colette's early play *La Vagabonde* in 1911.[42]

Long before Barney launched this iconic series of salons, she fell in love with Liane de Pougy (originally Anne-Marie Chassaigne). Born into a relatively poor family, and raised in a nunnery, Liane became extraordinarily wealthy from her lovers (her novel *My Blue Notebooks* recollects her affairs); she was known as a notorious demimondaine. Having danced in the Folies Bergères, she met many men whom she recalled in her novels. She was sexually liberated, and memorialized Barney in her book *Idylle Saphique* of the Belle Époque. A certain Comtesse Valtesse de la Bigne taught Anne-Marie or Liane the "profession." "Money was its goal and life-blood so clients must be rich, she must conceal vulnerability or sentimentality and must not fear publicity, reproach or blame, or voice principles, morals, or sectarian beliefs."[43] In 1899, Liane de Pougy met Natalie Barney, who was entranced by Liane's beauty and there began their "subversive display."[44]

The Sapphic group consisted of many fascinating and productive women. They initiated a cult with their outrageous lifestyles, moving from one love to another, and the exorbitant funds they spent.

> This generation of lesbians created frameworks that offered them, if not an escape, at least some play within the representational bounds of femininity. They inscribed themselves within genres such as biography, autobiography and portraiture—genres in which the codes of identity and social status have traditionally taken form. Lesbians modified the conventions of these genres in radical ways.[45]

One reads a great deal about them and their association with Romaine, Natalie, and to some extent Ida. Barney's many dalliances included Renée Vivien (Pauline Mary Tarn) and Élisabeth de Gramont, the Duchess de Clermont-Tonnerre. Vivien's mother was Hawaiian and her father was Scottish, and Vivien's appearance as a sweet, innocent, and charming young lady betrayed her intemperate life spent in and out of affairs. Everything about her intrigued her friends, although she claimed to wish for her death to find peace. She had the linguistic knowledge to translate Sappho into modern French (1903) and traveled with Barney to Lesbos to resurrect a women's artist colony. Unfortunately, Renée was addicted to alcohol and drugs and died of anorexia at the age of thirty, weighing sixty-six pounds. She became Natalie's daunting lover, as she overwhelmed her with flowers and poems that were unbearably sexually explicit. "It is tragic, since she had a poetic gift which might have deepened had she matured."[46]

At the same time (1910) that Romaine met Ida, Natalie Barney was introduced to Élisabeth or Lily de Gramont, the Duchess de Clermont-Tonnerre, a brilliant intellect who wrote four volumes of memoirs and dedicated her *Almanack de Bonnes Choses* to Natalie. They fell in love and had an affair that lasted seven years. Lily was one of the first Paris lesbians to crop her hair short and wear elegant dresses and feathered hats. She sported a lorgnette and was thought to be very beautiful. When her husband, the Marquis Philibert de Clermont-Tonnerre, discovered her peccadilloes, he locked her up. But she escaped with her two daughters to Natalie Barney's rue Jacob home. "Love between Natalie and Lily evolved into a lifelong friendship with components of respect and liking."[47] Both women were free of societal restrictions and lived their lives as they pleased; Lily "voiced feminist and left-wing views, and earned herself the nickname the Red Duchess."[48] Like Ida, the Duchess as well as Romaine transformed themselves into nurses during World War I, but not to the extent that Rubinstein availed herself of that painful role.

De Gramont also created the libretto for Ida Rubinstein's ballet, *Diane de Poitiers* (1934), as well as a study of Marcel Proust's writings (*Marcel Proust*, 1948, Flammarion), whom she knew quite well. When Élisabeth attended a screening of Rubinstein's film *La Nave*, she was enchanted by her acting[49] and adored Rubinstein, as she took to heart her elite fashionable style of dressing, her manners, and her home full of "calm and erudition."[50] Élisabeth de Gramont describes Ida's abode: "It is often the question of an Ivory Tower when speaking about artists. I only know one and that is the home of Ida Rubinstein where everything that reminds us of music is carefully put aside. I admire this proud tenacity."[51]

One of the most lauded and notorious of the women in this circle was the author of *The Well of Loneliness*, Radclyffe Hall. Marguerite Radclyffe Hall became "John" to her friends. She was born in 1886, a daughter of an English father and an American mother. She fell in love with an older woman, "Ladye," who encouraged her to publish her poems and to become a writer.[52] When she met the excitement of her life, Una Trubridge, they remained partners for years. Una was noted for her sartorial whimsy, in that she wore male attire and sported a lorgnette. She also fled her husband for this great amorous affair with Hall. Hall's groundbreaking novel re-creates the sort of secretive relationships that lesbians at that time had to endure and the resulting sadnesses they suffered. More than anything it makes evident their need to be recognized by their peers as serious people whose concerns and values were no different from theirs. Friendly with both Hall and Trubridge, in 1924 Romaine took a studio in London to paint Una's portrait, and to Una's dismay, it turned out to be a caricature. "Like Brooks, Hall did as she pleased, protected by wealth she had both inherited and earned from her writing."[53] This close-knit, odd, but vivacious posse of women briefly intrigued Rubinstein, but she never lost sight of her passion for the stage.

When Hitler's scourge eventually enveloped Europe, it became evident that many of these women in Paris with Jewish ancestry would be at risk for deportation. That meant that not only Rubinstein would have to flee, but also Lily de Gramont who had Jewish relatives, and Natalie Barney, who would never have admitted her Jewish heritage. At the same time there were those, like Brooks, Hall, and Barney who flirted with fascism, as did many aristocrats of the period.

The modern Parisian women with whom Rubinstein consorted before the war had much in common. For the most part they inherited huge fortunes or certainly could live very comfortably, were cosmopolitan, enjoying far-reaching travels, gourmet food, and consequential and challenging conversations. They envisioned their bodies as vessels of beauty, to be exposed, to be savored, and relished, therefore rejecting Victorian values and openly flouting middle-class boundaries around sexuality. In fact, satisfying their sexual interests was a known quality of their lives, and they freely gossiped about their latest conquests, be they with men or women. Rubinstein proved no different from these women, but she was very selective, and what she could not accept, what was anathema to her, was the wasting of time. She was obsessively laboring, thinking about her next project, and deeply concerned about the people with whom she worked and funded for her performances.

In Jacques DePaulis's biography of Ida Rubinstein, he recollected that Rubinstein is often invited to Barney's Temple de l'Amitié, but she rebuffs invitations in order to pursue her own interests[54]—"Elle s'excuse souvent de ne pouvoir s'y rendre"—although, she felt it important to be seen from time to time with these literary stars. After the war in 1917, she offered to play the starring role in a play dedicated to Natalie Barney by Lucie Delarue-Mardrus, for the inauguration of the Théâtre Fémina, *Sappho désesperée*, but the role of Sappho ultimately went to Madame Delarue-Mardrus.[55] Summing up years of difficult times, for Brooks and Rubinstein and herself, after attending Rubinstein's ballet evenings in 1928, Barney defends Rubinstein and all women: "We have all obtained what we wished for: Me, I have my salon, Romaine has become a great painter, and Ida a renowned dancer."[56]

After her sensational performances at the Ballets Russes, Rubinstein needed to discover another instrument for her talents. Her attraction to d'Annunzio depended on her astonishing sense of herself as a scintillating star,

Gabriele d'Annunzio, 1910. Photographer unknown. SOURCE: LEBRECHT MUSIC AND ARTS/ALAMY STOCK PHOTO.

an actress who wanted to create and perform in great works by formidable artists, with outstanding musical compositions that would inscribe her forever in the history books.

It was in the beginning of 1910 that d'Annunzio began to work seriously on the Saint Sebastian project, one that gained much traction after meeting Rubinstein. In a collection of letters between Debussy and d'Annunzio, the latter refers to Rubinstein passionately: "In writing, the poet cannot cease thinking about Rubinstein. Is she beautiful? She is, and in his eyes she is more than beautiful. He saw her, an image lost in the crowd of frivolous actresses in Paris, like a Russian icon in the middle of the Rue de la Paix with its trinkets. She is a fabulous being."[57]

After Rubinstein read a first draft of *Le Martyre*, she exclaimed, "I am still so moved by the extraordinary beauty that you have created for me. It must happen this spring, if it takes moving heaven and earth to achieve it."[58]

D'Annunzio responded as follows:

> There is in her being I don't know what great measure of youth, as if by a reverse marvelous calculation in the current or flow of her years. Before dancing, she is seated in silence, seated like a Sybil who is waiting for the goddess within herself or whom she hears inside herself. What sculptural and spiritual destiny crafts her like this? When she stares at me, without smiling, there is something in her more human and of such a sad gentleness. By what mysterious guise do you appear as more human while being more divine?[59]

Is he writing about his love for her?

> Do you remember? Do you remember? All the flames from the past are burning once again for my punishment. I don't know.... She stands erect beyond the dream, in the dream and she dances in the enameled room like the very rich binding of a Koran or of a sacred book from Iran. She dances, before us, absent from us beyond nature, beyond magic, beyond the music.[60]

The production of *Le Martyre de Saint Sébastien* was inspired by Medieval Mysteries or Miracle plays, combining the arts, and bringing together Christian and early images, mysticism and magic, tenderness and extreme violence, ecstasy and self-torture. D'Annunzio sought a new interpretation of religious values, in tune with the Parisian intellectual climate of the time, taking as his subject Sebastian, the young and handsome officer of the Praetorian Guards in the third century. The poetic drama that d'Annunzio skillfully imagines required that Rubinstein speak as well as move in her own unique way. One of the stunning moments were the movements that Michel Fokine created for her as Sebastian danced on hot coals, and "the mystic frenzy is at its height."[61]

Briefly, the lyric drama tells the story of Sebastian, a Roman soldier, who shoots an arrow toward heaven, but strangely, it disappears and does not fall to earth. Inspired by this miracle, Sebastian converts to Christianity. The Roman Emperor Caesar Diocletian who is attracted to Sebastian, demands that before abandoning Apollo for Christ he must prove the miracle. Sebastian dances on hot coals that turn into lilies, heals a sick woman, and when executed by multiple arrows, his soul flies to heaven.[62]

Included in the papers and letters of Rubinstein is a contract dated early 1910 between Jacques Rouché, at that time the director of *La Grande Revue* and Gabrièle d'Annunzio, author of the play *Fedra*, as the contract indicates, that will be presented at Rouché's theatre in French and will not be played anywhere else. Letters followed asking d'Annunzio to sign documents allowing for this play to go forward, as well as a letter criticizing d'Annunzio for not sending the play to be translated in time.

During the summer of 1910, Rubinstein traveled extensively, even to Africa, but stayed in touch with d'Annunzio. Since she hadn't heard from him, she feared that he would shift the role of Sebastian to another actress. Such was her wealth that when traveling afar, she always took with her a large staff, and tents with kitchens, bathrooms, and reception rooms.

In October or November, d'Annunzio moved to Arcachon, a quiet hideaway on the ocean near Bordeaux, suggested by Romaine Brooks to escape from the hurly-burly of Paris. In order to completely extract himself from the world, he takes on a pseudonym, Guy d'Arbes, and it is to Guy that Rubinstein writes on November 9, 1910. She thanks him for the books he sent her and goes on to inform him about some collaborators, Calvocoressi and Ducasse, and to let her know if they please him. Calvocoressi is a musicologist and critic who introduced d'Annunzio to Roger Ducasse, a young composer, and a student of Gabriel Fauré.

To Romaine Brooks's and d'Annunzio's retreat in Arcachon, Rubinstein arrives, covered in chiffons by the House of Worth with an enormous hat and feathers, hoping to hear more about the play. D'Annunzio read some lines from Sebastian that totally excite her and prove to her that d'Annunzio was the genius with whom she would tie her hopes for another sensational stardom. "As a present she took d'Annunzio a tortoise with a gilded shell. She practiced shooting arrows into pine trees, courted his approval of her

Ida Rubinstein as Sébastien in *Le Martyre de Saint Sébastien*, 1911.
SOURCE: THE CHRONICLE/ALAMY STOCK PHOTO.

performance and resisted his weak attempts at seduction."⁶³ It became clear that he was not really interested in her as a lover.

On November 10, Léon Bakst sent him copies of his designs, "far from being complete," as there will be five changes of decor and 500 costumes, an extraordinary number in the cast. Bakst then, in his letter to d'Annunzio, documents his biography, a kind of narrative résumé proving his credentials that includes some very interesting insights.⁶⁴ Although Bakst's credentials were impressive, he felt the need to impress d'Annunzio with further proof of his value because he perhaps suffered a slight insecurity.

Bakst was drawn to study in St. Petersburg as it represented the height of a diverse and cosmopolitan culture, but even after Bakst achieved some success as a painter, "he was denied a residency permit there because of his Jewish lineage. Perhaps his 'Orientalism' was part of a complex personal quest for self-perception, one combining ethnic and idealogical Jewishness, cultural Russianness and universal Europeanness."⁶⁵ Indeed Bakst symbolized the height of cosmopolitan chic, flaunting his singular talent for the exotic.

Bakst reveals that as a young artist he went against the grain of his teachers in St. Petersburg and ran to Paris to study with a Finnish Artist Albert Edelfeldt, "très honnête et très sage" ("Very honest, and very wise"). He taught him to think clearly and how to use pen and ink. Bakst said that gradually he developed his own colorful style, "more sensual, more vibrant, more sincere." The heart of his credo lies, he writes, in his search for the "most intense feeling of the work, I love the passion of color, and of form, of opulent textures and materials, gold and diamonds, and "I am driven by such an ardent desire to reassemble the most violent contrasts in order to obtain the impression of such richness and astounding passion."⁶⁶

In his appeal to d'Annunzio, he sums up: "Here are the elements that I adore: imperial color, beautiful and sensual shapes, blood, the odor of perspiration, the voice strangled by emotion, spectacles of profound, anguished emotions, and pride in the beautiful and splendid flesh."⁶⁷ These words perfectly describe the brilliance of his rich designs.

Soon on November 12, Rubinstein insists on the importance of using Debussy as their composer, "*frère*," and that she will definitely try to reach Debussy and have him meet d'Annunzio without brusquely taking him away from his work.

More pressure is put to bear on d'Annunzio. She writes on November 13 that she has to see him immediately as she leaves in the next days. "Please come today between 7 and 8 p.m., or tomorrow the same?

At the same time that she is desperate to receive the script of *Le Martyre*, she informs d'Annunzio that she is negotiating with various people to have them coach her acting, a certain Jeanne Julia Bartet and another coach, Marie Samary. Rubinstein knows the importance of guidance and training, especially when she is preparing a major role and wants to appear her best in the city of Paris.

Her chasing after d'Annunzio must have been terribly frustrating. She writes him that she is very chagrined not to have news of him, and not to know when he will be coming to visit her. "I have such a burning desire to see you and to hear you tell me about Saint Sebastian so that you can explain all that I am reading in order to 'know everything' and to prepare myself for our work and to enter into a state of grace."[68] She tells him that she's made all the exterior arrangements, that she signs for the theater with Gabriel Astruc tomorrow, but that the question of music "me tourmente." "Please write, my brother, to let me know that you are coming and that you will bring peace to a soul in pain."

By December 1910, Rubinstein returned to Paris to install herself in the opulent suites of the Carlton Hotel. "I am here in Paris. It is the idea of the young Saint that brought me here. I have only one desire. That is to play your Saint Sebastian.... It is my life." She addresses d'Annunzio as her *frère* and gives him notice of who she is seeing to move him to write the drama. In particular, she writes, "Let me know if the beginning or middle of May are of interest. I prefer the beginning ... I saw Rigaud. Everything is arranged very well. Your brother who is happy."[69]

It seems d'Annunzio will finally arrive in Paris. Debussy will also come, and Bakst will be invited as well. She indicates that she adores "la beauté, inouïe," "the incredible beauty," that he has sent her and that this production will take place in the spring, even if it is necessary to bring heaven and earth together?" Again, on the letterhead of the Carlton Hotel, she asks d'Annunzio if he wants another composer, Schmitt (Florent, winner of 1900 Prix de Rome) to be there in case Debussy refuses the job. She wants to meet with the producer Astruc, but thinks it would be better if d'Annunzio were there as well. In her invitation to Astruc, she thanks him for the "renseignements," the information he gave her on the Isadora Duncan school. There would be no better friend than Isadora if Rubinstein were to take an interest in her work. Apparently, Rubinstein met Isadora Duncan when Duncan was performing in Moscow in 1905, but to Rubinstein's chagrin, she was rebuffed and chased away, even though she was an aficionado and absorbed much of Duncan's free-body philosophy as a young student.[70]

Finally, Claude Debussy's wife sent Rubinstein a telegram to say that they would be there, "quoique souffrante" ("although suffering"). It is then Astruc's turn to write d'Annunzio to invite him to the Café de Paris, where the hosts will be Debussy and his wife. Rubinstein responds positively, adding that she will transmit the invitation to Madame de Goloubeff.

On December 11, 1910, Robert de Montesquiou contacts d'Annunzio, thanking him for giving him a name that connotes "tendresse et le convenable respect," and as well, Robert tells him that he must remain invisible, especially for d'Annunzio. This no doubt refers to the shocking fact that d'Annunzio owes enormous amounts of money to his creditors and has fled Italy to Paris to avoid them and to hide there. De Montesquiou alerts him that he will bring him to attend a special occasion that "peut servir notre cause" and that can serve our cause. "However, to be clear, one does not serve d'Annunzio, one honors him, so I say, Votre Robert."

Included in this correspondence is an interesting invitation that was sent to the acolytes of d'Annunzio, a "causerie" or discussion about his novel *Forse che si, Forse che no* (Maybe it's yes, maybe it's no), with the participation of the actress Madame Jeanne Julia Bartet from the Comédie Française on December 13, 1910, at l'Hôtel de la Revue "Les Arts" in Paris. Since it seemed that René Blum worked on a translation of this book, I wonder if Blum were not one of the invited.

The notes traveling back and forth are now occasionally via pneumatique, in December 1910 from Astruc to d'Annunzio, confirming their contract and informing d'Annunzio that the formidable Debussy will also receive a contract. One of Rubinstein's short telegrams, this one from Milan to d'Annunzio on December 25, 1910, tells him to "think big," that she is working daily with Fokine, that she is "burning" with a desire to perform the work, and that Rome will be next, signed Le Frère.

D'Annunzio writes brief notes as well. In an undated letter, Dossier 17 Archives Nationales, he reminds Astruc that Gerard d'Aganné is arriving and should visit with Astruc, perhaps during one of the performances? In another letter to Astruc, d'Annunzio writes that he'd like to dine that night with Astruc so long as there are no other guests. "You know that I am incognito and in a dangerous situation."[71] He goes on to say that he'll be at "Sebastian tomorrow evening, and to please arrange everything with Astruc's marvelous facility, Cordially, Gabriele d'Annunzio."

In a following letter, Rubinstein addresses d'Annunzio as Archer, which in French means bowman or it can also mean officer. She speaks about how *triste*, or sad, she is without news from him and asks him to visit with Fokine before Fokine travels to set a ballet in St. Petersburg. She sends him her tender thoughts and signs, Le Frère.

While d'Annunzio was struggling to complete the libretto, Rubinstein went on tour to Italy. Her performance as Cléopâtre in Rome, according to Vittorio Mignardi the director of La Scala was a "succès magnifique"; everyone was enchanted and especially by Fokine's choreography! She telegrams from Milan to d'Annunzio or Guy d'Arbres that Bakst is with her and that she wants to be remembered to Debussy.

With a sort of wonderment, Rubinstein received a letter from d'Annunzio in January 1911 that ignited her tentative hopes. D'Annunzio tells his dearly beloved "brother" that he was unable to see her in Milan, that his work would have been compromised, as he could not avoid visiting his mother and then on to his home in Florence. Thus, he told her that he did what he had to do; he worked! Here, he declares, are the first and third finished acts. "There you will see the plenitude of action and you will hear the cithara (ancient Greek stringed instrument) for the too beautiful Saint. I am working every night through to dawn." "You will see the gleam of dawn like a rosy glimmer, youthful sister with warm tears. Goodbye, goodbye. I shall think about you without respite, and I love you across the flame in my spirit."[72]

As we have noted, in Professor Garafola's personal collection these letters from this period to and from Gabriel Astruc, the theater manager and producer at the Théâtre du Châtelet, discuss contracts, and there are those to and from Rubinstein dealing with issues of hiring the necessary actors for *Le Martyre*, and payments to various parties for their participation in the production. One of the most important messages is from d'Annunzio to Astruc, certainly sometime in 1911, near the premiere of *Le Martyre*. D'Annunzio repeats that the role of the emperor is terribly important and must be played by M. Max, who might also play another role in disguise.

D'Annunzio tells Astruc to visit Debussy who completed the third act, the most important section musically. "His understanding is exceptional, it is a rare joy to work with such an artist."[73] Debussy cannot be equaled in his genius. Astruc wrote back to d'Annunzio that Debussy wishes a chorus of fifty or sixty voices that would augment the cost enormously.

But there were other issues with Debussy. It was not a fertile period in his compositional life; he was working on Edgar Allen Poe's *Fall of the House of Usher* with difficulty and apparently never finished it. The prospect of collaborating with d'Annunzio, this strange poet, did not enchant him. De

Montesquiou slid by the name of the composer Debussy, to convince Emma, his wife, of the brilliance of the Sebastian project and finally on November 10, 1910, the deal was sealed. "In the meantime, Rubinstein is in constant contact with Bakst and Fokine who it seems are excited to begin work on Saint Sebastian." Astruc confided in his letter to d'Annunzio of January 20, 1911, that one of his society ladies had reservations about this performance of Saint Sebastian, "They feared it would be an affront to Christianity." Certainly, they knew the church would intervene.

Ida Rubinstein as Sébastien in *Le Martyre de Saint Sébastien*, 1911. Photographer unknown.
SOURCE: JEROME ROBBINS DANCE DIVISION, THE NEW YORK PUBLIC LIBRARY FOR THE PERFORMING ARTS, ASTOR, LENOX, AND TILDEN FOUNDATIONS.

The reviews of *Le Martyre* were mixed; the production with amazing scene changes and an orchestra with 100 and a chorus ending up of almost 200 dazzled the audience but only for so long, as the play lasted five hours; it was given only nine performances.

"Critics called it decadent, flamboyant, incoherent; they had difficulty with d'Annunzio's French verse and Rubinstein's thick Russian accent. Jean Cocteau compared her to a stained-glass figure, miraculously animated. Lily de Gramont called it 'a symphony that makes you believe in heaven because it takes you there.'"[74] Vincent Cronin reported that the show was an "item," when Le Tout Paris filled the Châtelet on the first night. "Rubinstein, in her scarab-like armour danced faultlessly through the very long work, the audience's attention being held by miracles, magic, lavish costumes and spectacular stage effects.... Debussy's score: a melodic precision, a breadth of inspiration, a boldness of colouring and accent such as Debussy has never before exhibited."[75]

At the time that Rubinstein was making a splash in Paris, de Montesquiou helped to feather the way for her career by continuing to introduce her to poets, writers, actors, and composers. She never met Marcel Proust, but, as a close friend of de Montesquiou, Proust attended her performances and in his correspondence with him wrote the following on May 23, 1911 about *Le Martyre*.

> Everything that is foreign about d'Annunzio is hidden in Madame Rubinstein's accent. But for the style, how to believe that it is foreign? How many French could write with such precision? As I always conclude by coming to your approach or opinion, I discovered that Madame Rubinstein's legs (which resemble half way those of Clomenil, and half way of Maurice de Rothschild) sublime. That for me was everything! But I found the play boring, in spite of some moments, and the music, agreeable but rather thin, quite insufficient, rather crushed by the story, and the orchestra very immense for the few farts. In the temple of the third act, I was convinced that it was the march of the little joyous ones that they were playing. But in the end, under the sun's harsh rays, after the death of Saint Sebastian, there is a beautiful joyous number.[76]

In this testy, ironic, and slightly contemptuous account, Proust delivers a crushing blow to de Montesquiou who worked on *Le Martyre* and helped d'Annunzio with the French language.

Another very important theatrical critic and writer, the future Prime Minister of France, Léon Blum carefully responded to the famous poet d'Annunzio's lyric drama, reawakening and focusing on the language d'Annunzio chose in his startling and ennobling rendering of the play. In the magazine, *Comoedia* on May 23, 1911, Blum eloquently wrote,

> D'Annunzio has ... written his drama in a language that without a hint of archaism and by a wonder of science and taste forms a kind of synoptic condensation of the resources and all the charms of the French vocabulary at various moments of its history. It is at once the language of courtly epics of the Middle Ages, the language of Montaigne or Amyot, the language of Gautier or Banville, while the usages and rhythmic sequences recall by turns the means of the chansons de geste and mystery plays, the methods of the Parnassians or the more recent symbolist poets. In the shifts of art and thought, in the imaged memories that traverse and nourish the drama, Greek evocations blend with Asiatic ones, and the Christian mystery play combines with the most modern forms of sensibility and thought.[77]

Perhaps after the production, the most appreciative of *Le Martyre* was Rubinstein herself. She declared: "How could I attempt to express the gratitude with which the heart and spirit of an interpreter overflows when a poet of the stature and genius of d'Annunzio most willingly avows that ... she has not betrayed his ideas, and that she has served his dream well.? [sic]"[78]

As was mentioned earlier, brushing off Diaghilev, Nijinsky, and the ballet world in general with *L'Après midi d'un faune,* one year later, Rubinstein decided to produce her own play and act the role of the beauteous Hélène in Émile Verhaeren's *Hélène de Sparte* on May 14, 1912, thus incurring more wrath from the great impresario Diaghilev. Surely, behind this enterprise it was no surprise to her that her dancing was not up to the technique of the Ballets Russes ballerinas, and, in truth, her Russian roots in theater cannot be overestimated. She was carefully trained as an actress and loved the written word, finding the Symbolist qualities in Verhaeren's script enticing. Ballet dancing with Diaghilev was not an option.

Along with magnificent decors and costumes by Léon Bakst, the Théâtre du Châtelet premiere of the production on May 4, 1912 had music by Déodat de Séverac, a full orchestra and dancers, the famous actor Édouard de Max as Pollux, along with what it seems from the program a hundred people, many of whom are not named. The Russian Alexandre Sanin directed the play. "Bakst's vision of prehistoric Greek archeology was drawn from the Greek sites of Crete and Mycenae.... The backdrop representing the agora at Sparta, recalls the Lion's Gate in Mycenae.... Bakst insisted that his

Ida Rubinstein as Sébastien in *Le Martyre de Saint Sébastien*, 1912. SOURCE: LEBRECHT MUSIC AND ARTS/ALAMY STOCK PHOTO.

stage designs were a personal interpretation inspired by his travels through the Aegean."[79]

Émile Verhaeren's version of the myth begins with Hélène being retrieved from Troy by her husband King Ménélas, who returns her to Sparta where her brothers Castor and Pollux reside. Having forgiven Hélène for acquiescing to her abduction by Paris and years of exile, she and the King seem to have come to an understanding and a lasting affection. But trouble immediately arises, caused once again by her astonishing beauty, with the lascivious, anomalous attentions of her niece, Electra, and shockingly her brother Castor. Even in her older years, Hélène remained seductive. Unable to control his jealous rage or his lust, Castor murders his father, Ménélas. When Electra discovers this regicide, she kills Castor in revenge. Hélène once again disrupts a kingdom, but not without retribution, as her father Zeus appears during the conclusion to the play, and tells her that she cannot find relief in her mourning or pain. She cries out, "Je veux mourir, mourir, mourir et disparaître" ("I want to die, die, die, and disappear"). Zeus, knowing how right she was, insists that she must expire and be reborn, and thus he sends her up into the sky, or Le Néant, as Verhaeren wrote.[80]

André Levinson in his *Bakst: Story of an Artist's Life,* tells of Bakst's stage craft for Hélène: "Bakst designed a bare and harsh setting for the martyrdom of Helen, who is condemned to be coveted unto death by all who come in contact with her: the ground reduced to lime, stones that have a burnt smell, heavy gates of the royal fortress, smoke of woodpiles—in short, everything in this volcanic landscape is a latent menace."[81]

Critics said of Rubinstein as Hélène: "She comes to her interpretation each evening with living sympathy. Her poses are most moving."[82] The effect of Rubinstein's bodily gestures was stunning and inspired the artist Georges Tribout to create a booklet of sketches that depicted her in various postures as the tragic narrative plays out. When viewing these sketches of Rubinstein's "poses," the influence of Delsarte seems most evident, as they are not the way a typical actress expounds her lines on stage. Rubinstein uses her arms and torso, with deep bends lurching far forward and then back, throwing her arms high up in the air as her head sinks to the ground. She presented expressions of grief that would move the most cold-hearted person. She was instinctively creating a very personal emotive language. Lynn Garafola noted that, "Rubinstein gravitated to dance when new theories of movement were beginning to transform the Russian dramatic stage. Ozarovsky, with whom

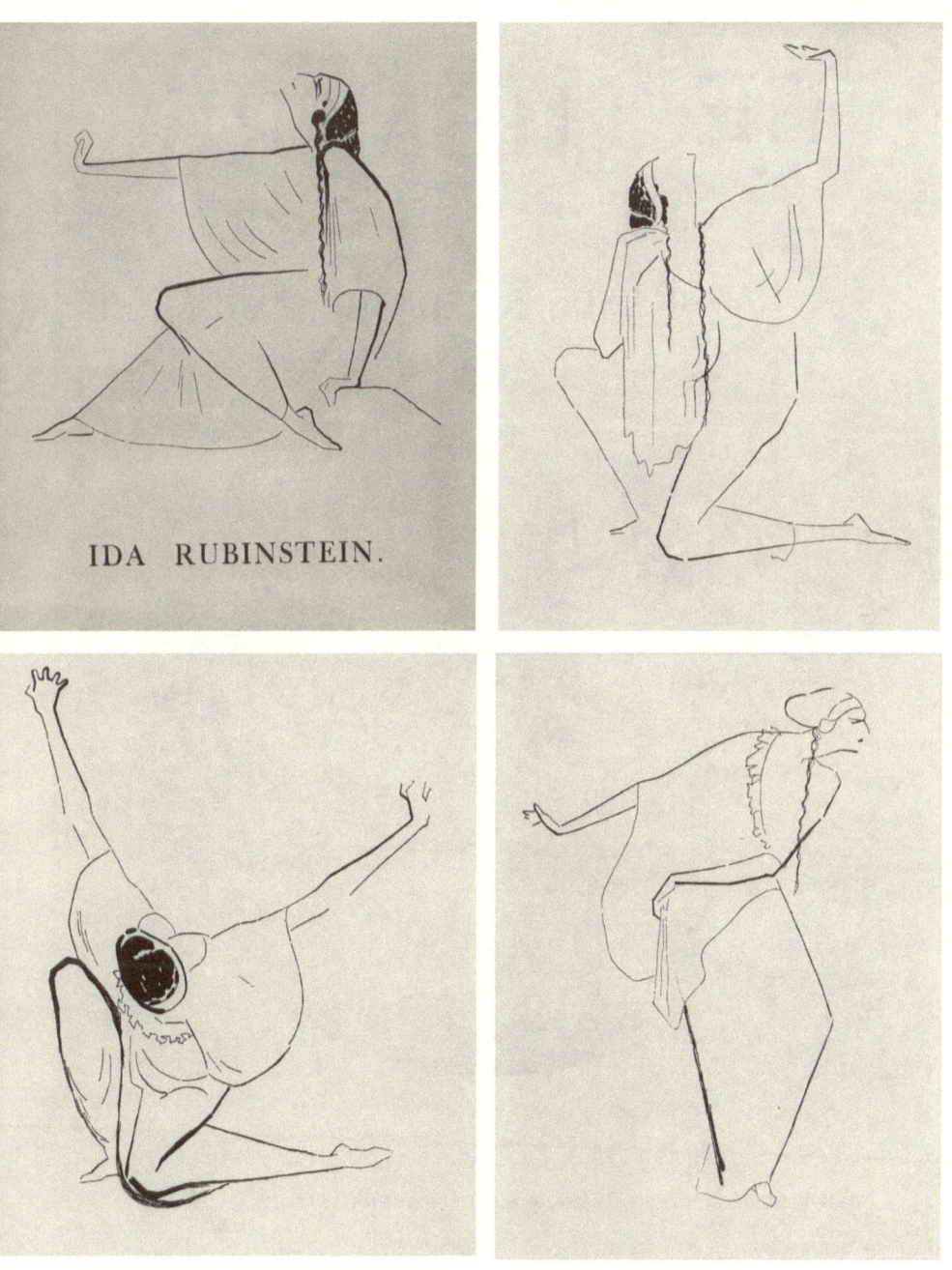

Ida Rubinstein as Hélène, 1912. Drawings by Georges Tribout. SOURCE: JEROME ROBBINS DANCE DIVISION, THE NEW YORK PUBLIC LIBRARY FOR THE PERFORMING ARTS, ASTOR, LENOX, AND TILDEN FOUNDATIONS.

Ida Rubinstein's Season, Le Théâtre, 1912. SOURCE: LYNN GARAFOLA.

she remained in contact, had lectured on François Delsarte as early as 1903."[83] Sadly, the play was only performed six times before disappearing.

Along with her singular appearances as "Le Martyre" in 1911 and "Hélène" in 1912, Rubinstein ventured to restage her interpretation of Oscar Wilde's *Salomé* again to music by Glazunov, with costumes and sets by Bakst. Once again, the Russian Alexander Sanin directed the production, at the Théâtre du Châtelet on June 13, 1912. The world was in love with Salomé. "Paris's 'Salomania' flared hotter than most. As the capital for art and entertainment of turn-of-the-century Europe, Paris was the main stopover for touring Salomés seeking to share in the choreographed blood lust.... Every vaudeville show seemed to include a Dance of the Seven veils; every hootchy kootchy dancer wiggling without underwear in some vaguely Eastern outfit was a Salomé in spirit."[84]

Wilde's play did not fare well in Paris, as the audience found it "invraisemblable" or untruthful and boring. At times the spectators were tittering and laughing at the narrative that they found obsolete. Rubinstein's remarkable attraction did not betray her, as one reviewer, Robert Flers, underscored, "She danced the dance of the Seven Veils with an audacity and shamelessness because they are hers innately, and reflect her nobility and distinction."[85]

It seemed that Rubinstein was destined to anguish Diaghilev, as the dates of the performances of *Hélène de Sparte* and *Salomé* (May 4-10 and June 12-19, respectively) coincided with Diaghilev's 1912 ballet season in Paris, thus creating another obstacle in their fraught relationship. They were scheduled to appear in the same Théâtre du Châtelet at practically the same moment; unfortunately, Diaghilev was obliged to arrange his performances earlier.

As with *Antigone* and *Hélène de Sparte*, great poetry fascinated Rubinstein. Her attraction to d'Annunzio and her respect for Vsevold Meyerhold led her to her next endeavor, the play *La Pisanelle ou La Mort parfumée*.

Never tired of collaborating together, Rubinstein and Bakst began working on d'Annunzio's *La Pisanelle ou La Mort Parfumée* commissioning the brilliant Vsevolod Meyerhold to direct the production that took place on June 11, 1913, at the Théâtre du Châtelet. Rubinstein admired his audacious and sensitive use of movement as an integral part of his dramatic strategies. Once again d'Annunzio explored the tension, indeed the clash of Christianity and obscure forms of paganism that resulted in the death of the lead character. Rubinstein's role as impresario was enhanced by her intense personality and strong will. Like *Le Martyre*, it was one of the first of her many theatrical projects involving a great number of participants that she helped to produce.

Ida Rubinstein in *La Pisanelle,* 1913. Profile drawn by Valentine Gross Hugo.
SOURCE: JEROME ROBBINS DANCE DIVISION, THE NEW YORK PUBLIC LIBRARY FOR THE PERFORMING ARTS, ASTOR, LENOX, AND TILDEN FOUNDATIONS.

She hired several hundred actors, and with the recommendation of Claude Debussy, his student Ildebrando Pizzetti was hired as the composer. Ever loyal to Rubinstein, Fokine agreed to choreograph the dances.

Rubinstein played the protagonist, Pisanelle, a beautiful, Italian courtesan brought to Medieval Cyprus for sale. She becomes the coveted object of a young King's affections; he mysteriously believes she is a holy pilgrim representing a Christian prophecy. Unfortunately, his lubricious uncle wants to make Pisanelle his private concubine. While Pisanelle is held in a convent, the uncle tries to seize her, but almost miraculously, she is saved by the King who furiously murders the uncle. As retribution, the mother of the King, angry that her son wants to wed the dancing courtesan, has Pisanelle killed by her slaves in the most dramatic scene, suffocating her with roses.

Rubinstein's role demands a very nimble dramatic approach, moving from a courtesan to a godly pious nun and then to a goddess. Obviously, Meyerhold was drawn to the choreographic possibilities of the narrative, and Fokine complied. But we have little sense of the "dance." In an article quoting Meyerhold on the dances, "Meyerhold à Paris," Gérard Abensour suggested that "The dances created by Fokine create a strong impression, although I am not totally in agreement with his conception."[86]

It seemed that Meyerhold was critical of Fokine, but we hardly know why. What we do know is that in d'Annunzio's stage directions for Rubinstein, her body, her effect in every scene, her towering presence even when not moving were astounding. Perhaps her most singular and compelling moment occurred in Act III. Preceded by a dance of the slaves who are soon to execute her, she appears before them, unsteady and wobbly as in a drunken state, she darts from one space to another, gloating and then speeding up her leaps and lunges more rapidly. Charles S. Mayer describes her in his *Ida Rubinstein: A Twentieth-Century Cleopatra*. "She appeared in a tight tunic of Parma violet, glittering with gold threads ... as she began the Dance of Perfumed Death. Then in an unforgettable sado-erotic coup d'oeil she was gradually smothered in blood red roses by slaves dressed in robes of clinging Indian red silks."[87]

Reviews were lukewarm. Most of the applause from critics went to Rubinstein. Quoted in Jacques DePaulis, Félix Duquesnel, the critic of *Le Gaulois* noted: "Her gestures have nobility, and her dance in the last act, elegant, discreet, a dance of attitudes rather than virtuosity, is moving and has reflections of sadness."[88]

Unfortunately, the Russian drama critic Konstantin Rudnitsky found the plot ridiculous and prurient.

In the first act Pisanelle was nearly naked, and she, the slave was being sold in the Famagusta harbor. In the second act the spice was that the courtesan turned out to be a saintly pilgrim. She was executed in the third act. But how? A fragrant death had been prepared; she was to be smothered in bouquets of roses that had been especially cut for this purpose by black Nubian women with golden sickles.[89]

According to Rudnitsky, the Russian critics who traveled to Paris for the occasion, purported that *La Pisanelle* was weak artistically and intellectually, but commented that Bakst created a major spectacle with incredible colors, archways, arcades, walls, sails, and pillows floating here and there. "Stupifyingly ornate and lavish," Meyerhold used hundreds of actors, making beautiful but empty poses. It was too opulent for Russian taste, even pretentious, in its effort to imitate "le style modern."[90]

A well-known Russian cultural icon, Marxist revolutionary, Anatoly Lunacharsky, found the interpretation of the play indecent, largely due to Rubinstein's influence. He describes the last ludicrous scene: "She is a dancer, and so this absurd dance finale has been devised. Then in the last scene, from backstage arrived a swarm of Negroes armed with colossal bouquets of crimson roses thrown in her face."[91] Other reviews such as in the *Russian Word,* found her mincing, simpering, and without talent, and A. R. Kugel remarked negatively that the play was a triumph of female snobbery.

French critics were less harsh. Emile Henriot in *Comoedia Illustré,* June 8, 1913, pondered how Meyerhold developed the script and score and how he used movement to evoke passions and emotional states. "According to M. Meyerhold, each of the actors must be seen as moving in a dance.... he evidently wished that every gesture be stylized, expressed in a pantomimic phrase suitable to the moment's need." Mary Fleischer in her accomplished book, *Embodied Texts,* reveals the strong movement-centered way Rubinstein played her part in *La Pisanelle,* "the crucial role that the body could play in conveying emotion and thought."[92]

On the whole, many critics testified that Meyerhold was not enchanted with the project and had no further associations with Rubinstein's productions, despite their early history together. It seems odd that Meyerhold voiced little interest in remaining in Paris, with extraordinary writers such as Mallarmé, Valéry, Apollinaire, and cubism shaking up the artistic scene.

Ida Rubinstein in *La Pisanelle*, 1913. Painting by Antonio de la Gandera for the journal *Comoedia illustré*. SOURCE: JEROME ROBBINS DANCE DIVISION, THE NEW YORK PUBLIC LIBRARY FOR THE PERFORMING ARTS, ASTOR, LENOX, AND TILDEN FOUNDATIONS.

Apparently, he needed to be in Russia to produce his work. But at that time, the Soviet authorities were against him as there was not enough socialist realism in his work, and crucially he was outspoken in his political views. One imagines that tragically, when Rubinstein discovered that Meyerhold was murdered by Stalin in 1940, considered an enemy of the country, and antagonistic to the Soviet people, she must have railed against the Stalinist gods!

Looking back on Rubinstein's Parisian years, one might say that her professional career, launched by Diaghilev in 1909, found its direction and tone from d'Annunzio's *Le Martyre* and *La Pisanelle* in 1911 and 1913; they were defining moments as she barely moved away from the large, splashy Bakst designs, the narratives suffused with mystical, mythical implications and Symbolist intentions, and always found herself bathed in the cynosure, in the light, no matter how many people were onstage.

CHAPTER THREE

The War and Benevolence

THE PERFORMANCE CAREER OF RUBINSTEIN was at its zenith at the time that World War I broke out. The war came almost by accident after the assassination in Sarajevo of the Austrian Archduke Franz Ferdinand and his wife by Serbian nationalists on June 28, 1914. This led Austria to declare war on Serbia on July 24, and Russia to respond with a general mobilization of its forces in support of Serbia, its ally. Germany then activated its army in response to Russia and on July 31 demanded that France declare itself neutral. Events accelerated; on August 1, Germany declared war on Russia, which was allied with France, and France, in turn, called up its forces. On August 3, Germany declared war on France and invaded neutral Belgium in order to outflank and bypass French defenses. The next day Britain declared war on Germany in support of its alliance with Belgium, and Europe found itself in a general war. All these momentous events caused enormous turmoil and harsh realities for those who lived through them. The tragic events of World War I penetrated every aspect of French life and culture and brought to an abrupt standstill theatrical life, as it was known before the war.

In 1914, Rubinstein had been vacationing with Romaine Brooks in Switzerland in the summer at the moment when war was declared in France.

At the time, Rubinstein was completely infatuated with Romaine Brooks, who eventually rejected Rubinstein; their affair ended soon after the beginning of the war. At the time of their affair, however, as mentioned earlier, Rubinstein's relationship with Romaine Brooks brought forth some astonishing portraits by Brooks. Brooks was captivated by Rubinstein and declared that she embodied the end of the century spirit, adding: "Rubinstein was very vain; a vanity that never surpassed her beauty." Brooks painted this odd and disturbing picture of Rubinstein, 'The Weeping Venus' (1917), which was said by Brooks to represent "the death of the old gods and the mutilations of the war."[1]

In *The Modern Woman Revisited: Paris between the Wars,* Joe Lucchesi ponders Rubinstein's relationship to Brooks and to the homosexual culture in Paris, seeing her penchant for playing travesty roles, such as Sebastian, as a titillating attraction for the Sapphic women, but also as a "dangerously gender-crossing figure."[2] Lucchesi also suggests the symbolism in Brooks's *The Weeping Venus,* her "softly lit, luminescent form lies on a moonlit balcony, head tilted to the side, several tears emerging from beneath the figure's closed lids."[3] Does this quiet, melancholic mood signal the sad demise after World War I of what was once an optimistic moment that became the heavy realization of meanness, brutality, and nihilism?

In another portrait of note, Brooks painted a glorified depiction of Rubinstein in the uniform of a Red Cross nurse, designed by Léon Bakst; it displayed her as a woman of firm conviction and determination, an angel of comfort who believed in her powers to protect and heal the sick and wounded.[4] Commenting on the painting, Brooks noted that, "Rubinstein went to war to recite poems to the soldiers at the front. My painting is a celebration for all the young women who sacrificed their careers, art and time for the battlefield."[5] It was a very different image of Rubinstein's previous extravagant, fashionable, exotic persona.

The news of the war breaking out was startling and affected Rubinstein's sensitive heart. Upon her return to Paris after her affair with Brooks, and almost immediately, she found ways to be useful, especially with her considerable financial means. For example, as Charles S. Mayer notes, "She donated four ambulances to the American Hospital in Neuilly near Paris, provided thirty beds at the Hotel Bristol for wounded English soldiers, had her own car transformed into an ambulance with which she would speed to the front lines to bring wounded soldiers back to Paris for treatment."[6]

Ida Rubinstein, portrait as a nurse in World War I, *La France Croisée*, 1914. Painted by Romaine Brooks. SOURCE: AMERICA ART, SMITHSONIAN MUSEUM.

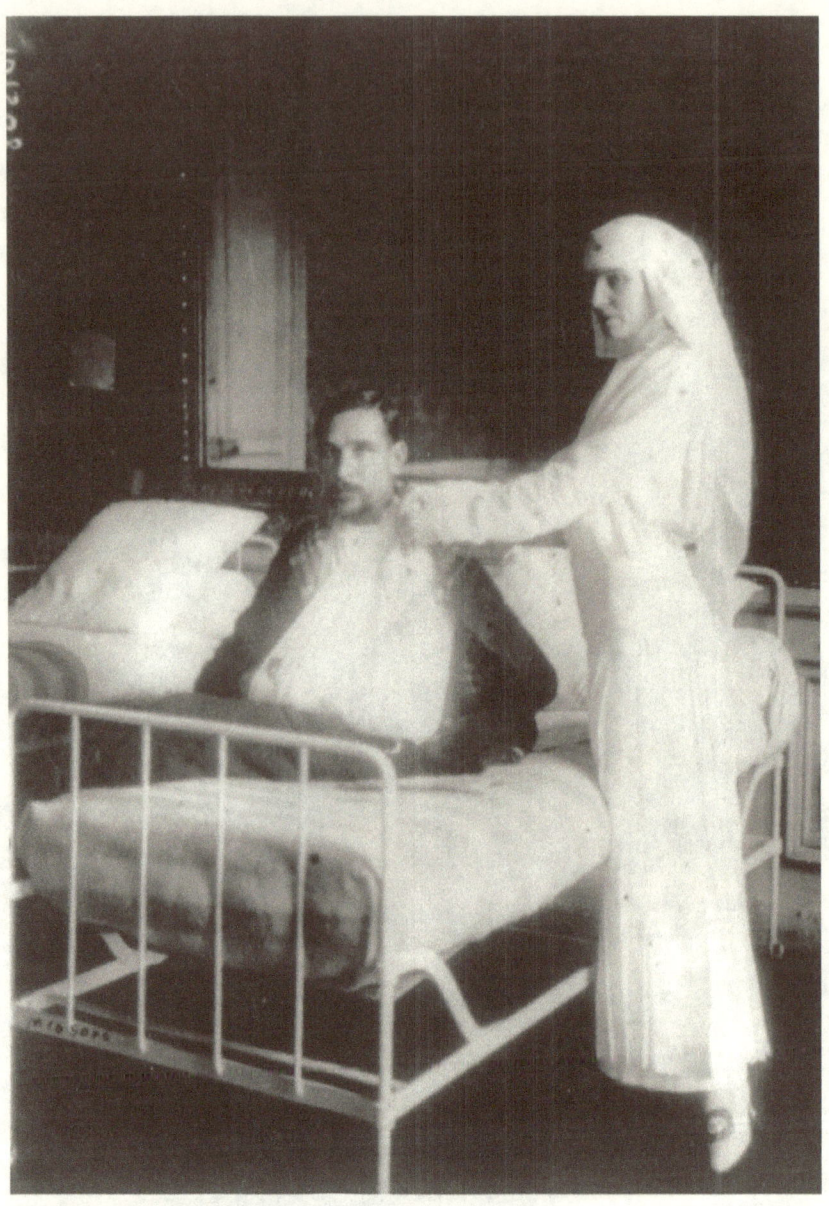

Ida Rubinstein, nursing a World War I soldier. Photo by M. Branger.
SOURCE: AUTHOR'S COLLECTION.

She remained in Paris to deal with the tragedy of thousands of deaths, trying to nurse and nourish the sick and wounded. Rubinstein threw herself into the war effort, having installed herself in the Hotel Carlton. It revealed a more compassionate side of her character.

She turned the Carlton Hotel into a hospital, to some extent inspired by the inimitable Sarah Bernhardt who transformed the Odéon Theatre into a hospital during the Franco-Prussian war in 1870. The hospital was filled with soldiers who suffered ghastly wounds, and lung and skin damage from flames and poisoned gas, suffocation, starvation, infections, and lost arms and legs. Her patients were disintegrating in front of her eyes. She read poetry and books to them, as well as letters from their parents telling them how much they were missed and how much they were loved. The injustice of this war found expression in a story that Rubinstein told, when she was taking care of a young man who lost his right hand, and the hospital had music playing in the background to assuage the patients. It was a mazurka by Chopin and the young man began to cry, because just as the war broke out, he was supposed to attend the music conservatory as a piano student. He would no longer be able to play Chopin. How the young were sacrificed![7] In four years close to 1,400,000 French died in the war. The English lost more than 600,000 troops.

Rubinstein's close friend and partner, Walter Guinness, generously helped finance the huge expenses of running the hospital at the Carlton. He was also engaged in the war effort, as a major with the Suffolk Yeomanry in Gallipoli, and Egypt.

In the Duchesse de Clermont-Tonnerre's (Élisabeth de Gramont) chatty book, *Robert de Montesquiou et Marcel Proust,* full of little, gossipy stories of the period, she insightfully states that "War offered artists the opportunity to reveal who they were."[8]

Rubinstein's lifelong champion, Robert de Montesquiou, as an old man at the time, discovered that he could stave off the solitude and frustration of not fighting in World War I by writing poetry. His poetic war elegies, *Les Offrandes Blessées* or *The Wounded Offerings,* contained, in their multiple strophes, the painful anxiety and profound exaltation of those left behind the wartime front. In spite of their unbearable sadness, they reaffirmed an instant, a nuance, an evocation of the monstrous drama. Here is an example of the first page of *Les Offrandes Blessées.*

Robert de Montesquiou, 1890. Photographer unknown. SOURCE: HIRARCHIVUM PRESS/ALAMY STOCK PHOTO.

Pale with reddening eyes full of tears, the body dressed in purple and crepe, the heart gripped in a vice, whose branches crush them. They carry an urn where floats a liqueur.

These are their tears, it is the blood of their loved ones that makes the beautiful vase feel heavier at each step,

Because the bright gravel have become rocks from which one hears an inextinguishable moan.

And these women of fright, ecstasy and prayer,

Who walk slowly in lost happiness,

Revive for us in their sad light,

Andromache, Ariane, Electre and Niobe. All four a teary quartet.

"Modern warfare with its chaos can hardly sustain a great epic poem. However, Montesquiou was able to adapt them."[9] Rubinstein declaimed the patriotic verses, really prayers of Robert de Montesquiou in the Théâtre de Sarah-Bernhardt. She offered her elegy of hope to those who attended her poetic orations wishing for a bright light to come. In a collection of Proust's correspondence, de Montesquiou extolled Rubinstein's reading of his poetry: "But there will be another artist, Madame Rubinstein who utters my verses in the most moving way."[10] During this trying time, de Montesquiou rediscovered his friendship with Rubinstein, and he remained close to her until his death. "Rubinstein caused him a little sadness, as she recited his *Offrandes* in different places, with a solemn beauty which perfectly suited the times."[11] Her readings became myth as they soothed many sullen souls.

In *Prince of Aesthetes,* Philip Jullian describes de Montesquiou's war poems, *Les Offrandes Blessées* (1914) as a collection that brings together, each in three stanzas of four lines, "offerings" categorized by the author as political, fairy tale, topsy-turvy, antique, fertile, resigned, lachrymal, boreal, hereditary sigillate, initialed, sacrificial, flagellatory, derisory, peccant, atavistic, and so on.[12] But unfortunately, de Montesquiou's pieces weren't as appreciated as he had hoped, so three years later he published in 1917 *Sabliers et Lacrymatoires,* a continuation of his *Offrandes.* They too did not receive good reviews. Having returned to his home in the Palais Rose, he tried to reconstitute his fanciful life of visits and salons.

During the war in 1917, Rubinstein enacted the role of Phèdre on the stage of the Opéra for the benefit of the Red Cross, and sonorously recited Racine's sumptuous poetry, dedicating her performance to Sarah Bernhardt who at that time was suffering from a terribly wounded and infected leg that

Ida Rubinstein as Phèdre, 1917. Costume by Léon Bakst.
SOURCE: ALAMY STOCK PHOTO.

needed to be amputated. Sarah had been traveling in the United States on tour, pleading for support for France during the war.

Robert de Montesquiou prodigiously influenced the career of Ida Rubinstein. Not only did he introduce her to d'Annunzio and to Romaine Brooks, but also to Sarah Bernhardt. In a sense he invested himself in the role of a Pygmalion, seeking to transform and elevate the qualities inherent in his choice friend, such as encouraging Rubinstein to visit the prestigious House of Worth where she soon became a faithful client.

D'Annunzio also cultivated a professional relationship with Sarah Bernhardt, choosing her to star in his plays. De Montesquiou arranged for Rubinstein to meet Sarah Bernhardt as he realized that in order to play major tragedienne roles she needed more attention to her voice, to not only work on her pronunciation, but also to perfect the phrasing and the meanings of the lyrical narratives.

Bernhardt and Rubinstein were in many ways soul sisters, despite their age difference. Both were superstars, attracting journalists and gossip columnists to their every move. In a way, toward the end of the nineteenth century, "Theatre was rapidly changing from an art form into a culture, into a culture industry with advertising, public relations and marketing as tools used to sell the commodity, be it the play, the actress, whatever."[13]

And Rubinstein and Bernhardt knew how to manipulate the forces that molded public opinion. Both women struck transgressive notes by playing male figures of grand importance, Greek gods and French historic heroes. Their beautifully lithe bodies looked tempting and sexually enticing in their male attire. Both women had Jewish backgrounds and suffered abuse and anti-Semitism from their critics and their caricaturists. What also tied them together was their lack of traditional parenting as they grew into women. Rubinstein lost her parents at an early age, and Bernhardt struggled as a child to just survive; her mother was born in the Netherlands and became a courtesan who rejected her needy child. Moving to Paris to seek more financial liaisons, Madame Bernhard put Sarah away in various pensions, and later installed her in a convent; her father was unknown. However, neither Bernhardt nor Rubinstein suffered the harsh and stultifying upbringings of Victorian parents that taught inhibitions and restraints. Their bodies became instruments of exploratory expression and fluidity onstage.

At this point in 1911, Bernhardt is sixty-seven and in full glory. She had traveled the world in triumph, with her "*voix d'or*," her "golden voice," where

the war and benevolence 91

Sarah Bernhardt, 1865. Photo by Nadar. SOURCE: GL ARCHIVE/ALAMY STOCK PHOTO.

crowds waited for hours to catch a glimpse of the divine Sarah. Bernhardt envisioned that Rubinstein should inhabit the role of *La Princesse Lointaine*, and that she would help her as she had a sustained an "amour du beau," a love of beauty. Sarah refused any payment for her work, one artist to another, regardless of the many hours they spent together. When Rubinstein and de Montesquiou were received by Bernhardt at her apartment, de Montesquiou introduced Rubinstein: "Je vous présente une rose de mon jardin," "I present to you a rose from my garden," and Bernhardt replied, "Une rose du jardin de Dieu." "A rose from God's garden."[14] At this very moment the two actresses became close friends and collaborators. The play by Edmond Rostand, *La Princesse lointaine*, interested Bernhardt for herself, as she wanted to play the travesty part, Jaufré Rudel; that would leave the lead role of the princess to Rubinstein. The project never came to pass. But their friendship endured and Rubinstein followed in Sarah's footsteps all along her career, playing roles such as Marguerite Gautier and Joan of Arc that ennobled Sarah. The critics praised Rubinstein for the improvement in the way she spoke her lines in French and the power she displayed in these roles. Rubinstein profited greatly from the careful guidance she received from Bernhardt. As mentioned earlier, in 1915 at the age of seventy, Bernhardt took a terrible fall onstage and severely injured her leg. For some reason it did not heal, and she was obliged to have it amputated, a tragic happening, as she lived for the stage. Having amassed many debts, she was unable to afford the operation. Rubinstein took over all the expenses of the clinic, while keeping secret her generosity.

But not all Rubinstein's critics believed in her beneficent and heartwarming care.

In a 1993 article, typical of former Soviet propaganda, judgmental and harsh, published in Russian by an art critic in St. Petersburg. The author not only criticizes Rubinstein's lifestyle but also takes jabs at her spectacular performances.

> When World War I broke out, both the French and the Russians lost interest in Rubinstein and her money, her hunts, her caprices. The war strictly could do without Modernism's ephemeral seductions, opposing them with the real rule of machines and technology. Rubinstein was mere flesh of the flesh of a disappearing style. After the war, whether she realized it or not, she tried to stop time, to preserve an epoch that appreciated her unusual beauty.[15]

However, this cynical and cruel assessment of Rubinstein's life and aesthetics ignored her incomparable courage during both wars, and especially the recognition given her by the French government in awarding her the Legion of Honor in 1934 and French citizenship for bravery and contributions to the war effort as she participated in the Association Générale des Combattants et Mutilés (Association of Fighting Soldiers and Gravely Wounded).

Rubinstein's colleague, Jean Cocteau, also found a way to be of service and shocked many of his performance friends when he "threw himself into the war effort in his inimitable way. He joined an ambulance unit spending much time close to the front lines, in constant danger from shellfire, dressed in an exquisite uniform designed by Paul Poiret."[16] Easily thought of as a shallow dandy, Cocteau displayed enormous bravery and was recommended for the Croix de Guerre.

Many of the aristocratic and idle rich in Paris knew not what to do and were thrown into a panic when the news came that the Germans were close to attacking Paris. Some of the women, notably Misia Sert, sought to transform large edifices into hospitals. Misia, of Polish descent, became a very close friend to Diaghilev, helping him to fund his company and staying by his side when he died in 1929. Misia was also able to form an ambulance unit with fourteen dress-shop delivery vans converted into motor ambulances, while enlisting the help of her future husband José Sert and Jean Cocteau as nurses. The ambulance procession leaving Paris is described by Vincent Cronin.

> She was at the head of the column in her large Mercedes and when the unit found and began to collect the first wounded, at Haye les Roses, Misia burst into tears.... They reached Rheims for the first bombardment and Cocteau described the much shelled cathedral as resembling a "piece of old lace." Her private Red Cross did excellent work and as the fighting receded from Paris, Misia handed over her ambulances to the Russian government which indeed was seriously short of such facilities.[17]

She and her wealthy women friends raised money for bandages and other necessities. Many simply fled Paris. The Sascha Guitrys left for Monte Carlo; Isadora Duncan fled to Trouville in Normandy and then to America. De Montesquiou, first tried to find a spot on the ship, *Venezuela,* which agreed to take passengers to Bordeaux. He spent twenty-four hours in the bottom hold, sitting on sacks waiting for the departure that never came. Finally, he found another way and went through the Hauts Pyrenées. Even if he couldn't follow strategic military methods, he profoundly sensed and followed the terrible drama. This almost sixty-year-old man was tortured by the idea of not being able to defend his country.[18]

Rubinstein's idolatry for d'Annunzio subsided during the war, with her obligations to the suffering in France. D'Annunzio was another personality who found expression in his nationalistic passion for Italy, but not by writing poetry. He returned there to fight for the Allies, became a war pilot at the age of fifty-two and participated in many perilous missions. In 1916, trying to flee two Austrian planes that bombarded him, his plane hit the ground near the Gulf of Trieste, causing severe injury to his head. He lost his right eye, but after some rehabilitation he went back to the war. D'Annunzio's activities after the war and the Paris Peace Conference in 1919 caused much consternation in the free world. He joined a right-wing party and set up the short-lived Regency of Carnaro in Fiume near Trieste, with himself as duce. He has been described as the forerunner of Italian fascism, influencing the notorious Benito Mussolini, which has unfortunately sullied his reputation.

Apparently, in late August 1919, Rubinstein flew to Venice to bring d'Annunzio a copy of de Montesquiou's poems, *Un Moment du Pleur Eternel*, and, always enamored of flying machines, "In 1925 d'Annunzio presented Rubinstein with an airplane so that she could visit him at his villa." D'Annunzio baptized her plane St. Sébastien.[19]

Not only did Rubinstein nurse the wounded during the war, but during and soon afterward she chose to put on benefit performances for impoverished Russians and for those who had fallen at the Battle of the Somme. It was probably somewhat true that she never recovered from the experience of such devastation. "She personally nursed the wounded, tended to the dying, changed the bandages on putrefying flesh, devoting all her energies to the ghastly mutilations brought into her hospital day after day."[20] Remarkably, it was not to be her last foray into the saving of lives.

the war and benevolence

CHAPTER FOUR

Between the Wars
*Fame, Some Shame,
and Pain from Losses*

SOON AFTER WORLD WAR I, in the autumn of 1921, de Montesquiou became quite ill, yet despite his fading health, he was rereading the proofs of his last poems, and cherishing the letters from the women he extolled and cared for.[1]

During this sad time, messages came from Rubinstein with the news of her voyage to Egypt. "It was in reply to Rubinstein that Robert de Montesquiou was to inscribe his last lines, on December 3, 1921: "This which will remain in your life, like the passing of a sorrowful man, threatened with not being able to bring to a successful end the manifestations of his art or the justifications of his equity. As far as you yourself [Rubinstein] are concerned, what hurt me cruelly was not to have been able to play my part in the marvelous Shakespearean conspiracy, which has set you on such a high pinnacle.""[2] Rubinstein had recently performed André Gide's translation of *Antony and Cleopatra* at the Paris Opéra.

De Montesquiou's funeral (December 11, 1921) took place at a church in Versailles, and the author Jullian describes her presence. "Rubinstein swathed in dark veils, stood as erect as a yew tree among the graves.... The first snow fell on the sheaf of orchids brought by Rubinstein. Where were the ladies who used to beg Robert to visit them; the young men who would fight for an invitation to his parties; all the actresses and the musicians whom he patronized?"[3] Only Rubinstein remained faithful to him in the end.

Despite the ravages of war's aftermath, Rubinstein never stopped performing, and continued to produce lavish productions, often with the financial support of Walter Guinness. But the huge responsibility of producing her own plays, and creating the means by which all the complicated issues came together, caused her to seek respite and beguiling adventure, and led her to travel far and wide, often to Africa as, for example, when she had written to de Montesquiou, "I am now on the shores of the lake at Bangwuolo, [Bangweulu]which I believe is the most beautiful place in the world. . . . I am writing to you here right at the source of the Blue Nile, in a mysterious forest full of orchids and violets, leopards and apes."[4] No doubt her wanderlust and hankering for adventure throughout her life found an escape in these dangerous yet fascinating trips.

Reenacting her interest in the Ancient Greek story of Phèdre, in another tribute to d'Annunzio's writing, Rubinstein decided to act and produce his *Phaedre*, on June 7, 1923, at the Opéra; it was originally performed at the Teatro Lirico in Milan in 1909. This was one of the last productions designed by Bakst, as he died the following year in 1924. The story based on Racine's adaptation of Euripides' *Hippolytus*, originally premiered in 428 BCE. The sites are neither Crete nor Egypt, but rather Troezen, in the Northern Peloponnese. For Phèdre, the daughter of King Minos, Bakst chose to costume and decorate the stage with "heavy, squat columns—references to archaeologist Arthur Evans's restoration of the so-called Palace of Minos."[5] But for Rubinstein's costume, Bakst combines early Greek geometric horse and bird panels with Dionysiac ivy ornaments and later snake bracelets, although Rubinstein did not perform with her breasts exposed.[6]

As with many of her plays, the critics found Rubinstein lacking in great dramatic artistry. Jacques Heugel in *Le Ménestrel*, June 15, 1923, bemoaned "the monotony of her voice, her narrow interpretation, only acceptable when Sarah Bernhardt plays a role, with her power of adaptation, near genius. Mme Rubinstein is not Sarah!" Another reviewer waxed poetic about her performance up to a point: André Beaunier in *L'Écho de Paris*, June 6, 1923. "Madame Rubinstein seems to float, pale and dreamy from a hot house where Maeterlink placed her. The flower comes to life and one might say she begins to run and leap like a leopard, half real half heraldic. You hear a beautiful voice, strong and serious, but you do not understand her words. It's a pity."

Rubinstein garnered critiques from both sides of the aisle. Nevertheless, she strove for a certain vision, an aesthetic that served to highlight her strengths and fulfill the destiny she saw for herself, somewhere between a muse and a martyr, a goddess and a heroine. She would remain true to her dream, even as it became harder to maintain with changing public tastes.

RUBINSTEIN'S CREDO: A GLIMPSE INSIDE HER BELIEFS IN *L'ART AUX TROIS VISAGES*

At the height of her fame, Rubinstein presented a fascinating, beautifully written essay on December 5, 1924, to a women's student group in Belgium. It was one of a number of her appearances in public, speaking about her work, reading poems and excerpts from the plays in which she performed. Her flowery prose, given to ornamentation, and steeped in romantic metaphors was later printed in *Conferencia: Journal de l'Université des Annales, Les Aspects de la Vie Moderne: L'Art aux trois visages.* Following the lecture, she performed a scene from d'Annunzio's *Le Martyre de San Sébastien,* accompanied by the music of Debussy. She had recently revived the lyric drama in 1922 and again in 1923 and 1924.

In the telling of her story, she discusses the philosopher-artists who most appealed to her, other than Friedrich Nietzsche, such as Stéphane Mallarmé and Paul Valéry. Like Mallarmé, Valéry conceives of dance as another language, akin to poetry, "where the power of expression goes beyond the statement of fact into the realm of infinite suggestion."[7] Having written considerably about dance in *L'Âme et la danse,* Valéry imagines the dancer as a metaphor in continuous transformation, "so that dancing as metaphor translates spirit into pure movement."[8] Valéry visualizes the dancer's soul: "Dance must therefore, by the subtlety of its lines, by the divineness of its upsurgings, by the delicacy of its tiptoe pauses, bring forth that universal creature which has neither body nor features, but which has gifts, days and destinies that has life and death"; When the dancer is moving, so Valéry continues, "She was celebrating all the mysteries of absence and presence; she seemed sometimes to be hovering on the brink of ineffable catastrophes."[9]

The scholar, Walter Putnam, sees Valéry's vision of dance and poetry as interconnected: "Dance represents for Valéry the poetry of action carried out by living beings, much in the same way that a poem is an act without any utilitarian purpose. Like all other art forms, including poetry, it is an act: when one starts to recite verse, it is the first steps in a verbal dance."[10]

To Valéry, and to Rubinstein, dancing is primarily a state of intoxication. "Our body, its arms and legs, performs a suite of patterns whose frequency produces a kind of inebriation that flows from languor to delirium."[11] According to Rubinstein, this euphoric experience has two main functions—revelation and liberation. The conditions that cause dissonance and conflict melt away and dissipate. The dancer and his or her body should just be seen in movement. Only the dancer can translate the ineffable, can portray the essence of so subtle a thing as love.

As Mallarmé had already discovered, dancing is admirably suited to the expression of essences. Here we are also close to Nietzsche's insistence on flight and inebriation through ecstatic dance. Though Valéry presupposes intellect as the highest of human attributes, he views the dancer's project as orderly and symmetric, "producing an effect of structural beauty,"[12] a magical moment for Valéry. The constant changes of patterns and movements reveal a divinity of thought, allying the dancer to godly acts. What caught Valéry's attention was the way the dancer's fluid impulses through space breaks it up and reforms it, thus reflecting the concept of time, or *la durée*. The dancer moves without really going anywhere, or accomplishing anything except a pure activity that could be considered the essence of inner life. Rubinstein marries these ideas to her own sensibility and understanding of how she developed a conscious approach to dramatic performance.

In Rubinstein's insightful essay, *L'Art aux trois Visages*, is a long meditation that essentially presents a discussion of her attitudes toward performance and theater; she lays out an aesthetic that fulfills her lifelong commitment to classical theatrical values enunciating the importance of a fusion of music, dance, and poetry.

She begins with a quote from one of the most beautiful poems by Charles Baudelaire, "Correspondances," "Nature is a temple in which living pillars sometimes give voice to confused words,"[13] which speaks to the way nature's secrets reveal themselves if we listen very carefully, and which imply a "profound unity" that Rubinstein intends to unmask in her discourse. This unity, though full of shadows, brings together drama, music, and dance; it is the art of the poem that Mallarmé invokes in his essay on Ballet: "All that which is Poetry—nature brought to life—leaves the libretto and freezes in cardboard equipment in the glittering stagnancy of purple and yellow muslin."

Rubinstein also looked to Mallarmé for her inspiration, though at times she differed with him about the inclusion of the other arts. "Mallarmé saw in ballet a magnificent independent art, which is more perfect as a means of expression than any other single scenic manifestation: 'In its perfect presentation ... such a vision comprises all, absolutely all the Spectacle of the future.'"[14] As a leader of the Symbolist movement, Mallarmé thought to evoke a moment or an idea through suggestion, where metaphor and symbolism take the place of exact description. Ballet and ballet as a dramatic form, then, is an art capable of projection into the most absolute thought, exactly as Volynsky proposed and d'Annunzio presented in his plays. For Mallarmé and for Volynsky, ballet is a metaphysical abstraction clothed in human form. Rubinstein refers to a quote from Mallarmé about the "magic circle" in her *L'Art trois visages,* exclaiming that, "I wish to exhibit the birth of this enchantment which for many centuries surrounded humanity with magical circles." These florescent spheres encompass and embrace the source of our imagination in the making of art.

Perhaps most telling is her next statement, especially in light of the staggering number of deaths from World War I. "In the face of the anguish and horrors of existence, the evocation of the dazzling splendor of the dream is the clarity that takes us toward death."[15] Here Rubinstein finds redemption in the glory and truth of the dramas that she mounts onstage.

> Art is truly a revelation. Revelation in all the magnificence and religiosity that the word suggests.... human beings rediscover their essences in a sob, or a sigh, or a gesture that comes close to the greatness of everything, and marks with its seal of beauty an identification with the Eternal, Art is also deliverance. Dance delivers us from heaviness, while music and poetry provide wings for our imagination.[16]

She continues this discussion by reiterating that nature is the backdrop of great drama, a series of indisputable forces that energize performance, while the three arts create a narrative in which the "wings of our imagination take flight." She explains, "The color of the sky, the murmur of fountains, the tenderness of verdure, the gushing of the sap, the swelling of earth herself. Here is the first inspiration: this universal cadence, this music of the spheres, where humanity finds itself carried away, seized by the Dionysiac intoxication symbolized by the rituals of Bacchus."[17]

She reflects on and references Nietzsche's mythic battle between the Apollonian and the Dionysian dialectic rooted in Euripides' *The Bacchae,* and reaffirms that the singing and the dancing and the poetry advance together to create its shocking finale. "The arts are strongly allied to recreate in the soul of the spectator the intoxication from which they gushed forth."

No doubt that she always returns to Aristotle's principles of Pity and Terror from his *Poetics* for her fundamental guide to tragic drama. She links the poet Gabriele d'Annunzio to the greatest theatrical artists, asserting that he was a chief modern proponent of the tragic chorus that expressed the "florescence of his lyricism." Her work with him on *Le Martyre* represented one of the highest points in her career, despite the problems of the production, notably its five to six-and-a-half-hour length.

The essay then takes on a cautionary mood. She warns, "Take care, watch out." The Dionysian moment, the disordered surge of the Bacchante, may find its limitations in the demands of rhythm. Perhaps the inventions of a director or choreographer might miss the depth of a brutal moment. Rubinstein still revels in her stance about transcendence: "Thus all the bodily symbols enter into play in order to translate this revelation, not the facade of the word, but all the attitudes and the gestures of dance, rhyming the movements of all the limbs."[18]

Rubinstein harkens back to the "beautiful book, Nietzsche's *Birth of Tragedy*," as she seeks the origins of the tragic lyric drama in the Dithyramb. Then she points to another great artist in the past, Friedrich Schiller (1759-1805), who stated that "the preparatory condition for poetic creation, was music, a certain state of the musical soul or spirit precedes and engenders in me the poetic idea."[19] She observes that the melody is the first and universal element of poetry, as do Schiller and Nietzsche, who find that the intense substance of the melody comes from the poem and the chorus, the life breath of music and dance. "Greek tragedy," she appraises, "is thus, in its origins, the Dionysiac choir whose effusions overflow and spread in images very much like the pindarienne odes. The choir according to the picturesque expression of Nietzsche, becomes the 'maternal lap of the dialogue.'"[20]

Judging those playwrights who succeeded Euripides, Rubinstein bemoans the disappearance of the tragic chorus in ancient Greece; the drama thus lost its mysterious depth and religious character. Stripped of the beneficence that music and dance bring to the narrative, the dramatist must then create a divine language in the rhythms of words that he confers on his heroes, if he is to reach the public.

Interestingly, Rubinstein cites the great American transcendentalist Ralph Waldo Emerson (1803-1882), whose tract on Shakespeare, recalls the stunning poetry of Hamlet's soliloquies. She agrees that these speeches beautifully project a poetic magic that invites the spectator to inaccessible places. But then she criticizes the romantic writer, Madame de Stael (1766-1817) for positing the radical notion that Greek tragedies are inferior to contemporary tragedies, "because a knowledge of the passions has evolved, and that with this understanding, tragedy has to follow the human spirit."[21] Rubinstein alleges that it is immature to debate whether Corneille or Racine has surpassed Aeschylus. All great poets obey the same Dionysiac calling, not from their complex or intriguing plots, but rather from the melody that emerges from the passionate verses.

In this illuminating booklet, she affirms that theatrical art is a revelation of the mysterious and the godly, finding its sources in the divine. She sees both the artist-performer as well as the spectator as participants in a ritual where one loses oneself and ultimately finds deliverance. Nevertheless, it is strange that she finds transcendence at the heart of her life in performance, while at the end of her life, she seeks solace in prayer. Her inability to keep pace with the extraordinary and diverse advances in modern theater later undermined her very reason for being.

RUBINSTEIN'S CONTENTIOUS CRUSADE IN THE WORLD OF BALLET

To return to the ill-fated choices Rubinstein made as a mature artist, one has to begin with her passion to appear onstage as a ballet dancer in classical pieces way after she appeared with the Ballets Russes. Rubinstein made the mistake on April 26, 1922, of putting on toe shoes in the ballet *Artemis Troublée*. Léon Bakst conceived the narrative as well as the designs, spending many hours at the Louvre studying the shapes and images for the antique scenario; he created a decor in the fashion of the paintings of Poussin. John Bowlt deduced that, "*Artemis Troublée* similar in plot to Hyppolytus, and Phèdre, was inauspicious, with critics referring to Rubinstein's title role as bearing the clear imprint of dilettantism."[22] The composer for the score was chosen by Rubinstein to be Paul Paray, his first ballet. The work was an adaptation of a poem, "Adonis troublé." Apparently, the music failed to enhance the ballet. Émile Vuillermoz in *L'Excelsior*, remonstrated that "the music possesses none of the artistic virtues that would have permitted it to fully express what was on the stage."[23]

But it was Rubinstein who also suffered insults. Adophe Boschot in his *L'Écho de Paris* criticized the stature of her long body and exclaimed that she towered above her nymphs, as much as by a head.[24] But André Levinson found

Ida Rubinstein, 1925. Photo by Phyllis Abbe. SOURCE: CONDÉ NAST LICENSING.

her "contour" captivating, her poses created with an "impeccable aplomb," her form as "svelte as a lyre," and with the "sculptural charm of a Bernini."[25] However, in the same *Comoedia* article from May 3, 1922, and in spite of his praise, he deplores, "her dance movement, in itself, jerky and irregular, her jagged attitudes, her arms often without beauty, her very long back hunched over and undulating." In other words, she could no longer do classical ballet. The ballet was quickly forgotten.

Conversely, Rubinstein was the toast of Paris when she acted the role of Marguerite Gautier in *La Dame aux Camélias* on November 27, 1923, just eight months after the death of her mentor and friend, Sarah Bernhardt. Bernhardt's son generously arranged for Rubinstein's production to play in the Théâtre Sarah-Bernhardt. The sets were opulent with magnificent furniture and a painted ceiling; her lush, expansive dresses provided by the House of Worth.

The critics deemed it a veritable triumph. It was in a sense a perfect, iconic role for her, a beautiful woman, fading and dying but gracious to the end. They found Rubinstein "belle et élégante" with "une grâce et distinction parfaite" or "Beautiful and elegant, with a perfect grace and distinction." André Beaunier, on November 29, 1923, in *l'Écho de Paris,* declared that she demonstrated a true "science d'attitudes, une grâce de cygne expirant" "A true science of gestures, the grace of a dying swan." The famed actor, writer, and director, Sacha Guitry, coached Rubinstein in this symbolic role of the dying diva. DePaulis writes that Michael de Cossart listed this play as a great success and that in the ten following years Rubinstein played the role in France and abroad more than 100 times,[26] a fact that amazes and proves how she realized the character of Marguerite Gautier in an attractive and touching manner. Rather than a shallow courtesan, Rubinstein emphasized Marguerite's thoughtful and intellectual side, along with an aristocratic lucidity hardly found in other portrayals of the role.

Rubinstein created two other pieces before her ballet season in 1928: *Orphée* (June 11, 1926), strangely called a "Mimodrame lyrique." She relished the profound grandiosity of the myth; and was acclaimed in the role of Orpheus, so much so that the author and composer, Roger Ducasse wrote, "Orphée, he is you, he lives and is revived in you. Yes, you have created him, Madame.... In the writing of this work, I presented in my mind and my heart your gestures, your moves, your glances, and even your silences."[27] Playing a male hero once again provided Rubinstein the breadth, power, and complexity that she sought in all her roles.

Soon after the *Orphée,* Rubinstein embarked on a new project, *L'Impératrice aux Rochers* on February 18, 1927, after a few delays and much anxiety on the part of the director of the Opéra and the composer, Honegger, the mystery play by Saint-Georges de Bouhélier, saw the light. The stage was filled with chorus, acrobats, figurants, jugglers, cavaliers, and so on, and needed many rehearsals to integrate everyone and everything designed by Alexandre Benois.

Told in octosyllables, the lyric drama lasted more than five hours with many changes of scene; it must have been a crashing bore. It told the tale of Vittoria, the Christian empress, loved deeply by the emperor Aurélien, but his brother Othon also loves Vittoria and will stoop to anything to deceive and conquer. Wounded by a stray arrow, the emperor eventually recovers and makes a pilgrimage to the Terre Sainte to thank God for his recuperation. A series of absurd and unlikely events ensue; the brother-in-law is attacked by leprosy, and Vittoria becomes a recognized empress. According to DePaulis the play "bored the spectators to a languorous sleep."²⁸ After five performances, the production disappeared from the stage; it was a spectacular failure. Rubinstein was undaunted by the bad reviews; she had accomplished what she wanted, to create a performance that was beautiful. That was all she claimed to achieve. And the stage was indeed exquisite, as were her thirteen gowns once again created by the House of Worth. The many plays and concerts she produced between the wars, despite some serious reprimands from the critics, only served to push her forward to create her own ballet company, a dream she sought since working for Diaghilev.

For Rubinstein's season of ballet in 1928/29, she hired Bronislava Nijinska, a decision that elevated Nijinska to high realms for her brilliant and groundbreaking choreography, but left the diva Rubinstein in a distant realm of disgrace. All the ballets were designed by her friend of many years, Alexandre Benois, who was the sole creator of the sets and costumes. They were extravagantly produced, and carefully conceived to give Rubinstein the beauteous surroundings that she always demanded. Rubinstein danced in every ballet, displaying her aging forty-five-year-old body that sadly revealed her lack of early training as a young child. The season brought forth fourteen new productions, including ten original scores and four with preexisting compositions.

> As an engine generating all new choreography and new musical compositions, Rubinstein and her company rivaled and in some ways surpassed all other existing troupes, including the Ballets Russes and the Paris Opéra's Corps de Ballet. In fact, three years after Diaghilev's death in 1929, her troupe was the only significant company producing and touring new works—no small feat during the early years of the Great Depression.²⁹

Rubinstein, as Louis K. Epstein further noted, utilized ideas from groups and their works that preceded hers, but she hoped to "surpass" them as she put together an international company that included Nijinska, Fokine, and Massine, as well as a number of former Ballets Russes dancers.³⁰ Knowing how important it was to appeal to a wider community, she engaged her troupe to perform in Monte Carlo, in La Scala in Milan, and in the Vienna Opera House. For the most part, Rubinstein used the Diaghilev formula for conceiving her works; they were relatively short one-act pieces with an emphasis on sumptuous scene decors, while directing the librettists, composers, and choreographers. "From the beginning then, Rubinstein cast herself as Diaghilev's equal in terms of her ability as impresario to bring together brilliant collaborators and guide their artistic visions."³¹ The scenarios that she chose were purposely old fashioned. Rubinstein insisted on discovering narratives that harkened back to former times, to mythology and fairy tales with their somewhat predictable moral messages. The stories required monumental edifices for the scenery to background the often absurd vicissitudes of her characters.

In order to grasp the huge scope of her accomplishments before delving into more detailed analyses, what follows is a brief summary of the run of the season.[32]

On November 22, 1928, she performed at the Théâtre National de l'Opéra in Paris. Rubinstein first starred in Nijinska's *Les Noces de Psyché et de l'Amour*, a ballet in one act, in the role of Psyché. Benois wrote the libretto to music by Johann Sebastian Bach and orchestrated by Arthur Honegger. Rubinstein had the starring role, dancing with her leading man, Anatole Vilzak.

Other Nijinska ballets danced by Rubinstein exhibit a range of diversity for the ageing dancer. Also on November 22, was *La Bien-Aimée*, a ballet in one act by Nijinska in which Rubinstein played La Bien-Aimée with Vilzak in the role of the Poet. The score was by Franz Schubert and Franz Liszt, orchestrated by Darius Milhaud. Last, there was *Boléro*, A ballet in one act, to music by Maurice Ravel sets, and costumes by Alexandre Benois; also choreographed by Nijinska. Rubinstein had the starring role.

Five days later on November 27, the company performed *Le Baiser de la Fée*, choreographed by Nijinska, an allegorical ballet. Igor Stravinsky composed and conducted it with Rubinstein as the Fairy, Vilzak as Rudy, and Schollar as his Fiancée.

On November 29, she presented *Nocturne*, choreographed by Nijinska, a ballet in one act to the music of Alexander Borodin, orchestrated by Nicolas Tcherepnine, with sets and costumes by Alexandre Benois. Rubinstein danced the Young Girl, with Vilzak as the Fiancé. Also on November 29, she debuted *La Princesse Cygne (The Swan Princess)*, a ballet in one act from the Opera *Tsar Saltan* to the music of Nikolai Rimsky-Korsakov. Nijinska choreographed, Rubinstein naturally starred as the Swan Princess, partnered by Anatole Vilzak.

Five days later on December 4, Léonide Massine premiered his *David* with Rubinstein's company. A ballet in one act to the music of Henri Sauget, with sets and costumes by Alexandre Benois, starring Rubinstein as David, with Alexis Dolinoff as Saul. In his book, *My Life*, Massine wrote about Rubinstein in his ballet, *David*, "It was difficult to get her to move gracefully. As she was dancing the part of David, the whole ballet was centered on her; I had very little opportunity for original choreography."[33] Rubinstein excelled at playing

between the wars

androgynous roles, despite Massine's complaints. The ballet *David* began with strains of song eliciting a longing for spiritual purity. The dance becomes a prayer, accompanied by "the music that is simple but the all-white-note texture still produces arresting dissonances."[34]

Soon after, on January 15, 1929, in Monte Carlo at the Théâtre de Monte Carlo, the company presented *La Valse*, a choreographic poem by Maurice Ravel with sets and costumes by Alexandre Benois and principal dancers Rubinstein and Anatole Vilzak. *La Valse* was performed in Paris on May 23, 1929.

This exhausting schedule pushed Rubinstein to drive not only herself, but her dancers and choreographers to achieve her dreams of leaving a legacy in the ballet world. When Rubinstein embarked on the adventure of this 1928/29 season of ballet in Paris, it was the year before Diaghilev died, and seemed to be a grand snubbing of the old impresario and certainly her attempt to imitate his glory. But this really was a turning point in her career, a most disastrous and desperate move to insinuate herself into the canon of modernist ballet.

Her company was pieced together from many distant countries—Russia, England, Bulgaria, Romania, Poland, America, Yugoslavia, and Switzerland. Oddly enough, there were no French dancers. In preparing for performances, Rubinstein was an avid proponent of rehearsals and expected all the dancers to respect the long hours and days of work. Nina Tikanova in her book, *La Jeune Fille en bleu,* described the complicated and often fraught atmosphere and events of the moment. They joked that their group should be called, La Compagnie des Répétiteurs d'Rubinstein. Tikanova revealed that Rubinstein did not rehearse with the company; rather, she worked in another studio with Anatole Vilzak, her star partner, or alone,[35] keeping herself isolated from their curious, and probably judgmental eyes. She was viewed by the dancers as someone beyond their dreams, with an extravagant sense of self and lifestyle, arriving at rehearsals in a Rolls-Royce with a red carpet thrown down for her entrance.

By this time, "she was looking worn, with badly dyed red hair, a very thin and gaunt face and flat feet, none of these are characteristics of a ballerina in fine form."[36] The dancers were impressed that she was able to rent the grand opera house whenever she wished. The director, Jacques Rouché, tried to arrange the performance schedule according to her liking. "Imagine Rubinstein, a foreigner and a Jew, who has such influence!"[37]

David Vaughan, in *Dancing Times* article, "A Peruvian in Paris," writes about a young Fredrick Ashton's impression of Rubinstein's company, as he joined it looking for more experience and a rather good salary. He noted that "it was generously funded by her lover, Walter Guinness."[38] Rehearsals began August 1, 1928, ample time before the opening, with a fee of 1,000 francs a month. The male dancers were instructed to wear clean shirts and were issued bottles of eau de cologne. There was ballet class from 9 a.m. to 10 a.m., rehearsal to 1 p.m., lunch and then rehearsal till 6 p.m., a dinner break and another three hour rehearsal from 8 p.m. to 11 p.m., a grueling schedule. Ashton admitted that this regime helped his technique improve, but he confessed to a wicked game of imitating both Rubinstein and Nijinska to amuse his fellow dancers.[39]

Acknowledging Rubinstein's impassioned desire to create her own ballet company and to make a historical statement with some of the finest choreographers of her generation, a few of these ballets will be examined in greater depth. In spite of tepid reviews, many outstanding qualities and characteristics can be observed in Rubinstein's groundbreaking season.

For *Les Noces de Psyché et de l'Amour,* Nijinska's choreography was well received. The ballet unites all the Greek gods to the chamber music by Bach, reinterpreted by Honegger who enhances the majestic tones with saxophones and "unusual instrumental combinations."[40] "Les Noces" presented a well-worn traditional tale telling of the gods on Olympus who are celebrating the marriage of Psyché and Cupid. Rubinstein danced the role of Psyché who arrives onstage dressed in a simple tunic of white satin, while the other gods appeared in an unparalleled magnificence. Using the language of pantomime, Psyché recounts the puzzling story of how Cupid suddenly kissed her on the shoulder, how he flew away to seek someone other than himself to adore her, but returned to her so that they could be reconciled forever and united before all the great divinities. The ballet with all its sumptuous costumes was received as a palatable re-creation of a Louis XIV spectacle, with a notable kudo to Nijinska.

A second ballet, also by Nijinska, *La Bien Aimée,* or *The Beloved,* was a duet in which Rubinstein played the Beloved, with Vilzak in the role of the poet. The music of Schubert and Liszt was orchestrated by Darius Milhaud. Milhaud worked with Listz's Soirées de Paris, which had been piano transcriptions of waltzes by Schubert. The story unfolds with the pianist Schubert (Vilzak) seated and dreaming about the women he loved in the past—peasant girls, young women wanting to have fun, and especially the cruel one whom he adored but who ran away—a seasoned Romantic tale. The composer created an ingenious addition to the orchestration, a mechanical piano that

between the wars 109

offended many in the audience, sensing it to be out of place. The French music critic, Henri Prunières, found Milhaud's use of the mechanical piano intriguing. "It plays sometimes alone, sometimes with the orchestra. An effect is produced which many critics condemned as bizarre, but which is not lacking in savor."[41] It posed a challenge on tours, as they were obliged to transport a pianola, not an easy feat.

The sensation of the evening was the seventeen-minute ballet, *Boléro*, choreographed by Nijinska, with sets and costumes by Benois. It was of course composed by Maurice Ravel, a very close friend of Rubinstein's. Ravel famously said, "I have written only one masterpiece. That is the Boléro. Unfortunately it contains no music."[42] Rubinstein asked him to create a Spanish composition, with Benois's startling décor consisting of a huge table that takes up practically the whole stage, on which the dancers beat their heels and move fluidly, not constricted by the table's height and space.

Maurice Ravel realized the controversy that this unusual, highly repetitive score might cause and wrote the following:

> It constitutes an experiment in a very special and limited direction. I issued a warning to the effect that what I had written was a piece lasting about seventeen minutes and consisting wholly of 'orchestral tissue without music' of

Ida Rubinstein Ballet Company with Maurice Ravel, 1929. SOURCE: GETTY IMAGES.

one long, very gradual crescendo. There are no contrasts; there is practically no invention except the plan and the manner of execution. The orchestral writing is simple and without the slightest attempt at virtuosity.... I have carried out exactly what I intended, and it is for listeners to take it or leave it.[43]

Levinson, in his book *Les Visages de la Danse*, describes the scintillating performance.

> Twenty men, fascinated by the sensual sorcery of one woman, with the undulation of her arms and the shifting of her torso, and swishing of her Basque skirt, by her lovely foot movements tracing circles on the floor, she, the dancer, designs the contours of the melody. The twenty men stamp their feet and beat the palms of their hands, marking the accents that form a percussion of diverse rhythmic tones. Each beginning phrase causes an intensity of effect. The premier dancer, M. Vilzac, crouches, twists and writhes, tormented by his sexual attraction and the incessant rhythms.[44]

In her intriguing study of the ballets by Ravel, *The Ballets of Maurice Ravel*, Deborah Mawer recalls that "Despite not winning the composer's full approbation, Rubinstein's flamenco cabaret created a sensation that produced abundant newspaper coverage in French, and English, not just for the premiere but also for subsequent performances in 1929, 1931 and 1934."[45] She clarified her understanding of this presentation by quoting Henri Prunières, the respected editor of *La Revue Musicale*.

> One was immediately taken captive, transported by an art which partakes of magic... Madame Rubinstein understood that the strength of the score was such that the dance must appear as a kind of visual projection of this radiant music... on a platform, she performed a type of very stylized bolero, amid the encouragement and impassioned quarrels of the spectators.[46]

Howard Sayette, ballet master of the Oakland Ballet provided me a DVD of *Boléro* from 1995. He had the extraordinary advantage of help from Nijinska's daughter, Irina (b. 1913), with her exceptional knowledge, as she oversaw the remaking of *Boléro* before her death in 1991. At the time of the performances, Rubinstein was taking lessons and studying with the famed ballerina Rosita Mauri in 1928, who no doubt also assisted with the Flamenco style and movements in this ballet. Mauri survived many years at the Paris Opéra, teaching advanced classes in ballet from 1898 to 1920.

Watching this re-creation of *Boléro* tells us about an aging Rubinstein and her trust in Nijinska, whose powerful choreography allows her to enhance and exploit the most cogent abilities of Rubinstein, her sensuality, her musicality, her gestural acuity, her fluid back, and her stunning confidence in her body's emotionality. Given the lasting power of the score as well as the dancing, it seems propitious to offer a glimpse of this radical piece.

The curtain rises on a shadowy Cabaret, with a flood of light pouring onto the single scenic object, a huge table in the center of the stage that serves as the cynosure for this unusual ballet. The starring female dancer is perched on top of the table, dressed in a ruffled Flamenco skirt and heels, her hair slicked back with a rose on the side of her bun. When the music begins, she moves her arms fluidly in circular motions, forming Spanish poses, gesturing at times with jabbing moves associated with that of a bullfighter, punctuating the space near her. She arches her back in a serpentine manner, not only displaying a lithe flexibility but also an ecstatic and sensual obeisance.

The stage whitens with more light on a group circling the table as well as other dancers moving back and forth, serving as a kind of percussive chorus while she pummels the surface of the table with her feet, taking snapshot poses in rhythm with the music. A chorus of male dancers begins to clap hands in a one and two beat. The stage is churning with people, perhaps twenty men and women, some dancers with guitars and capes. While she is elegantly situated, a male dancer alights onstage to join her, both bending their torsos forward and back, a greeting and acceptance of each other. She turns and pirouettes, bourrées, kicks, and turns. Our eyes are focused on her motioning feet, jabbing and stamping on the tabletop. She and her partner place their arms in a lyre-like pose, the wrists of the hands touching high above their heads.

When four men jump on the table, they begin to throw her in the air with her arms arched high above her head. She looks like a geyser shooting up through space. The repetition of the melodies and rhythms drive the moves with deep back bends, turns, and men lifting her high in the air. As these actions repeat, and the music reaches a crescendo, the many dancers onstage continue their background swirls and parades while the Flamenco/Spanish ballerina continues to be thrust vertically into the air. At the finale of the music, she is flung backward so that she is in a deep arched back, with her face to the ceiling tilting back to the audience, her body held high on the table, a vision of a goddess flying and being worshiped.

In the *New York Times*, Prunières commented on Ravel's score.

> Maurice Ravel's *Boléro* is an amazingly successful work.... I know of no music more haunting. With it what takes place on the stage can only be a kind of visual projection of the music itself. Mme. Rubinstein and her colleagues have well understood. We see a milling crowd of characters escaped from a Goya painting. The effect is most graphically picturesque and fits marvelously with the music. Our gratitude is due Mme. Rubinstein for having given pictorial vitality to such a score and presented such a superb spectacle.[47]

Other ballets caught the attention of the press as well and illustrated Rubinstein's acute sense of aesthetics. The music for the Stravinsky ballet, *Le Baiser de la Fée*, was inspired by the thirty-fifth anniversary of Tchaikovsky's death. Stravinsky, always concerned about his remuneration, charged 6,000 dollars, a huge fee at the time; Rubinstein accepted readily. It was decided to base the ballet on the fairy tale by Hans Christian Anderson, *La Reine des Neiges (The Snow Queen)*. The story begins with a fairy kiss on a baby boy, a fatal moment, as twenty years later, the beautiful fairy kisses him again, fatally, and carries him off from the earth to be with her forever. Strolling along in Paris before the performance, Stravinsky noticed a poster for the season with his name spelled incorrectly and was enraged. Despite this mishap, he conducted the first performance. However, the original choreography played very few times and disappeared without a trace of objection.

The season received mixed reviews, for the most part not adulatory in Paris, but quite positive on tour to Brussels, Monte Carlo, and Vienna. In the newspaper, *Le Temps*, on November 24, 1928, Henri Malherbe described an evening's ballet.

> It is impossible to witness more sumptuousity, and taste in the organization of a choreographed divertissement. Madame Rubinstein seems refined, and supple, in her affect and manner in all three ballets. She is surrounded by a troupe of dancers with accomplished virtuousity. She is worthy of all the praises for her supreme effort, her choices and her example.[48]

Feeling that the critics were ill equipped to review the ballet season, Tikanova admonished that few of the critics of ballet are dancers, nor do they critique only dance, but are usually musicians or musicologists. However, there was André Levinson who dedicated himself to dance. In his assessment of Rubinstein's season, in *Comoedia* on December 8, 1928, he astutely observes in *La Princesse Cygne*, "It is the principle of scenic decoration that dominates in this performance and not the choreographic design. One hesitates to put so much emphasis on the value of the décor."⁴⁹ Levinson is critical in some ways of all the ballets including *Nocturne, David,* and *La Princesse Cygne*. But he recognizes the innate talents of the choreographers and dancers.

> In all of these ballets, it is only on rare occasions that the dancers have an opportunity to shine. But a simple glissade assemblée, an elementary movement in the technique can be enchanting if it is accomplished with bravoura by Ludmilova. What beautiful work does Nikolaeva and Mlle. Schollar, who was acclaimed in *Le Baiser de la Fée,* has thus a perfect musicality and an elegant carriage and pretty pointe work.⁵⁰

Levinson delights in the ballerinas. Madame Rubinstein enjoyed some critically positive reviews, but they were modified by some stinging comments. For example, in *La Presse* on December 5, 1928, Jane Catulle Mendès writes: "Madame Rubinstein remains admirable in all that conveys her art of plastique (or mime and gesture), with a slow and continuous melody of poses and of hieratism. She is worthless in her attempts at classical dance, no matter her effort and her intense application, because her long body structure is contradictory to it. In sum, these ballets bring nothing new to the art that they wish to serve."⁵¹ Ouch!

But the most damning renunciation came from a renowned music and dance critic, Émile Vuillermoz, in *L'Excelsior* on December 3, 1928, clearly noting,

> After having discreetly examined its professional conscience, critics were obliged to awkwardly tell Madame Rubinstein that her obstinacy in choosing to reserve every major role for herself in each of her ballets and her impertinent disdain for elementary ballet technique that she must possess in order to justify this diabolical perseverance, takes away from this season of ballets a great part of its artistic significance.⁵²

Thus, the brilliance and magnificence of her season was abnegated by her egotistical need to be center stage instead of choosing with her usual good taste other dancers for the spotlight.

Serge Diaghilev, her lifelong rival, reacted to this 1928/29 season of ballet with vicious and relentless anger and contempt. Apparently, he made some malicious anti-Semitic remarks as well. Scheijen reveals the highlights in a letter from November 23 that Diaghilev wrote to Serge Lifar. He complained,

The performance was nothing but provincial boredom. Everything was interminably long, even the Ravel that went on for a whole 14 [really 16] minutes. The worst of all was Rubinstein herself.... she appeared with Vilzak but no one in the theater, not even I, recognized her. Hunched with disheveled red hair, hatless, in ballet shoes (all the others were in helmets, feathers and high heels), in order to appear shorter. She was a total failure. She can't dance at all. She stands on her toes with bent knees and Vilzak keeps moving her along.... All that's left of her face is a huge open mouth and a mass of clenched teeth that represents a smile. Pure Horror.[53]

Diaghilev also had nasty words for Stravinsky's score for *Le Baiser*. "He made an ill advised choice of music by Tchaikovsky, tiresome and lachrymose, allegedly brilliantly orchestrated by Igor. I say 'allegedly' because to me its sounds gray and the whole style is moribund."[54] Scheijen continued this examination of Diaghilev's cruel remarks. When interviewed by a writer for a Russian émigré journal, Diaghilev aimed poison darts at Rubinstein,

Rubinstein herself doesn't realize that the art of dance is the most difficult, the most delicate and the most cruel art. It doesn't forgive mistakes. The hunched figure of poor Rubenstein with her feebly bent knees, the complete confusion of her classical spasms, made a second-ranking but trained dancer in her company seem like the heroine of old fashioned adagio dances devised a century ago.[55]

In many ways Diaghilev spoke the truth, but ignored any regard for Nijinska's or Benois's fine work, or the creative intelligence of the other composers.

Months earlier, Diaghilev's animosity toward Rubinstein had mounted when he heard that she was going to start her own ballet company. Feeling relieved and assured of his company's successful future after the disbanding of the Rolf de Maré's Ballet Suedois in 1925, he suddenly felt threatened by Rubinstein, sneeringly calling her new project, "Les Ballets Juifs" ("the Jewish Ballet Company").[56]

But it is noteworthy that history has preserved its respect for *Boléro*, for one of its most perceptive observers, Agnes de Mille, noted: "The history of ballet contains many chronicles of great sums spent to frame the posturing of some theatrically speaking amateurish figure—none of whom lasted long. And although they commissioned the great to serve them, few of their efforts counted. Ravel's *Boléro*, ordered by Rubinstein in 1928, is probably the most noteworthy exception."[56]

between the wars

Ida Rubinstein's Ballet Company on tour, 1929. Bronislava Nijinska in center, Frederik Ashton second on her left. Photographer unknown. SOURCE: JEROME ROBBINS DANCE DIVISION, THE NEW YORK PUBLIC LIBRARY FOR THE PERFORMING ARTS, ASTOR, LENOX, AND TILDEN FOUNDATIONS.

Soon after the 1928 season, on January 15, 1929, Rubinstein presented *La Valse* to another hypnotic score by Maurice Ravel, which he titled *A Choreographic Poem*. He described the context of his music as inspiring the site of swirling clouds that open up to reveal dancing couples spinning on the stage. As the clouds disappear, the couples continue their swirling, moving to the ebb and flow of the majestic score. Apparently Benois made the mistake of creating an overloaded, rococo decor with heavy costumes in the style of the seventeenth century, diametrically opposed to the ethereal and simple directions that Ravel stipulated. In a way, this completely undermined Nijinska's choreography, confusing and irritating the critics and viewers.[57]

Ravel completed the score for *La Valse* in 1920, and in a version for two pianos it received its first hearing in a private home in Paris. "In the audience were Diaghilev, Stravinsky, Poulenc, and Massine. Following the performance, Diaghilev proclaimed the work a masterpiece, but said it was unsuitable for staging because, in his words, 'It's not a ballet. It's a portrait of a ballet—a painting of a ballet' and so he refused to produce it."[58] Fortunately, Rubinstein disagreed. Marcel Schneider evoked the words of Ravel in describing his haunting score: "It was a kind of apotheosis of the Viennese waltz which to my mind evokes a fantastic and fatal whirling."[59]

A more recent reconstruction of Ravel's and Nijinska's *La Valse* was initiated by Millicent Hodson and Kenneth Archer, the team that also brought back Stravinsky's and Nijinsky's *Le Sacre du Printemps* for the Joffrey Ballet in 1987. Hodson and Archer conceived *La Valse* as taking place during World War I at the time Rubinstein was involved in her relationships with Romaine Brooks and Gabriele d'Annunzio. Hodson and Archer emphasized, in their description, that when Rubinstein heard of the outbreak of World War I, according to an account by Brooks, she threw herself on the ground and prayed, identifying with destiny not as a theatrical role, but as a spiritual reality. As a consequence, it was this scene that prompted Brooks to paint the well-known *La France croisée*, which portrayed Rubinstein in a Red Cross cape as leader of women's auxiliary troops.[60] Nonetheless, however the ballet was conceived, its brilliant score secures the success of its movement ideas.

As with *Antigone* and *Hélène de Sparte*, great poetry fascinated Rubinstein. And her affinity for beautiful prose inspired her to perform in Shakespeare's *Antony and Cleopatra*, Dostoyevsky's *The Idiot*, and Alexandre Dumas's *La Dame aux Camélias*. She was naturally drawn to poetic dramas, especially sung poetry, and when she read Paul Valéry's verses for his melodrama *Amphion*, she was captivated.[61] It was a ballet melodrama for reader, solo voices, chorus, and orchestra, combining elements of oratorio, spoken drama, and ballet.

In the program for the Paris Opéra's opening night of *Amphion*, June 23, 1931, we note that the composer Arthur Honegger and Léonide Massine were responsible for the music and the choreography, while Alexandre Benois created the décor, which Valéry disliked. Paul Valéry wrote: "I have tried in *Amphion* to coordinate, the words, the song, the orchestra, the mime, the dance and the décor as well, so that these diverse elements can adjust themselves one to the other. That is what my goal was. Arthur Honegger and Madame Rubinstein have marvelously understood me." Valéry wrote a preface to his Mélodrame, *Amphion*, in which he recounts the genesis of the narrative ballet. He describes the male god Amphion, played by Rubinstein.

> A beautiful personage who will create a relationship between architecture and music as ordained by Apollo, dressed and standing as nobly in the midst of the most poetic scene with rocks and streams at the foot of mountains, let there be a dense and hideous forest, with a glimmer of a dark and mysterious pool reflecting the sky. Our hero comes to life and begins to move and act. He has a lyre in his hands that gleams. Stirred by the divine strings and songs, the rocks begin to move and roll along drawn toward a place where the whole pile of them assembles, gradually becoming a building, composing the shape of a temple. That is the essence of *Amphion*. Thus *Amphion* is a "hymne à la gloire de la construction et de l'homme constructeur."[62]

The ballet allowed Valéry to put in practice his dramatic theories. Sylvie David-Guignard describes the essence of the ballet in her article, "Amphion: from Greek myth to Valeryian melodrama." She continues: "The melodrama of *Amphion* bathes in an Apollonian light; its protagonist, far from ordinary humanity, incarnates the spirit of creativity.... All is symbol, abstraction and priestly ritual. Apollo awards Amphion the lyre that sings forth beloved music and the 'laws of music.'"[63] Louis K. Epstein further elucidates: "Music inspires architecture, symbolizing music's role as foundation for and summit of the cultural hierarchy."[64]

Valéry's notes concerning the dancers, particularly in the episode of the construction of the temple, demonstrate that Valéry also attributed great importance to the choreography and noted that the rocks played by male dancers should rise and move freely, either with heavy jumps or rolling down the hills, as they direct themselves from one side of the stage to the other. Light and shadow also intensify the scenic flow, with the stage almost in obscurity as Amphion dreams; slowly as he awakens and we hear Apollo's intonations, the light rays almost explode and the stones and rocks turn into the Theban temple.

Véronique Fabbri noted problems with the decor, "Valéry's ritual tone for Apollo, for the Muses suffused the script. In letters sent to friends, Valéry was not pleased with Benois' decors, finding them too realistic, not sufficiently geometric."[65] Also, the landscape of the stage was filled with opposing aesthetics and seemed to be confusing. One critic, Henri Malherbe, lamented that "the designs, though naturalistic in inspiration, contradicted the symbolic intention of the poet, which was to free himself from the pseudorealistic style."[66]

There is some description of Massine's movement choices. For example, Vicente Garcia-Márquez notes that, "As always with Rubinstein, the choreography [for *Amphion*] relied more on pantomime than dance."⁶⁷ In a further description, Levinson felt that "Massine's choreography though relegated to semi-darkness since all the light was directed towards the protagonist and surrounded by all sorts of obstacles, manifested originality, although it was compressed by the uncalled-for tyrannical necessities of a paradoxical mise-en-scène." The choreography's 'counterpoint of movement' and 'monumental gymnastics' were not 'exempted of grandeur,' and 'Massine's Russian constructivism' was justified by the libretto."⁶⁸

One can well imagine how Massine would have moved the "*pierres et rochers*" ["stones and rocks"] around the stage, giving the very skilled dancers quite original and expansive contemporary moves. In the program, the dancers' list includes among the sixteen male dancers Alexis Dolinoff, Pierre Vladimiroff, and Roman Jasinsky, with twelve women including Larina, Lipskaia, Nina Verchinina, and Maria Kouznetzova. In the course of the narrative, the dancers seem to be part of the stage design. Levinson complained about Rubinstein's narcissism, "How sad that Mme Rubinstein, who stages so many important productions, continues to spoil everything by becoming the star."⁶⁹ Émile Vuillermoz chimed in with the same objection. "Why does she persist in personally engaging in battles in the fields of choreography and diction out of which she would not be able to emerge victoriously?"⁷⁰

Other critics were also unimpressed with Rubinstein's performance as well as her vision of the mise en scène. The *Journal des Débats* underlined the difficulty of "seeing everything and hearing everything." But Massine's choreography floated above the negative reaction. According to Fabbri commenting on Massine's work in *Paul Valéry, le poème et la danse*,

> The choreography seems to have been appreciated. It was conceived, no doubt at the same time he was working with the Ballets Russes and probably pushed along very quickly. He also seems to have arranged a great place for acrobatics that was agreed upon by the poet and the choreographer.⁷¹

Perhaps the last word came from Valéry himself who wrote a letter in 1933 to the editor of the magazine *Marsyas*, Sully A. Pèyre who had criticized Valéry's poem *Amphion*. Valéry defended his conception for the ballet that Rubinstein disavowed.

> You have read a libretto with eyes that were searching for a poem. I published this text, perhaps wrongfully. But the execution of the work was such that in doing so that would establish my intention. I could not impose my

views, which were the simplest in the world, and I had the tedious experience of watching a Russian ballet when I had conceived of a kind of religious ceremony.[72]

But in spite of the misinterpretation of his work the poet was full of praise for the composer Honegger in a letter he sent to the *Revue Musicale* June 14, 1942.

Rubinstein pushed forward her belief in *Amphion* by taking it on tour with the other ballets from 1928 and 1929. There was a cast of 100 that included a chorus of eighty-five, practically an inundation to the London theater. Nothing deterred Rubinstein from her theatrical philosophy that united the poet's word to music and dance, according to the ancient formula. This conceit corresponded with many writers in the theater and gave credibility to her role as an ardent animatrice.

A VIEW OF RUBINSTEIN AND HER PERFORMANCE PERSONA

There is no doubt that Rubinstein worked diligently to achieve her artistic vision, but her choices raise several questions and often confounded her public. When contemplating the force of Rubinstein's performance person, her ambiguous sexuality and her enthusiastic self-promotion as a dandy puzzled and intrigued the socially literate community of her time. In a sense she lived a double life; one was her image as the beauteous, exotic diva, the other was the mystifying, sexualized boy/girl of *Le Martyre*.

Her androgynous presence was substantiated by her connections with a Sapphic group in Paris, but also by the way she shaped her male roles. As the mythic male/female god/goddess, she reigned supreme in these roles, notably as Sebastian (in many different performances), Sémiramis, Orphée, and Amphion, though it was not unusual for actresses and dancers to take on male roles at the end of the nineteenth and early twentieth centuries. In her personal life, her brief passion for Romaine reflected a moment in time, in the early twentieth-century Paris when women wanted, "not only to be active but, above all, to be sexually active: to actively desire, to freely choose the objects of desire, to cross established boundaries of propriety dictated by gender, race, class, age and marital status."[73]

Most revealing, however, Rubinstein had no interest in defining herself as a Sapphist, or as any sexual object at all. Rather, she tasted the energy and passions of these women and used this sexuality in her interpretations of the roles she played. In *Hélène de Sparte,* when Electra tells Helen (Rubinstein's role) that she has fallen in love with her, Electra is rebuffed. But when reading Verhaeran's play, there is the distinct impression that Helen represented and encouraged her personification as a love figure for both women and men.

Fernand Nozière, an occasional passionate supporter of Rubinstein, tried to come to terms with some conflicting and troubling opinions of her: "One hates or loves her. She creates an almost religious atmosphere wherever she is. She needs an audience that appreciates high-class art, noble art, not banalité or realité, but beauty and elegance."[74] Of course when Diaghilev first saw her in St. Petersburg, having been told by Bakst that she was fascinating, Nozière reflected, "How could he not be dazzled by the beauty she emanated?" And, Nozière found her interpretation of Helen of Sparta one year after *Le Martyre* to be a deeply moving and unique personification. He concluded: "Ah, this is not the blond Helen, it is the Helen of darkness, it is the evocation of a savage and brutal epoch."[75]

Charles Mayer commented on the dual qualities of Rubinstein's stage presence, not in terms of her sexuality but rather as a multitalented artist. "She clearly understood her own value as a performer. 'I consider myself an actress and a dancer. I think the dance is a part of drama. It is an expression of drama. The real dancer must be dramatic. She cannot dance unless she has drama in her soul. I love to combine dancing and drama.'"[76]

One of her leading male dancers, Keith Lester, recalled how Rubinstein effectively accomplished her roles.

> With painstaking practice, however, and after spending hours each day in front of her bedroom mirror to perfect her poses, she developed a special affinity for gesture as an expressive enactment of inner emotions, a notion central to the movement and acting aesthetics of French music and drama teacher François Delsarte. This practice ... presaged a lifelong dedication to beauty and her own physical appearance.[77]

So convinced was she of her intense and subjective understanding of the roles she played that she pronounced in an interview with Pierre Van Taassen of the *New York Evening World*, on June 23, 1926.

> I do not need to rehearse. For I am Saint Sebastian the moment I step on the stage. I live his life and I know his innermost feeling in that play; every movement and every word comes from me spontaneously. I am, as it were, impregnated with the soul of Saint Sebastian. In that role I am completely master of myself. I can actually see clearly what is going on around me; I experience the most sublime ecstasy, although I remain quite lucid.[78]

As mentioned earlier, Rubinstein did not flinch when onstage with her nearly naked body. She did not fear what people would say about her "oriental performativity." Critics assumed that her religion affected the way she moved and acted. Russian critic and ballet historian Valerian Svetlov related her distinctive style to her Jewishness: "She has the suppleness of a serpent in the physical form of a woman; her dance presents the stereotypical voluptuous charm of oriental grace full of the indolence and reserve of an impulsive passion. The entrancing languor of her dance ... is permeated with the spirit of the passionate and cajoling dances of the biblical Jews."[79]

A number of recent writers about early twentieth-century performance have theorized about her "decadence" and attributed it to late nineteenth-century malaise and nihilistic attitudes that flowed over into the new century. Patricia Vertinsky quotes Edward Said, who wrote about Rubinstein: "One of the first 'Salomés' to disrobe on stage was the young Russian Jewish artist Ida Rubinstein, whose 1908 performance of the 'dance of the seven veils' in her own staged production of Oscar Wilde's Salomé is said to have precipitated an outburst of Orientalism, anti-Semitism and misogyny."[80]

Charles Batson reflected further on her exotic persona: "Playing the Orient, meant playing up sexual promise, and threat, unlimited desire. Rubinstein staged on her body the game of cloaking and exhibition that marked her public persona, promising yet blocking full access."[81]

Batson explores Rubinstein's titillating qualities: "When she portrayed Zobéide in *Schéhérazade,* the long open seams on her garments from time to time exposed her torso and legs, teasingly telling the eyes to watch her. The Parisian public had thrilled to stories of Rubinstein's striptease as Salomé, to her undressing as Cleopatra, and to her erotic exposure in *Schéhérazade.*"[82] Indecency was trendy, but for Rubinstein the body was sacred, all the while her behavior upended the bourgeois blinders she refused to uphold.

In his illuminating study of decadence at the fin de siècle, Eugen Weber expostulated on the many expressions of decadence: "The apparent collapse of established ideals, the reaction against scientific materialism and rational explanations, encouraged interest in mystery and the supernatural, appreciation of faith for the sake of faith."[83] Weber spoke about mysticism, something Rubinstein seemed attracted to, and deliberated that it became a means of "being original—a Christian decadence" and brought together one's private obsessions with public ones. It fought off the sense of decay and distress that haunted this period. There were fears of the moral and physical degeneration of the French nation, especially after the loss of the

Ida Rubinstein, 1920s. Drawing by Arthur Grunenberg. SOURCE: JEROME ROBBINS DANCE DIVISION, THE NEW YORK PUBLIC LIBRARY FOR THE PERFORMING ARTS, ASTOR, LENOX, AND TILDEN FOUNDATIONS.

Ida Rubinstein as Basiola in Gabriele d'Annunzio's film *La Nave*, 1921. SOURCE: THE PICTURE ART COLLECTION/ALAMY STOCK PHOTO.

war to the Prussians in 1870, and the immediate fierce response of the Paris Commune.

It was not only the unveiling of her beautiful body that seemed to arouse the word *decadent*. Karl Toepfer studied nudity in *Empire of Ecstasy: Nudity and Movement in German Body Culture 1910–1935*, and wrote that: "The more the naked body becomes, the more the body dominates perception, the more the body assumes an abstract identity. Modernity signifies a tendency toward abstractness of form."[84] It seemed that modernism and decadence were often tied together.

Many writers and artists did not appreciate being identified with decadence and created the new form, Symbolism. The decadents represented an earlier stage of development on the path toward Symbolism; Symbolists argued that subjectivity, spirituality, and mysterious internal and external forces were sources of the truth rather than what is derived from the observation of outward appearance; the truth cannot be represented directly.

Rubinstein's dive into Symbolism seemed to go along with the Symbolist credo put forth in 1886, in its effort to avoid being labeled decadent.

One of the more profound descriptions of Rubinstein as a personality and as a performer was offered by Colette in *Candide*, a literary and political weekly with a patently nationalistic and an anti-Semitic stance, very popular during the interwar period. Nevertheless, Colette, the brilliant literary figure of the period, wrote for them and pondered the quixotic and complex Rubinstein in an essay/review published December 13, 1922. Colette chronicles with wisdom and clarity Rubinstein's persona, whom she confesses she did not know personally. She begins her piece with the comment, "I imagine that Rubinstein has a great soul, much larger than her body, and this soul, given the slightest shock, responds with all of her being. A material sign inserts itself into the body of Rubinstein, and is sufficient to illuminate her, to create an illusion of her."[85]

Then she qualifies this comment with a strong diagnosis. "Madam the Dancer, this is not you! Yes, you are a mime, who enchants us, and lives in your surprising body, where grace propagates itself slowly all the length of your body and surrounds it in circular waves."[86] So Colette understands the heart of the problem with Rubinstein. Yes, she is an astounding performer, but much more a mime than a ballet dancer. Lynn Garafola emphasized that her training as an actress enhanced the glorious possibilities of gesture in creating a role.

> Vasilii Geltser taught her plastique, and Meyerhold taught her "plastic motion," influenced by François Delsarte whose ideas reached Russia in the beginning of the twentieth century. So boundaries between acting and dancing were eroded. Fokine made the "fully expressive body" a cornerstone of his new ballet. But it was Isadora who embodied the ideal; and she met Isadora on her trip to St. Petersburg and followed Isadora's principles.[87]

Colette knows what derisive remarks had been made about Rubinstein in the past, and defends her explaining that, "She puts up with criticisms, ones that caricature her, offering heavy handed remarks, and nasty parodies. No matter what the criticisms, she keeps on working."[88]

But Colette also can strike a harsh note. "She cannot really dance the way she wants to. She attacks the stage, this year with classical ballet, which resists her efforts. I imagine that she cannot accept advice from those who know classical technique, no counsel, who might be the first to say that classical ballet is a profession, not the creation of a role."[89] Colette cautions Rubinstein, but we know that it is to deaf ears. "More often than not she is a hardy female pony, nourished, but whose tiny size and specialized athleticism permit her to move rapidly. She is a sturdy creature, who appears very light and airy. She is a flame that generates infinite curves."[90] Such were Colette's insights into Rubinstein's theatrical being.

Always curious about where her talents as an actress could reach, after World War I, Rubinstein appeared on the silver screen in 1919, in a film about St. George by the Italian film director Giulio Aristide Sartorio, to little reaction.[91]

Perhaps more successfully, she looked to d'Annunzio for his Italian film scenario of *La Nave,* directed by the playwright's son. It is an interesting way to ponder Rubinstein's performance persona and to examine carefully her role as the toxic heroine Basiliola, the only film we have in which she dances.[92] There are subtitles in Russian that apparently were translated from the Italian by M. Bronstein in 1910. The whole silent film with added music takes place in one hour and twenty-four minutes and presents many scenes in which Rubinstein appears. But perhaps the episode that best describes her dancing and acting ability, as well as her poignant movement talent is when she seduces her enemies. She dances a short solo, in a vast, teeming melodrama filled with heavily populated scenes and overly dramatic acting.

The story takes place in early medieval times (552 CE), with the prediction that Venice will become the most exceptional and prosperous city in Italy. Here the ship, *La Nave,* is the symbol of Venice's power over the Adriatic. The stage is filled with the populace of the city, emitting a rarely seen energy and gestural excitement. Some are wearing medieval peasant outfits and others are dressed in capes or white robes with black stripes on the lower sleeves; they are rarely absent from the stage. While Basiliola is dancing, behind her is the bestial and ferocious chorus. There is music in the background by Ildebrando Pizzetti, although there are no spoken words.

The character of Basiliola seems to represent the old pagan religious beliefs, while the huge chorus symbolizes the rise of Christianity along with the Gratici brothers and their mother who hovers over them. Basiliola was the queen or highborn daughter of a man belonging to the Faldero faction. Her father Orso and her four brothers were blinded, and had their tongues cut out by followers of their enemies, Sergio and Marco Gratici. In the end, Basiliola wreaks her vengeance on them by seducing them, but finally she dies, throwing herself on a burning altar, punished for her crimes, her old world beliefs as well as her startling sensuality.

Rubinstein makes a glorious entrance, standing proudly at the bow of her ship as it comes into port; she's surrounded by women and holds herself imperiously. She is clothed in filmy material, her silken cape blowing in the wind held by her arms out to the side; the crowd announces that she is a Siren of the sea, and that she has just returned from dancing at the court of Theodora, as they suspiciously gaze at her.

She makes her next important entrance when she speaks to her enemy Marco telling him "I am from the Faldero crown, the daughter of Orso. You know me very well. Your predatory eyes have tried to swallow me." She throws her arms high in a gesture of triumph telling him that her father called her Basiliola, but "you shall call me Destruction!! Oh Gratici, for you I will dance a victory dance."

But Basiliola not only seduces and eventually finds ways to defeat her enemies, Marco and Sergio, she also decides to kill all those who blinded and cut out the tongues of her brothers. Supported by a flank of soldiers, she had these terrible men thrown into a pit. While standing on top of the pit, she kneels down and aims her bow and arrow at her enemies, and swiftly and accurately kills each one as they shout insults at her. When she notices Marco observing her grotesque actions, she begins to laugh at him. Trying to escape, he grabs her bow and breaks it in half. Still the quintessential seductress, she covers up her bosom with a kittenish look. Softening his demeanor, he then shelters her with his cape, as she takes her bejeweled headdress and crowns him with it. The crowds never cease their amusement, regaling and laughing as they have been given permission to celebrate and indulge themselves. Rubinstein appears to have completely dazzled everyone and moves with confidence as she brandishes a sword above her head. The music then begins and she commences her dance.

Now adorned in a light-colored, bare-midriffed, and jeweled bodice with a gauzy, tulle-like skirt, she puts on a string of pearls and a forehead band, and wafts her way onto the screen, her loose, long hair framing her delicate features and aquiline nose. While crouched over, Rubinstein moves in an elfin manner, flitting from one side of the camera to the other. At first glance, she appears to be playing a gypsy flirt, with her bare stomach and baubles and the sweeping skirt; the layers seem to swirl like a Romantic tutu. Indeed, at one point she seductively sinks back on her bent knee and arches over her front leg, very much like the dying swan. She throws her arms up, her long, willowy body like a winged bird about to take flight. Then she crosses her arms on top of her head, folding them sensually, casting her eyes down with a come-hither look.

Though the camera barely shows her feet, it almost seems that she's wearing pointe shoes and moving on the tips of her toes, and despite her height she appears light as a feather. Often jumping from one side of the stage to another, she now appears catlike, twisting her body with her arm in front, the other above, and the head tilted questioningly. Then she hops, taking one foot in back and then the other, upstage (or backward) toward the gathering of people drawn to her magnetism. Her face is magical, smiling fully at times, and then barely opening her lips, but always with an air of superiority and control of the gaping crowd.

One of the hostile brothers, Sergio, is seen watching her, laughing and speaking silently to her insistently. Musicians playing old instruments accompany her movements. What the viewer sees is the ease with which she manipulates her long, slim figure, perched high on her toes at times, wispily taking her whole lanky frame into diverse spaces. The last glance we catch of her dance is when she opens her arms wide and sinks slowly to the floor, her gaze cast upward, as the mysterious Sergio calls back to her. Then she rises on her toes to rush toward the camera, forward and back with her arms flying up and down, flung out to the side. She is the sublime siren, the femme fatale, perhaps the Salomé of her youthful performances. Indeed, the composer of the score for the film quotes Richard Strauss's theme music for the opera, *Salomé* during Rubinstein's dance.

In this cinematic display, she reaffirms her reputation as a brilliant actress and inimitable performer, even in these short episodes, and these many years later. How would we characterize the realization of her dramatic intentions? As we know from her writing in *L'Art aux trois visages,* and her attachment to the ideals of Greek tragedy, she begins with the thought that all human beings have an innate sense of art, and of being an artist, and that we seek understanding and revelation through the experience of heroes in a dramatic narrative, with music and dance. The observer in the audience ties him- or herself to the events onstage and lives through the heroes, finding his or her own deliverance. Rubinstein feels this synchrony with the audience in her life as an actress and a dancer, and knows that the wonderment she creates in the moment and onstage is at the heart of her contribution to performance.

It seemed, however, that Rubinstein's luck was running out, as in April 1934, at the age of fifty-one, the critics were heartless in their reviews of Stravinsky's *Perséphone,* one of her last roles. As she aged and suffered these biting critiques, she became more and more melancholy. Though Perséphone was predominantly a speaking/acting role, her dancing, which relied on her usual gestural vocabulary, simply could not rise to the occasion. She was faulted for her exaggerated facial and physical effects, remindful of the theatrical representations of a played-out Symbolism. Her makeup and florid hand gestures derived much influence from the movie stars of the silent film period. Also, in *Perséphone* she had to save her breath for her recitations, so it was apparent that she kept her movements to a minimum. A dancing partner, Keith Lester, wrote about Rubinstein's shivers before going onstage: "Her look of glazed horror frightened me; if we had not been through the passage of temptation carefully with Kurt [Jooss], I might have thought that this was a full Stanislavsky rendering."[93]

Rubinstein commissioned a brilliant cadre of artists to work on *Perséphone* for her Paris ballet season in 1934, despite the grim economics of the time and the threat of impending war. Igor Stravinsky, André Gide, Rubinstein, Jacques Copeau, Kurt Jooss, and André Barsacq are the protagonists in this sweeping *melodrama, Perséphone.* (It was the poet Paul Valéry who previously used the term *mélodrama* for two works he created for Ida, *Amphion* [1931], and *Sémiramis* [1934].) Opening on April 30, 1934, *Perséphone* received but three performances at the Paris Opéra.

Perséphone faced relentless problems from the melodrama's origins to its first performance, but also philosophical and musicological traditions and underpinnings that shaded and influenced its exalted purpose. Each of the artists projected his or her intellectual codes and individual theories onto the work. Perhaps all artists are outliers to some extent, but this group certainly represents those who were exiles from their countries, or from their cultures, and were decidedly melancholy.

Charles Joseph included *Perséphone* in his book *Stravinsky's Ballets,* titling one of his chapters "Terpsichorean Hybrids," because the ballet/melodrama contains a sung and spoken text with music and choreography.[94] Rubinstein had met Stravinsky when she danced with Diaghilev's Ballets Russes in 1910, and had worked with the composer unsuccessfully in 1920, as he dropped out of the play *Antony and Cleopatra*. For her 1928 season, however, together they had created the ballet *Le Baiser de la Fée*.

She had long been a follower of Gide's writings and poetry and when she invited him to do something for her season in 1934, he mentioned his "small ballet" titled *Proserpine* or *Perséphone*, written in 1909 (but conceived even earlier), and based on the Homeric *Hymn to Demeter* (650–550 BCE). Gide had made several versions of the myth, playing with various elements in its dramatic path and had spent over forty years contemplating its features.

In Rubinstein's production, nearly 100 choristers sang onstage, and in the third scene fifty children joined the chorus. Ten dancers were assigned as the Nymphs. The first tableau begins in the setting of a cathedral rather than a Greek temple, with Eumolpus of the Eleusian Mysteries chanting to Demeter, Perséphone's mother (played by the youthful Nathalie Krassovska), that her daughter ate "the seeds of the pomegranate." (Mercury, played by Anatole Vilzak, will later give these seeds to Perséphone.) Demeter entrusts Perséphone to the Nymphs who follow Perséphone into the underworld. Drawn to the narcissus, she sees the underworld through it, wandering between life and death, almost in a daze, but united with the beauty surrounding her.

The second tableau takes place in the underworld, opening with Perséphone asleep on a large ornate bed. Gide allows his heroine to feel the welcoming presence of Hades, rather than his threat. Sadly, Demeter grieves and searches for Perséphone and this lamentation disturbs Perséphone; the souls of the Shades are disheartened and their "inquiétude" affects Perséphone.

The rebirth of Perséphone in the third tableau sees her as the seed of spring. She affirms herself as she partners with Triptolemus—a character, invented by Gide, who represents the first cultivator of agriculture. Luxuriously dressed and content, she appears proudly on Hades's arm and announces her destiny as Queen of the Dead, and there she teaches the Shadows to live in peace with their fate. She finally walks out of Hades and into Demeter's outstretched arms. The Gods agreed that Perséphone would stay above ground nine months of the year (spring through autumn) and in Hades for the three months of winter.

In the book, *Modernist Mysteries*, Tamara Levitz describes the vicissitudes that Rubinstein had in producing "Perséphone," and unravels the complicated issues encompassing several major battles among artists who were intellectually and culturally at odds with each other. In describing the making of this sung drama, the author concentrates on "breaking away from the text-based accounts of historical meaning, or what [Foucault] called the 'regime' of 'scientifically true statements.'"[95] In such a Foucauldian analysis, one places in the forefront the way power relations come to light as things change. And things were constantly changing for Rubinstein. Levitz examines the many drafts that Gide penned; the stage notes indicated by Jacques Copeau, the director and founder of the Théâtre du Vieux Colombier; and the musical distinctions noted by Stravinsky.

Perhaps the most contentious problem of the production was the uneasy and troubled relationship between Stravinsky and Gide. When Gide first heard the musical score for *Perséphone,* he realized that his poetry, his cadences were being ignored, and that Stravinsky had deliberately bypassed his text, creating almost a contradictory sonic environment. Their clash really began at Rubinstein's home at a dinner on October 20, 1933, where the first run-through, in a roomful of luminaries from Paris's artistic high society took place. Paul Claudel, Paul Valéry, Arthur Honegger, Igor and his son Soulima Stravinsky, Jacques Copeau (a friend of Gide's), and Rubinstein were there. Stravinsky and his son played a piano transcription of two of the three tableaux in *Perséphone.* Gide was disheartened when he heard the music at this dinner, despite the fact that Rubinstein paid enormous sums of money to bring these artists together for *Perséphone:* 200,000 francs to Gide, 180,000 francs to Copeau, 25,000 francs to Barsacq for his stage and costume design, and three installments of 25,000 francs (and perhaps more) to Stravinsky. In 1934, 1 US dollar was worth 50 French francs.

The work lacked a choreographer, although Michel Fokine was choreographing the ballet *Diane de Poitiers* for Rubinstein's 1934 season. The problem was that Stravinsky held an antipathy toward Fokine and refused to work with him. Stravinsky proved to be very contentious. Eventually Kurt Jooss was hired to come in, as Copeau strongly championed him, and at an earlier time Jooss had choreographed Stravinsky's *Pulcinella.* Jooss began work in January 1934.

Little is really known about how Jooss moved bodies around, and what exactly Rubinstein did in her solo as Perséphone. At the time there were so few critics who understood dance, and apparently the most famous, André Levinson, disliked Jooss's dances. At a later time, Stravinsky mentioned that Rubinstein did not dance Perséphone's solo, but rather declaimed the text and that was as it should be. But there are some photographs of the dancers, and some descriptions that suggest Jooss was influenced by Isadora Duncan's

between the wars

Greek representations, as well as by his major teacher, Rudolph von Laban. Jooss had recently escaped with his company from the Nazis, after having received a 1932 distinguished award for his ballet *The Green Table* at the first Paris choreographic competition, organized by Rolf de Maré.

Jooss seems to have been the only artist without rancor toward others working on the project. In a way he was in luck, as Stravinsky's attraction to church music and ritual inspired him to ask the choreographer to superimpose movement on closed vocal numbers. So Jooss used physical gesture to advance the action and to realize the musical intention. "This blatant theatrical approach differed from Gide's notion of musical expression."[96]

Levitz does provide some clues as to how Jooss worked. Using a balletic vocabulary as his base, he played with improvisation, suggesting to his dancers dramatic narratives and gestures derived from Ancient Greek vases and other artworks, as well as some everyday movement. This method would seem to have been particularly relevant to the liturgical aura of the work. Developing ritual-like movement, "[Jooss] sculpted these gestures to both individual and collective moves in unison and coordinated them exactly with Stravinsky's musical rhythms, in a style reminiscent of Émile Jaques-Dalcroze."[97] One of the key moments for dance occurs when Perséphone makes her descent into Hell. Jooss choreographed this episode to Stravinsky's saraband—a Baroque dance form that the composer used to signify a memory that could not be recaptured.

It seemed that the production of *Perséphone* was doomed from the start. Its resplendent scenery and hordes of people and children onstage, the beautiful songs and lyrical music, and the fervent acting could not erase its heavy conception. Although only fifty minutes long, and critics praised the noble presence and inimitable poses of Rubinstein, it only received three performances.

After her professional disappointment during the 1934 season with *Perséphone,* Rubinstein's reputation improved with Élisabeth de Gramont's ballet *Diane de Poitiers,* composed by Jacques Ibert and choreographed by Michel Fokine. Apparently de Gramont brought to life the epoch of Henry II and his mistress Diane, with splendid decor by Alexandre Benois and choreography by Fokine. Ibert explained how he pruned his musical resources from common folk tunes of the sixteenth century. De Gramont situated Rubinstein's role perfectly and it received rave reviews: "The enormous success of *Diane de Poitiers* brings a lovely brightness to the 1934 season."[98] De Gramont was invited to work again in 1938, with Ibert on a ballet, *Le Chevalier*

Errant, commissioned by Rubinstein, however the ballet was never produced. Probably Rubinstein was too occupied with her other performance pieces with Paul Claudel.

Soon after the rather sad eventuality of *Perséphone,* Rubinstein teamed up with her esteemed partners Paul Valéry, Arthur Honneger, and Michel Fokine to create an innovative and daring piece, *Sémiramis,* which harkened back to themes resembling her first role as Cleopatra. It was presented at the Paris Opéra on May 11, 1934. Honneger and Valéry became fast friends working on *Amphion* and were delighted to collaborate once again. *Sémiramis* told the story of a Babylonian queen who fought and conquered foreign lands, stole their precious objects, and took slaves. Among the prisoners is an attractive man with whom she falls in love. However, he soon tries to take over her regime and flaunt his superiority; this incenses her and she immediately has him killed by her ferocious Amazons. Brutality seemed a common theme in many of Rubinstein's productions.

There was a fifteen-minute speech for Rubinstein that concluded this drama, as well as a more intriguing declamation of the slave chorus in Act I that sounded like wordless singing. "*Sémiramis* provided Honegger with an opportunity to experiment with a new musical technology, the ondes Martenot, or musical waves invented by M. Martenot, which he introduces in the fifth scene of the ballet-melodrama to set off the queen's choice of a slave."[99] This early electronic instrument sounded otherworldly, and "supported Rubinstein's attempt to return to the kind of self-exoticizing, mythologizing spectacle that first launched her Parisian career."[100] The music contained beautiful passages praised by critics, but the poetry, drama and dance failed to entrance the audience. Rubinstein was faulted for her inability to render Valéry's poetry elegantly, but she did receive some reviews that were encouraging. In *La Revue Musicale* edition from 1934, Suzanne Demarquez testified that "Mme Rubinstein found in Sémiramis a role that perfectly expresses her 'plastique.' Her appearance on the chariot of war, the triumphant movement of her rising toward the throne and the deathly gesture which resolves in a tender supplication, all are visions that one will keep in one's memory for a long time."[101]

However, Vuillermoz wrote in *L'Excelsior* (May 14, 1934) that he disliked Fokine's choreography for the production, nor did he appreciate the voice, diction, and delivery of Rubinstein as the Queen. Charles Mayer quotes Honneger who discusses the flow of the piece from a magazine article, "Valéry et la musique," *Style en France,* on June 1946.

The first two tableaux, filled with nothing but movement and music, gave way in the third to a long monologue by the heroine. The music was then supposed to recede and become a sonorous background against which the spoken voice would stand out. There was an obvious risk in the use of such a form. The audience expecting the ballet to take up again, laughed during the recitation of the text because it seemed too long. And yet this was the elite of Parisian society who, as is well known, "adores Valéry."[102]

Her efforts with poetic drama were radical and provocative, but essentially, they did not work as good theatre, although they gave inspirational opportunities to the composers, choreographers, and the poets. The audiences realized their breakthrough efforts, respecting Rubinstein's legacy but leaving her with a troubled reputation.

RUBINSTEIN'S SWAN SONG

In 1938, after many years of acting in dramas with Greek or French heroines, and trying her luck with running a ballet company, her final theatrical triumph resulted in the Oratorio, *Joan of Arc at the Stake*, or *Jeanne d'Arc au Bûcher*, also by Paul Claudel with music for chorus composed by Arthur Honegger. Once again, a Jewish woman playing a Christian Saint provoked vitriolic outbursts, certainly because at this moment Jews were the targets in Europe. It was a supreme irony that her last, signature gift to the stage was her role as the iconic Christian female martyr, Joan of Arc.

The first performance in May 1938 took place in Basel, Switzerland, under the direction of Paul Sacher, followed by a concert in Orléans, France, in May 1939, and finally in Paris at the Palais de Chaillot, the next month in June 1939. Audiences raved as she as Jeanne offered them solace and hope in the face of an invading enemy when many artists lost their sense of meaning in a world of fraction and fracture. Playing Jeanne who saved France on the eve of the German invasion was a stroke of genius. She was determined to continue her performances of *Jeanne d'Arc* in spite of the looming threat and was able to broadcast on Radio Paris a live performance of *Jeanne d'Arc*; she began touring it to several Belgian cities.

Many of her reviews for "Jeanne" were highly complimentary, as they found her musicality and the sonority of her voice with the poem and music as sublime. But there were some scandalous remarks found in newspapers known for calumny and poor taste. For example, one author could not help himself from describing the Oratorio in the following terms:

> After the enemy's conquest of Orléans, Jeanne d'Arc played by the Jewess Rubinstein came on the scene. The next week, May 8th, M. Albert Lebrun and the Archbishop of Westminster came to save the city of Orléans. The deciding damage was to be the performance of *Jeanne d'Arc* with the participation of the Jewess Rubinstein, the Free Mason, Jean Hervé and the musical composition by Arthur Honegger.[103]

The vituperative comments continued through 1939, as when Marcel Jouandeau in *Le Peril Juif,* an anti-Semitic publication known for its incendiary comments about Jews wrote, "Almost all the conductors of our orchestras in Paris are Jewish, here one only plays Jewish music. Monsieurs Honegger and Milhaud etc. not only have a good hand, they have the whole hand!"[104] The writer assumed that Honegger was also Jewish, which he was not. Suffice it to say, Rubinstein's last, rather brilliant performance capped a complicated and extraordinary career.

EACH OF THE WORKS discussed in this book featured different aspects of Rubinstein's passion for the spotlight, and each brought out different qualities in her performance fulfilling her vision of specialized aesthetics. Though Rubinstein may have been bereft as a child growing up without parents, her character and temperament dictated that she have boundless confidence in her abilities, not only as an impresario hiring some of the greatest artists in the modernist movement to work with her, but also as an actress encouraged by her mentor Sarah Bernhardt, and as a ballerina, cushioned by her financial control over those choreographers whom she encouraged to feature her at her best. Although this period of her life did not reach the peaks of the prewar years, she still maintained a formidable stage presence in spite of her often anachronistic themes. Indeed Meryle Secrest recounts Romaine Brooks's poignant, disarming interpretation of Rubinstein's legacy.

> The degree to which Ida Rubinstein ceased to be long, thin, hieratic, with almond eyes, a mixture of Queen Nefertiti and the mosaic of Torcello, and became a pathetic, forgotten figure, can be charted in the cycle of changing tastes, which decrees that one generation will find ludicrous posturing the art which its parents have idolized; and also what Romaine had long suspected to be Ida's stubborn lack of good sense.[105]

But we must remember that Romaine was bitter and vindictive toward the end of her life and even refused to see Rubinstein when she moved to Vence. And as for the invectives hurled toward Rubinstein by French critics, there is the issue of their vanity that emboldens their criticism like armor against the foreigner. "Their insinuations and outright insults reflected the threat they felt she and her art posed to French culture. One of the most common subtexts revealed the prejudices they carried concerning the purity of art and the corrupting influence of money. Her Jewish heritage likely provoked a number of nasty references to her wealth."[106]

CHAPTER FIVE

War Again and the Menace of Anti-Semitism

AT THE OUTBREAK OF WORLD WAR II, Rubinstein did not want to leave Paris. On May 24, 1939, she received the Grand Cross of the Legion of Honor, its highest award, for her work in response to the war; she had set up a wing of a hospital in Étiolles near Paris, where she nursed French soldiers before she escaped to London. It was rather naive of her not to see the threat she faced, being born a Jew. Guinness was instrumental in protecting Rubinstein from the dangers of remaining in Paris in 1940; the Germans entered Paris on June 14, and were ferociously bombing London in September 1940. The Vichy government's Statut des Juifs in Paris on October 3, 1940, forbade Jews from holding important positions in French life. Guinness convinced her that she had no choice but to escape Nazi Europe.

Absurdly, she stayed until May 1941, when the Germans launched a blitzkrieg against Belgium and the Netherlands and sent troops across the border to France. Luckily, she fled before the *rafle* or round up of 743 Jewish intellectuals and artists in December 1941, including Colette's husband, Maurice Goudeket, who was lucky to be released from the camps, and René Blum, for whom she had worked in Monte Carlo and would not survive Auschwitz. Guinness talked her into flying to Algeria, still a perilous locale, and arranged for her departure in the spring of 1941, in a plane from Casablanca to Portugal, and there, from Lisbon to London. Guinness's and Rubinstein's relationship began in 1909 or 1910, so there was no question as to their loyalty to one another; sadly their intimate letters and information about them have disappeared. Guinness's wife, Lady Moyne, died in 1939, but even this event did not alter the secrecy of their affair.

All that Rubinstein owned in her opulent Paris home at 7 Place des États Unis disappeared into Nazi coffers. She was completely dependent on Guinness now.

During the war, she began the remarkable, if not new activity of healing the wounded and sick. Despite her love of theater, she refused any interest in attending theatrical performances, but rather immersed herself in "charitable works." She began by visiting French pilots who had been shot down and rescued. Once again Rubinstein used her extraordinary finances to construct her own wing in the hospital at Camberley near London. She also worked at the British Legion Sanatorium at Preston Hall, Kent. Talking freely and consoling the young pilots became her major occupation; she was obliged to physically help with the nursing. She never appeared at society functions. However, she did host a champagne party, including the wounded who could attend to celebrate the shooting down of a thousand German planes. Soon after she was made godmother to the Free French Air Squadron.

One of the most devoted soldiers to Rubinstein was a French pilot, Roland Leblond, Commander of the Légion d'Honneur. He recounted his story that he fought for the English (his father was in the RAF), when his Spitfire was shot down and he had to bale out offshore near Cornwall. Wounded, he was taken to a French hospital where Mme Rubinstein visited him. From the end of 1945 through to 1947, she came to see him many times. He was twenty-four, she was in her sixties, but they became good friends. When he left the hospital, he was still in very bad shape. They then began to write. She was going through particularly bad times but still found time to write very comforting letters. M. Leblond, who lived in Menton, France, had a photograph of his Alsace Free French Division; of some 200 young men only 17 survived, many of whom were badly wounded. Rubinstein gave her devotion to these men. After she died, Leblond often visited Vence to lay flowers on her grave.

Shortly before the gathering storm of World War II, Walter Guinness (aka Lord Moyne) continued his odysseys to uncharted areas without Rubinstein.

Apartment on the Place des États Unis in Paris. SOURCE: AUTHOR'S COLLECTION.

His intrepid explorations have aroused interest, especially in anthropological circles. In a recent publication of the British Museum, "'Some Friends Came to See Us': Lord Moyne's 1936 Expedition to the Asmat," Nick Stanley recovers the photos and commentary of Lord Moyne, the passionate, inveterate adventurer who loved living in parts of the world others had not visited. Prior to Lord Moyne's expeditions, there had been only fleeting recorded interactions between the Asmat people of South New Guinea and European explorers. Moyne's three visits (1929, 1935, and 1936) took place over a seven-year period and document an era during the Asmat's activities that since has been severely impacted by travelers to the area. His observations and photos recall a time past. "Moyne was making a claim to have achieved friendly relationships despite the mutual suspicion in which both they and the Asmats held each other."[1]

Moyne's account of his third voyage was published in September 1936, after his return to England. *Walkabout* is a book that contains ninety-seven photographs, thirteen of which relate to the Asmats and their native handicrafts, all taken by Lady Vera Delves Broughton. Both Guinness and Rubinstein relished the sometimes fierce interchanges they had with exotic locales and hunting wild animals. Sharing far-flung places brought them together without being hounded by the curious and gossip-seeking populace. How sad that they never lived together in peace.

Atrocities to Jewish populations during World War II cannot be overemphasized, and it seemed that Lord Moyne unwittingly participated in one of the sad events that plagued this moment, as he was instrumental in the story of the *Struma*, a refugee ship from Romania. It is a historical abomination and remains a vivid reminder of what horrible deeds the Holocaust perpetrated. In 1942, fleeing Romania, nearly 800 Jews were aboard the *Struma*. It was interned, and quarantined by Turkey offshore for seventy-one days, then set adrift without power and torpedoed by a Soviet submarine in the Black Sea in 1942. Stalin ordered his submarines to sink all neutral ships in the Black Sea to prevent supplies from reaching Germany. The war in Europe had already been underway for several years, and Jews originally from Hungary, Austria, and Czechoslovakia crammed onto the squalid, former cattle boat, with bunks stacked ten high, with no kitchen, and only eight toilets. There were no life preservers. The crew was mostly Bulgarians. Refugees paid up to 1,000 dollars to a criminal who promised visas to Palestine, and a seaworthy ship, neither happened. Only one person survived the blast.[2]

Against this backdrop, Rubinstein and Guinness continued their secret love affair when something very ironic and devastating happened to him, related to the tragedy of the *Struma*. Late in his career, in 1941, Guinness was appointed by Prime Minister Churchill, to be the British minister resident in the Middle East, and was regarded as one of the architects of Britain's strict immigration policy limiting Jews from coming to Palestine. There is no evidence that Lord Moyne was anti-Semitic, but in the face of Arab resistance to Jewish migration into Palestine, and the British government's fear that this might bring them to support the Germans in the war, led him to enforce the policy of no Jewish immigration to Palestine, including the refugee ship, the *Struma*. The Jewish radical organization, Lehi, or the Stern Gang in Palestine waited until 1944 to take revenge on Lord Moyne, and two young gang members killed him when he was in Cairo. The Jews in Palestine thought that Moyne was hostile to Jewish settlement, due to his support of an Arab federation in the Middle East. But this opinion has been contradicted. Nevertheless, it became apparent that the gathering storm of fascism and Nazi power crushed any hopes Rubinstein may have had for the future. She had known Guinness for thirty years; he was her lover, ally, friend, confidante, and travel companion.

After that loss, and her deepening sense of alienation from the world around her, she retreated into herself and spirituality, spending months at a time at the Medieval Abbey of Hautecombe, a Benedictine Monastery. These reclusive journeys into isolation continued until she died. When she returned to Paris from London at the end of 1944, she discovered that her apartment and all her belongings were lost to the Vichy and Nazis. Paris had become a wasteland, emptied and moribund. Finding little comfort there, she looked for a change in 1948 and moved to Biarritz where she stayed until 1952. By this point she had retreated into a very solitary life, practically a hermit. She had already lost de Montesquiou, Bakst, d'Annunzio, and Ravel. And after Guinness's assassination, she became very much alone in her mourning, completely leaving her sense of Judaism as she delved into the quietism and mysteries of the Catholic religion. Then finally she decided to move to the south of France, to Vence, where she died in 1960.

RUBINSTEIN AND ANTI-SEMITISM

Although Rubinstein originally identified as Jewish and her family's wealth was known to be philanthropic, evidently Judaism held little attraction for her. Nevertheless, her Jewish origins obviously concerned many writers of her generation. We must remember that Rubinstein never changed her noticeably Jewish last name, despite her susceptibility as a major female star to both misogynist and anti-Semitic attacks on her background.

Rubinstein's childhood and life began and was framed by virulent pogroms in Russia, the Dreyfus Affair and later, the Holocaust. It is difficult to imagine that these events did not affect her deepening sense of isolation and unadmitted despair. There is also no doubt that she lost many of her Jewish friends who disappeared in the mayhem of Nazi brutality. She never considered her Jewish origins important to her art. But there is this powerful statement and warning raised by Vladimir Jankélévitch in *Modern French Jewish Thought*.

> To cease to be a Russian Jew, it is not sufficient to be a naturalized Frenchman. The fact of being Jewish is a fact that is effaced neither by naturalization nor by conversion. How can we define something whose essence is so indefinable? There is a virtue to this alibi, a consititutional alterity that belongs to Jews. This indeterminate attribute that a Jew has of never being absolutely present, but always absent in some way is not anything stable or objective.[3]

Karina Dobrotvorskaya, in the *St. Petersburg Theater Journal*, could not forget Rubinstein's background decades after her death and wrote,

> Rubinstein possessed a geometric body, a biblical face, the viscous plasticity of the feline family. For a cat—she was too grand and too tall. As a tigress—too graphic. A lean lioness. A greedy, imperious and insatiable one. She stubbornly did not wish to notice that her thinness and the splendor of her bejeweled clothing merely underscored the defect of the diamond which on closer inspection was only glass.... She was fabulously rich, amazingly beautiful, exceedingly wealthy, and completely without talent. It seems that the name Rubinstein brings only this to mind. Even the remarkable portrait by Serov, imprints an eccentric decadent woman, bare [naked] and with rings on her toes.[4]

This outrageously unfair review points to pervasive patterns that have dehumanized Jewish performers with comparisons with animals, objectified them physically, and rendered them to a crass stereotype. In short, Dobrotvorskaya offers nothing less than a distortion, a caricature of a human being.

Dobrotvorskaya goes on to discuss Rubinstein's complex persona: "The phenomenon of Rubinstein existed in contrasts of the exquisite and the ugly, face and body, of a young and feminine idealized tsarina and the daughter of a Kharkov Jewish millionaire."[5] Not an accident that her wealth and religion are continually cited, as the ugly part. Though Dobrotvorskaya acknowledges Rubinstein's shrewd commissioning of great modern composers, she attacks her on many levels. This biting article by Dobrotvorskaya suffers from a backward-looking, Soviet-style Marxism and harbors anti-Semitic assaults. Unfortunately, it only exacerbates and contributes to the long line of negative critiques that Rubinstein received during her life, most of which centered on her Jewishness.

The history of France in the late nineteenth and early twentieth centuries cannot ignore the power and consequences that the Dreyfus Affair (1894-1906) produced. It began when Rubinstein was eleven and ended when she was twenty-three. Upon her arrival in Paris in 1909, she could not help but know the attitudes that prevailed at the time. Maurice Blanchot in his essay, "Intellectuals Under Scrutiny" from 1984, comments on the Dreyfus Affair: "That appalling affair, during which were uttered against the Jews and those who stood by them, words as violent as the most violent of those with which the Nazis worked themselves up in order to justify a final solution."[6] This extraordinary moment in French history, and therefore in the forces of European politics, stands out as a barometer of intellectual madness. "Valéry, Mallarmé and Gide all took the side of the unjustifiable against Dreyfus, all in the name of justice, according to them."[7] Valéry wrote later in his *Notebooks* about his inept decision. How ironic that Valéry had worked so patiently and attentively with Rubinstein on their ballet *Amphion* (1931)!

Anti-Semitism followed Rubinstein from her earliest youth to her mature professional life. In James Loeffler's *The Most Musical Nation: Jews and Culture in the Late Russian Empire*, he observed that the anti-Semitic writings of Wagner infiltrated the Russian musical press continually from 1880 on. When Gustave Mahler's Fifth Symphony premiered in St. Petersburg in 1913, another critic, Mikhail M. Ivanov, attacked the work as "decadent foreign rubbish by a Viennese Jew."[8]

Rubinstein's dear friend and mentor, Sarah Bernhardt also struggled with the way she was treated because of her Jewish background. When she was extolled for her performance as Joan of Arc, *La France Chrétienne*, an openly anti-Semitic paper, disagreed: "This Jewess will deliberately play the role of Joan of Arc in the wrong way; she will present her as a hysterical woman who has hallucinations; she will make her behave in the most extravagant way; she will turn the holy girl into a mad and grotesque virago."[9]

Pierre Birnbaum seconds these comments about the aura of hate surrounding Jewish figures in the late nineteenth and early twentieth century. He of course points to the Dreyfus Affair and how anger toward Dreyfus mounted relentlessly, promoted by the publication *L'Action Française*, which fomented this fury.[10]

Let me begin with some critical comments that hit hard at her Jewish background, beginning with her early career and culminating with World War II: In Rebecca Rossen's book, *Dancing Jewish*, she recounts that Rubinstein danced the lead role in two versions of her *Salomé* (1908 and 1912), both moments of insidious remarks about her Jewish origins, either by the clergy or the press. Rossen discloses, "When she starred in the Ballets Russes' *Cléopâtre* and *Schéhérazade*, Jean Cocteau described her 'the great ibex of the Jewish Ghetto.' Although she was not an innocent party in her framing; her typecasting as a Jewish/Oriental dominatrix revealed growing turn-of-the-century anti-Semitism and the ways in which stereotypes about Jewishness are inseparable from gender and sexuality."[11]

After 1909, in both Paris and Russia, assaults on Rubinstein proliferated as she became more of a starring personality in a number of plays, especially when she collaborated with Gabriele d'Annunzio and Claude Debussy in *Le Martyre de San Sébastien* (1911). Michael de Cossart wrote in his biography of Rubinstein that on May 8, 1911, the Cardinal della Volpe questioned why "the two main organizers of this profanation were Jewish in origin?"[12] He was referring to Gabriel Astruc, the theater producer and to Rubinstein. He neglected to mention Léon Bakst's participation. The Monsignor in Paris, Léon-Adolphe Amette, carried out the Vatican demand and forbade all Catholics from attending the play.

Indeed, the original Catholic censors of the play may have had good reason to ban it. Rubinstein's legs were not only very visible, they were bare and of such perfection to attract the male emperor Diocetian's lascivious glances. Also, the Saint mimed the Passion of Christ set in deliberate parallel to the death and rebirth of Adonis. Only five days before the premiere of the play, it was put on the Index. A season in Rome was also canceled as Rubinstein's "Jewish" presence might have incited public outrage.

In addition at the time, Astruc confided in his letter to d'Annunzio on January 20, 1911, that one of his society ladies had reservations about this performance of Saint Sebastian, that they feared it would be an affront to Christianity. Certainly, they knew the church would intervene. Astruc, himself a Jew, told d'Annunzio that "They will try to insinuate that you are creating a sacrilege, and they will try to quickly prove that for the second time I crucified God."[13]

An article by Barbara Jepson makes an insightful point suggesting that, "The Catholic church also may have objected to Rubinstein's bare legs, and to the portrayal of a male Catholic Saint by a Jewish female dancer. Debussy and d'Annunzio both published a statement that they were not practicing Catholics but insisted that *Le Martyre* was intended to glorify Sebastian and all Christian heroism."[14]

In Lynn Garafola's "Circles of Meaning," she describes the context in which Rubinstein carved out the role of Sebastian and her unique cross-over talents as actress and dancer. Garafola emphasizes that in this role Rubinstein defied theatrical standards as a woman playing a Saint and being unquestionably a Jew. "She was criticized for her Eastern otherness and exotic modernism, a mirror of Jewish taste." *Cosmopolitanism* was the dirty word. "She was as beautiful as she was rich, with raven hair, and almond eyes of the anti-Semite's classic Jewess."[15] Garafola went on to acknowledge that her public persona ripped apart proper behavior, and that she divorced her husband in order to marry d'Annunzio; she seemed to have a number of lovers, proving that "Jewish women were 'hot,' undependable and fickle."[16] These were quotes originally from a gossip-y 1911 *New York Times* article.

Similar issues emerged one year later, in 1912, when Rubinstein took the acting role of the beauteous Hélène of Sparta, the libretto written by Emile

Verhaeren, a Belgian Symbolist poet. Two reviews that brought to light her immigrant situation were cited by Daniel Flannell Friedman: "The critic Judith Clavel in *La Vie* denounced the author Émile Verhaeren for abandoning his work to Jewish foreigners, notably the director, Alexander Sanin, Léon Bakst and Rubinstein."[17] In the fascist right-wing journal, *L'Action française,* Léon Daudet railed against the Jewish foreigners in the production, "The French public should rise up against Jewish foreigners, against their mercantile obscenity, and their obscene mercantilism; we must tear our theater from its servitude to them."[18] French cultural and economic protectionism were rampant during the interwar years. Epstein sheds light on the prejudices faced by musicians at this time.

> The government required subsidized orchestras to employ no fewer than 95% French musicians and the Ministry of Fine Arts agonized in internal memoranda over how to encourage French conductors and soloists to deny their services to foreign institutions.... Money for cultural endeavors was scarcer than ever. No matter that Rubinstein was merely following in the footsteps of primarily French writers, composers and visual artists, that she funded and guided an impressive flowering of French creative activity, that her spectacles helped France's most prestigious institution, L'Opéra, stay solvent—all this seems to have been obscured by the xenophobia, anti-semitism and misogyny of a culture that longed for the pre-war social order.[19]

It was no secret that Rubinstein was reviled for flaunting her extravagance and wealth, the proverbial Jewish entrepreneur. A producer with sumptuous tastes, Rubinstein rented the Théâtre de L'Opéra almost every year from 1919 to 1934. Pascal Lécroart delves into the criticisms to which Rubinstein was subjected, and concludes that "her talents were formidable and that those who wrote favorably about her counter balance the judgments of journalists at the time who were afflicted with xenophobia and anti-Semitism."[20]

In 1931 André Levinson hurled insults at Rubinstein in *Le Temps:* "Has not the National Theatre the obligation to incorporate in its repertoire representative works of contemporary dance masters? And yet we have allowed a Russian patron and dilettante the job of staging this Valse of Ravel with the aid of a foreign corps de ballet."[21]

Not only was she ridiculed for her religion and her money, but gender issues also thwarted her reputation: Stravinsky called her a "particularly vain woman" (in a letter to Paul Hindemith, April 16, 1932). Diaghilev included her in the category of "sluts who think themselves dancers."[22]

In a fascinating, rarely written about moment in 1934, Charles Mayer informs us that Rubinstein, who was then past fifty years old, came across a Biblical theatrical group from Palestine in Paris, the Chel Players. Intrigued by them, she imagined that her next endeavor would have a Biblical theme. It seemed surprising and ironic that she would seize on a Jewish topic, given her disinterest in Jewish traditions. She sought the help of Darius Milhaud and Paul Claudel, but Claudel declined this idea, opting to transform the Jewish scenario into one that dealt with Jesus Christ. In 1925, he had constructed a play, *Le Festin de Sagesse*, about Jesus's sharing a Sabbath meal in the house of a leading Pharisee from the Gospel of St. Luke. Claudel's influence was paramount. Mayer confirmed that Rubinstein never performed it and that it did not see the light until 1946.[23] It is interesting to note that later in life Rubinstein read the Bible with great passion. DePaulis highlights this phenomenon: "Every day and even more toward the end of her life, she immersed herself in the sacred pages."[24]

During these times of failure and success, Rubinstein focused almost exclusively on her work and showed little interest whatsoever in politics or religion. Moreover, she certainly displayed no observance of Judaism. Gradually though, some years after the Russian Revolution and World War I, a phenomenon occurred in France and Europe, a resurgence of conversations about the importance of spirituality and religion. Rubinstein fell under the spell of Paul Claudel's poetry and religiosity, collaborating with him on a production of his *Les Choéophores* (1935), in which she played the lead role of Clytemnestra, and in 1936 she converted to Catholicism. Rubinstein entreated a Dominican priest, père Antonin Motte, the prior of the monastery of Saulchoir near Tournai. She was intent on learning how to live a cloistered life, wanting an internal quiet that would assuage the turbulence surrounding her and decided to escape occasionally to the Château de Sourches where the calm, beauty, and silence eased her nervousness. Was it her certain knowledge that being born a Jew would haunt her and prevent a peaceful aging, especially in light of events in France and Germany?

CONCLUSION

Despite the almost insurmountable issues presented here, Rubinstein's legacy deserves to live on through her significant groundbreaking contributions to subsequent twentieth-century zeitgeist. Between the wars, she had produced and starred in twenty-nine plays or ballets in major theaters throughout

Ida Rubinstein, 1930s. SOURCE: COURTESY SUEDDEUTSCHE ZEITUNG PHOTO/ALAMY STOCK PHOTO.

Europe. It was an astonishing output. In addition, along with La Argentina, Isadora Duncan, Anna Pavlova, and a few others, she became another great woman producer, hiring the most talented, even revolutionary designers, composers, writers, and choreographers: a wonder woman for her time.

Véronique Fabbri eloquently praises Rubinstein's unique contribution to the theater.

> Unlike many of her contemporaries Ida Rubinstein possesses, all at once, a solid musical formation, and a no less profound understanding of dance, even if she were not "accomplished," and especially a knowledge of poetry and of prosody to which Valéry like Claudel were sensitive. The capacity to practice these different arts could only help her to project their essence and to maintain it.[25]

Fabbri goes on to comment on Rubinstein's magical and generous legacy: "Ida Rubinstein's professionalism, her force of will to be the most complete artist possible, anticipates the formation of theatre artists after the war; she offers especially to poets like Valéry, rare possibilities of pursuing the relationship between poetry and the dance."[26]

While the famous entrepreneur impresario Diaghilev is praised for his brilliant taste and savoir faire, Rubinstein suffers disgrace for her largesse and abundant finances, as Epstein confirms. "Yet her entirely defensible, even laudable aesthetic predilections manifest again and again in the works she commissioned, rendering her work as animatrice inseparable from her creative collaborations, and the works they produced."[27] Her ability to bring together felicitously several art forms was praised by the scholar, Andrew Sheppard, as he envisioned her "an innovator in dance, music and drama as they coalesce in Modernist Theatre."[28]

Rubinstein's contribution to her interwar ballets cannot be underestimated. She capitalized on the legacy of hiring new composers, scene designers, and poets to enhance her productions, and only in the 1930s was ballet "officially recognized as contributing to France's cultural future as well as its past."[29] A thirst for new music among ballet companies gained passionate advocates and audiences.

I had mentioned earlier that while she embodied heroic characters, underneath the surface, she was a deeply tragic and unappreciated figure. Even though she converted to Catholicism, she had to flee Paris during the Occupation. Under the Vichy regime, she lost her French citizenship (*dénationaliser*) as a result of the Nuremburg laws.[30] While in England during the

1940s, she paid large sums to build and work in hospices to save French soldiers wounded during the war. But she never recovered her stardom. After the war, she wasted away in the South of France, very isolated in her religious fervor, almost starving herself to death. After Guinness died, Rubinstein lived another sixteen years. But having lost her lover, many friends, and her home, she therefore, retreated into herself. She died in 1960 at the age of seventy-seven, abandoned by the press and her friends.

EPILOGUE

Why Remember Ida Rubinstein?

RUBINSTEIN ENCOURAGED, worked with, and supported financially some of the world's greatest choreographers, composers, directors, dancers, poets, and designers. This formidable list includes the following:

- André Gide translated *Antony and Cleopatra* and wrote the libretto for *Perséphone*.
- Igor Stravinsky composed the music for *Perséphone* and *Le Baiser de la fée*.
- Paul Valéry wrote the poetic narrative for *Amphion* and *Sémiramis*.
- Paul Claudel wrote the poetic narrative for *Les Choréophores*, and *Jeanne d'Arc*.
- Vsevolod Meyerhold directed *Salomé* and *La Pisanelle ou la Mort Parfumée*.
- Arthur Honegger composed the music for *Amphion*, and *l'Impératrice aux Rochers*.
- Florent Schmitt composed the music for *La Tragédie de Salomé*, et *Antoine et Cléopâtre*.
- Claude Debussy composed the music for *Le Martyre de San Sébastien*.

- Maurice Ravel created the music for *Boléro* and *La Valse*.
- Déodat de Séverac composed the music for *Hélène de Sparte*.
- Darius Milhaud composed the music for *Les Choréophores* and orchestrated the music for *La Bien-Aimée*.
- Jacques Ibert composed the music for *Diane de Poitiers*.
- Roger Ducasse composed the music for *Orphée*.
- Gabriele d'Annunzio wrote the libretto for *Le Martyre de San Sébastien*, *La Pisanelle ou la Mort parfumée*, and *Phaedre*.
- She worked multiple times with both Léon Bakst, her primary designer until his death in 1924, and Alexandre Benois until her last performance in 1940.

These choreographers created her ballets:

- Michel Fokine: *Salomé, Le Martyre de San Sébastien, La Pisanelle ou la Mort parfumée, Sémiramis,* and *Diane de Poitiers*.
- Léonide Massine: *David, Les Enchantements d'Alcine,* and *Amphion*.
- Bronislava Nijinska: *Les Noces de Psyché et l'Amour, La Bien-Aimée, Boléro, Le Baiser de la Fée, La Valse, Nocturne,* and *La Princesse Cygne*.
- Léo Staats: *Istar* and *Orphée*.
- Kurt Jooss: *Perséphone*.
- Nicola Guerra: *Salomé* (1919) and *Artémis troublée*.

APPENDIX

Productions by Ida Rubinstein

List Assembled by Lynn Garafola

PRODUCED WORKS

Antigone

    COSTUMES: Léon Bakst
    STAGE DIRECTION: Yuri Ozarovsky
    FIRST PERFORMANCE: St. Peterburg Lydia Yavorskaia's New Theater, April 16, 1904
    PRINCIPAL PERFORMERS: Ida Rubinstein (Antigone)

Salomé: Tragedy in one act by Oscar Wilde

    MUSIC: Alexander Glazunov ("Dance of the Seven Veils")
    SETS AND COSTUMES: Léon Bakst
    STAGE DIRECTION: Vsevolod Meyerhold
    CHOREOGRAPHY: Michel Fokine
    FIRST PERFORMANCE: St. Petersburg, Conservatory (Grand Hall), December 20, 1908 (only the "Dance of the Seven Veils" was performed)
    PRINCIPAL PERFORMER: Ida Rubinstein (Salomé)

NOTE: The premiere of the full work, scheduled for November 3, 1908 at the Mikhailovsky Theater, St. Petersburg, was canceled because of censorship.

Le Martyre de Saint Sébastien (The Martyrdom of Saint Sebastian): Mystery play in five acts by Gabriele d'Annunzio

MUSIC: Claude Debussy
SETS AND COSTUMES: Léon Bakst
STAGE DIRECTION: Armand Bour
CHOREOGRAPHY: Michel Fokine
CHORUS MASTER: D. E. Inghelbrecht
CONDUCTOR: Andre Caplet
FIRST PERFORMANCE: Paris, Théâtre du Châtelet, May 22, 1911
PRINCIPAL PERFORMERS: Ida Rubinstein (Saint Sebastian), Adeline Dudlay (The Distraught Mother), Vera Sergine (The Sick and Feverish Girl), Maxime Desjardins (the Emperor), and Henry Kraus (the Prefect)
PRINCIPAL SINGERS: Rose Féart (One Voice), Ninon Vallin, and Yvonne Courso
NOTE: This work was revived at the Théâtre National de l'Opéra on June 17, 1922 (see below).

Hélène de Sparte (Helen of Sparta): Tragedy in four acts by Emile Verhaeren

MUSIC: Déodat de Séverac
SETS AND COSTUMES: Léon Bakst
STAGE DIRECTION: Alexander Sanin
CONDUCTOR: Louis Hasselmans
FIRST PERFORMANCE: Paris, Théâtre du Châtelet, May 4, 1912
PRINCIPAL PERFORMERS: Ida Rubinstein (Helen), Vera Sergine (Electra), Edouard de Max (Polius), Maxime Desjardins (Menelaus), Roger Karl (Castor), and Dorival (?) (Zeus)

Salomé: Drama in one act by Oscar Wilde

MUSIC: Alexander Glazunov
SETS AND COSTUMES: Léon Bakst
STAGE DIRECTION: Alexander Sanin
CHOREOGRAPHY: Michel Fokine ("Dance of the Seven Veils")
CONDUCTOR: Louis Hasselmans
FIRST PERFORMANCE: Paris, Théâtre du Châtelet, June 12, 1912 (répétition génerale); June 13, 1912 (premiere)
PRINCIPAL PERFORMERS: Ida Rubinstein (Salomé), Odette de Fehl (Herodias), Edouard de Max (Herod), and Roger Karl (Jokanaan)

La Pisanelle ou la Mort parfumée (La Pisanelle or The Perfumed Death):
Comedy in a prologue and three acts by Gabriele d'Annunzio.

> MUSIC: Ildebrando Pizzetti
> SETS AND COSTUMES: Léon Bakst
> STAGE DIRECTION: Vsevolod Meyerhold
> CHOREOGRAPHY: Michel Fokine
> CONDUCTOR: D. E. Inghelbrecht
> FIRST PERFORMANCE: Paris, Théâtre du Châtelet, June 11, 1913
> PRINCIPAL PERFORMERS: Ida Rubinstein (La Pisanelle), Suzanne Munte (The Queen), Eugenie Nau (Oriour la Devine), Jane Thomsen (Dame Eschive), (?) Neith-Blanc (Altafior), Louise Marion (Odiart la Chamaigre), (?) Delve (La Saraquille), Marcelle Schmitt (Penthésilée), (?) Barella (Sister Julienne), Edouard de Max (Prince of Tyre), (?) Joube (Ober Embrias), Jean Hervé (Sire Huguet), (?) Puylagarde (Psillud le Crétois), Camille Gorde (Le Léopardier), (?) Desfontaines (Maître Ancel), Paul Baume (Almoner), (?) Taldy (Le Bailli de la Secrete), (?) Mendaille (Le Baile de Venise), Camille Mars (Zan Corner), and Jean Durozat (Bishop of Lemisse)
> NOTE: In the program and publicity for the season, Pizzetti was called Ildebrando da Parma.

Phèdre: Tragedy in five acts by Jean Racine

> FIRST PERFORMANCE: Paris, Théâtre National de l'Opéra, June 27, 1917 (Act IV only)
> SETS AND COSTUMES: Léon Bakst
> PRINCIPAL PERFORMERS: Ida Rubinstein (Phèdre), (?) Prozor (Oenone), Edouard de Max (Thésée), and (?) Escande (Hippolyte)
> NOTE: Only Act IV was given.

L'Imroulcaïs, le roi errant (L'Imroulcaïs or the Wandering King):
Drama in 3 parts and 12 tableaux by Femand Nozière, based on the poems of Imroulcaïs, as translated by Edmond Doutte

> MUSIC: Camille Erlanger
> FIRST PERFORMANCE: Paris, Théâtre Sarah-Bernhardt, February 17, 1919 (gala)
> PRINCIPAL PERFORMERS: Ida Rubinstein (Ocem Djoundab/Oum Djonbab); Mmes Bèrangère; and Sida ben Saïd; MM. Andre Cahuzac, Joube (lmroulcaïs), Grétillat, Paul Daubry, Campana, Lacoste, Geo Derval, Perdon, Lagrange fils, Fraticelli, Dalsace, and Piquard
> NOTE: Additional performances were given at the same theater on February 22 and 24.

La Tragédie de Salomé (The Tragedy of Salomé):
Ballet in one act after a poem by Robert d'Humières

    MUSIC: Florent Schmitt
    SETS AND COSTUMES: René Piot
    SCENE PAINTING: (?) Bertin
    CHOREOGRAPHY: Nicola Guerra
    CONDUCTOR: Camille Chevillard
    FIRST PERFORMANCE: Paris, Théâtre National de l'Opéra, April 1, 1919
    PRINCIPAL DANCERS: Ida Rubinstein (Salomé), Christine Kerf (Herodias), (?) Even (l'Emeraude), G. Franck (le Saphir), Camille Bos (la Perle), Georges Wague (Herod), Paul Baron (Jean), and (?) Bourdel (le Bourreau)
    SINGERS: Antoinette Laute-Brun, Leonie Courbieres, and (?) Dagnelly
    NOTE: This ballet was first produced at the Théâtre des Arts in November 1907, with Loie Fuller in the title role. On April 22, 1912, at the Théâtre du Châtelet, the work was revived with new choreography by Ivan Clustine and with Natalia Trouhanova as Salomé. The following year (June 12, 1913), a version choreographed by Boris Romanov with Tamara Karsavina in the title role was presented by Diaghilev's Ballets Russes at the Théâtre des Champs-Elysées.

Antoine et Cléopâtre (Antony and Cleopatra): Tragedy in six acts and fourteen scenes by Shakespeare, translated by André Gide

    MUSIC: Florent Schmitt
    SETS AND COSTUMES: Jacques Dresa
    SCENE PAINTING: Georges Mouveau
    CONDUCTOR: Camille Chevillard
    FIRST PERFORMANCE: Paris, Théâtre National de l'Opéra, June 13, 1920 (répétition générale); June 14, 1920 (premiere)
    PRINCIPAL PERFORMERS: Ida Rubinstein (Cleopatra) and Edouard de Max (Antony)
    NOTE: Léon Bakst worked closely with Rubinstein in the genesis and early planning of this production.

Artémis Troublée (Confused Artémis): Ballet in one act by Léon Bakst

    MUSIC: Paul Paray
    SETS AND COSTUMES: Léon Bakst
    CHOREOGRAPHY: Nicola Guerra
    CONDUCTOR: Camille Chevillard
    FIRST PERFORMANCE: Paris, Théâtre National de l'Opéra, April 28, 1922

PRINCIPAL DANCERS: Ida Rubinstein (Artemis), (?) Jasmine (Alkippe), (?) Severin (Zeus), and Josef Svoboda (Acteon)

Le Martyre de Saint Sébastien: Mystery play in five acts by Gabriele d'Annunzio.

MUSIC: Claude Debussy
SETS AND COSTUMES: Léon Bakst
SCENE PAINTING: Orest Allegri
STAGE DIRECTION: Armand Bour
CHOREOGRAPHY: Michel Fokine
CONDUCTOR: Henri Defosse
FIRST PERFORMANCE: Paris, Théâtre National de I 'Opéra, June 17, 1922
PRINCIPAL PERFORMERS: Ida Rubinstein (Saint Sebastian), Suzanne Desprès (la Mère douloureuse), (?) Greyval (la Femme voilée), Madeleine Vincent (la Femme muette), (?) Rochemay (la Femme aveugle), Maxime Desjardins (the Emperor), Henry Kruass (the Prefect), Pierre Bertin (Sanae), (?) Perras (Marc), (?) Maury fils (Marcellien), Edmond Menaud (l'affranchi Gudène), Henry Verlay (Theodote), (?) Lagrange (Vital), and (?) Maxime (le Héraut d'armes)
PRINCIPAL SINGERS: Jane Laval (Une Voix), Jeanne Montfort, and Yvonne Courso (les Gemeaux)
NOTE: This was a revival of the work first produced on May 22, 1911 at the Théâtre du Châtelet (see above), somewhat cut and with a number of new costumes and design elements by Bakst. The production was revived in 1923 and 1924, and performed on tour in Brussels (1924), Milan (1926), and London (1931).

The Spirit of Venice: Series of tableaux depicting a reception given by the Doge of Venice to the Persian Embassy in the eighteenth century.

FIRST PERFORMANCE: Paris, Théâtre National de l'Opéra, June 24, 1922
PRINCIPAL PERFORMERS: Ida Rubinstein (Adriatic), Edouard de Max (Doge), Cecile Sorel (Venice), Prince Kaner of Kapurthala (Persian Prince), and Hubert Stowitts
NOTE: This was presented at the Grand Prix Ball, organized by Princess Murat as a benefit for Russian refugees in France and other charities.

The Dying Swan

MUSIC: Camille Saint-Saens
FIRST PERFORMANCE: Paris, Théâtre Edouard VII, April 21, 1923
PRINCIPAL DANCER: Ida Rubinstein

NOTE: This was performed at a charity matinee in aid of Russian refugees in France. Another performance, also in aid of Russian refugees, was given at the Théâtre des Champs-Elysées on June 14, 1923.

Phaedre: Lyric tragedy in three acts by Gabriele d'Annunzio

MUSIC: Ildebrando Pizzetti
SETS AND COSTUMES: Léon Bakst
STAGE DIRECTION: Armand Bour
CONDUCTOR: Philippe Gaubert
FIRST PERFORMANCE: Paris, Théâtre National de l'Opéra, June 7, 1923
PRINCIPAL PERFORMERS: Ida Rubinstein (Phaedre), Suzanne Despres (Astymone), M. Moreno (Aethea), M. Berry (Gorga), (?) Sylvie (Hipponoe), (?) Greyval (Eunone), Maxime Desjardins (Thesée), (?) Yonnel (Hippolyte), Paul Capellani (Eurythos), and (?) Chambreuil (le Prêtre)
NOTE: This was a revival of the work first produced on April 9, 1909 at the Teatro Lirico, Milan. In 1926, for Rubinstein's Italian tour, Pizzetti's music was replaced by a new score by Arthur Honegger.

La Dame aux Camélias (The Lady of the Camelias):
Play in five acts by Alexandre Dumas

STAGE DIRECTION: Armand Bour
SETS AND COSTUMES: Alexandre Benois
SCENE PAINTING: Oreste Allegri and Georges Mouveau
FIRST PERFORMANCE: Paris, Théâtre Sarah-Bernhardt, November 27, 1923
PRINCIPAL PERFORMERS: Ida Rubinstein (Marguerite Gautier), Ernest Ferny (Armand Duval), (?) Chameroy (Saint-Gaudens), (?) Deneubourg (Comte de Giray), (?) Puylagarde (Gustave), Jeanne Delys (Prudence), Lucienne Marsac (Olympe), and (?) Mauloy (Georges Duval)
NOTE: Rubinstein performed Act V at a charity matinee for Russian refugees at the Théâtre Edouard VII on April 21, 1923. Another "preview," also in aid of Russian refugees, was given at the Théâtre des Champs-Elysées on June 14, 1923.

Le Secret du Sphinx (The Secret of the Sphinx):
Dramatic poem in four acts by Maurice Rostand

SETS: (?) Perronnet and (?) Bertin
COSTUMES: Erte
FIRST PERFORMANCE: Paris, Théâtre Sarah-Bernhardt, February 20, 1924
PRINCIPAL PERFORMERS: Ida Rubinstein (Âme du Sphinx), Gilda Darty (Isabella Monti), (?) Fresnel (Une Jeune Égyptienne), MadeleineThomas;

MM. (?) Yonnel (Paris Eglano), Roger Puylagarde (Marcellus), (?) Chameroy, and (?) Deneubourg (Prince)

NOTE: February 20, 1924 was the date of the dress rehearsal, opening night was on February 21.

Istar: Dance poem in one act by Léon Bakst.

MUSIC: Vincent d'Indy
SETS AND COSTUMES: Léon Bakst
CHOREOGRAPHY: Léo Staats
CONDUCTOR: Philippe Gaubert
FIRST PERFORMANCE: Paris, Théâtre National de l'Opéra, July 10, 1924
PRINCIPAL DANCERS: Ida Rubinstein (Istar), (?) de Malkazouny, Odette Joyeux, Germaine Dugue (Visions of Childhood), Colette Salomon, (?) Sarazotti (Visions paradisiaques), (?) Delsaux (Vision rampante), (?) Ryaux (le Bonheur terrestre), (?) Ferouelle (Vision sacerdotale), Serge Peretti (Vision céleste), (?) Pacaud, (?) Durozoy (Visions guerrières), and Paul Baron (Vision de feu)
NOTE: This ballet was first produced on April 22, 1912, at the Théâtre du Châtelet with choreography by Ivan Clustine and with Natalia Trouhanova in the title role.

L'Idiot (The Idiot): Play in five acts and six scenes by Fernand Nozière and Vladimir Bienstock after the novel by Fyodor Dostoyevsky

STAGE DIRECTION: Armand Bour
SETS AND COSTUMES: Alexandre Benois
SCENE PAINTERS: Oreste Allegri (Scenes 1, 2, and 5) and Nicolas Benois (Scenes 3 and 4)
FIRST PERFORMANCE: Paris, Théâtre de Vaudeville, April 1, 1925
PRINCIPAL PERFORMERS: Ida Rubinstein (Nastasia Philippovna Barachkoff), Gina Barbieri (Nina Alexandrovna Ivolguine), Claire Nobis (Aglaé Ivanovna Epantchine), Louise Dauville (Daria Alexievna), Camille Vernades (Barbara Ardalionovna lvolguine), Paul Capellani (Parfène Semenitch Rogojine), Pierre Blanchar (Prince Léon Nicolaievitch Muichkine), Armand Bour (General Ardalion Alexandrovitch Ivolguine), Ernest Ferny (Totzky), Rouviere (Ferdychtchenko), Jean Fleur (Lebedeff), Maurice Benard (Ptitzine), Julien Lacroix (Semen Parfenovitch Rogojine), and Lucien Nat (Zaliojeff)

Orphée (Orpheus): Lyric mime-drama in three acts by Roger Ducasse

MUSIC: Roger Ducasse
SETS AND COSTUMES: Alexander Golovin

CHOREOGRAPHY: Léo Staats
CONDUCTOR: Philippe Gaubert
FIRST PERFORMANCE: Paris, Théâtre National de l'Opéra, June 11, 1926
PRINCIPAL DANCERS: Ida Rubinstein (Orpheus) and Marie-Louise Didion (Eurydice), Suzanne Lorcia, (?) Damazio (Bacchantes), (?) Ryaux (the god Hymen), and (?) Denizard (Thanatos)
PRINCIPAL SINGERS: Andree Marilliet (A Young Girl), Madeleine Lalande (A Young Woman), Charles Cambon (An Old Man), and (?) Madlen (A Young Man)

L'Impératrice aux Rochers (The Empress of the Rock): Mystery play in five acts and thirteen scenes by Saint-Georges de Bouhelier

MUSIC: Arthur Honegger
SETS AND COSTUMES: Alexandre Benois
SCENE PAINTING: Oreste Allegri and Nicolas Benois
STAGE DIRECTION: Alexander Sanin
CONDUCTOR: Philippe Gaubert
FIRST PERFORMANCE: Paris Théâtre National de l'Opéra, February 17, 1927
PRINCIPAL PERFORMERS: Ida Rubinstein (Empress Victoria), Suzanne Despres (the Virgin), (?) Clervanne (Lalage), (?) Rueff (Francesca), Andree Marilliet (a Voice), Jacques Gretillat (Othon), Maxin1e Desjardins (Pope), Jean Herve (Emperor Aurelius), (?) Benglia (Sultan of Marocco) Richard Wilm (Lorenzo), Andre Wasley (Beaudoin), (?) Lesieur (le Braconnier), Max Chartier (the Old Counselor), and Maurice Dorléac (the Chaplain)

Les Noces de Psyché et de I' Amour (The Marriage of Cupid and Psyché): Ballet in one act by Alexandre Benois

MUSIC: Johann Sebastian Bach, orchestrated by Arthur Honegger
SETS AND COSTUMES: Alexandre Benois
SCENE PAINTING: Helene (Benois) Braslawsky
CHOREOGRAPHY: Bronislava Nijinska
CONDUCTOR: Walther Straram
FIRST PERFORMANCE: Paris, Théâtre National de l'Opéra, November 22, 1928
PRINCIPAL DANCERS: Ida Rubinstein (Psyche), Anatole Vilzak (Amour), Ludmilla Schollar, Nadine Nicolaeva (Legat), Joyce Berry, Anna Ludmilla, Alexis Dolinoff, and Serge Unger

La Bien-Aimée (The Beloved): Ballet in one act by Alexandre Benois

MUSIC: Franz Schubert and Franz Liszt, orchestrated by Darius Milhaud
SETS AND COSTUMES: Alexandre Benois

CHOREOGRAPHY: Bronislava Nijinska
CONDUCTOR: Walther Straram
FIRST PERFORMANCE: Paris, Théâtre National de l'Opéra, November 22, 1928
PRINCIPAL DANCERS: Ida Rubinstein (la Bien-Aimée); Anatole Vilzak (Poet)

Boléro: Ballet in one act

MUSIC: Maurice Ravel
SETS AND COSTUMES: Alexandre Benois
SCENE PAINTING: Oreste Allegri
CHOREOGRAPHY: Bronislava Nijinska
CONDUCTOR: Walther Straram
FIRST PERFORMANCE: Paris, Théâtre National de l'Opéra, November 22, 1928
PRINCIPAL DANCERS: Ida Rubinstein (Danseuse), Anatole Vilzak, Alexis Dolinoff, Eugene Lapitzky, and Serge Unger
NOTE: A second version, with choreography by Michel Fokine, was produced for Rubinstein in 1934.

Le Baiser de la Fée (The Fairy's Kiss):
Allegorical ballet in four tableaux by Igor Stravinsky

MUSIC: Igor Stravinsky
SETS AND COSTUMES: Alexandre Benois
SCENE PAINTING: Georges Mouveau
CHOREOGRAPHY: Bronislava Nijinska
CONDUCTOR: Igor Stravinsky
FIRST PERFORMANCE: Paris, Théâtre National de l'Opéra, November 27, 1928
PRINCIPAL DANCERS: Ida Rubinstein (Fairy), Anatole Vilzak (Rudy), Ludmilla Schollar (Fiancée), Nadine Nicolaeva (Legat), Anna Ludmilla, Joyce Berry, Alexis Dolinoff, Eugene Lapitzky, and Serge Unger
SINGERS: Andree Marilliet and Louis Arnoult

Nocturne: Ballet in one act

MUSIC: Alexander Borodin, orchestrated by Nicholas Tcherepnine
SETS AND COSTUMES: Alexandre Benois
SCENE PAINTING: Hélène (Benois) Braslawsky
CHOREOGRAPHY: Bronislava Nijinska
CONDUCTOR: Walther Straram
FIRST PERFORMANCE: Paris, Théâtre National de l'Opéra, November 29, 1928
PRINCIPAL DANCERS: Ida Rubinstein (Young Girl), Anatole Vilzak (Fiancé), Ludmilla Schollar, Nadine Nicolaeva (Legat), Anna Ludmilla, Joyce Berry, Eugene Lapitzky, and Serge Unger

La Princesse Cygne (The Swan Princess):
Ballet in one act from the opera *Tsar Saltan*

MUSIC: Nikolai Rimsky-Korsakov
SETS AND COSTUMES: Alexandre Benois
SCENE PAINTING: Oreste Allegri
CHOREOGRAPHY: Bronislava Nijinska
CONDUCTOR: Walther Straram
FIRST PERFORMANCE: Paris, Théâtre National de l'Opéra, November 29, 1928
PRINCIPAL DANCERS: Ida Rubinstein (Swan Princess), Anatole Vilzak (Guidon), Ludmilla Schollar, Nadine Nicolaeva (Legat), Anna Ludmilla, Joyce Berry, Alexis Dolinoff, Eugene Lapitzky, and Serge Unger

David: Ballet in one act

MUSIC: Henri Sauguet
SCENARIO: Andre Dodelet
SETS AND COSTUMES: Alexandre Benois
SCENE PAINTING: Oreste Allegri
CHOREOGRAPHY: Léonide Massine
CONDUCTOR: Walther Straram
FIRST PERFORMANCE: Paris, Théâtre National de l'Opéra, December 4, 1928
PRINCIPAL DANCERS: Ida Rubinstein (David), Alexis Dolinoff (Saul), Nadine Nicolaeva (Legat), Anna Ludmilla, Joyce Berry, Eugene Lapitzky, and Serge Unger

La Valse (first version): Choreographic poem by Maurice Ravel

MUSIC: Maurice Ravel
SETS AND COSTUMES: Alexandre Benois
SCENE PAINTING: Oreste Allegri
CHOREOGRAPHY: Bronislava Nijinska
CONDUCTOR: Gustave Cloez
FIRST PERFORMANCE: Monte Carlo, Théâtre de Monte-Carlo, January 15, 1929; Paris, Théâtre National de l'Opéra, May 23, 1929
PRINCIPAL DANCERS: Ida Rubinstein, Anatole Vilzak, Alexis Dolinoff, Eugene Lapitzky, Serge Unguer, Anna Vorobieva, Mona Stal, Klavdia Lotova, and (?) Oulianovska
NOTE: A second version, with new choreography by Nijinska and new designs by Benois (executed by Nicolas Benois), was produced in 1931 at the Paris Opéra; a third version, with choreography by Michel Fokine, in 1934, also appeared at the Paris Opéra.

Les Enchantements de la Fée Alcine (The Enchantments of Fairy Alcine):
Ballet in 1 act by Louis Laloy, after Ariosto

> MUSIC: Georges Auric
> SETS AND COSTUMES: Alexandre Benois
> SCENE PAINTING: Hélène (Benois) Braslawsky
> CHOREOGRAPHY: Léonide Massine
> CONDUCTOR: Gustave Cloez
> FIRST PERFORMANCE: Paris, Théâtre National de l'Opéra, May 21, 1929
> PRINCIPAL DANCERS: Ida Rubinstein (Fée Alcine), Ruth Varpotiec (Angélique), Anatole Wiltzak (Roger), and Eugene Lapitzky (Tancrède)

Amphion: Ballet in one act by Paul Valéry

> MUSIC: Arthur Honegger
> SETS AND COSTUMES: Alexandre Benois
> SCENE PAINTING: Nicolas Benois
> CHOREOGRAPHY: Léonide Massine
> CONDUCTOR: Gustave Cloez
> FIRST PERFORMANCE: Paris, Théâtre National de l'Opéra, June 23, 1931
> PRINCIPAL DANCER: Ida Rubinstein (Amphion)
> SINGERS: Madeleine Mathieu, Nelly Marty, Mady Arty, (?) Kirova (Voices of the Muses), and Charles Panzera (Voice of Apollo)

Diane de Poitiers: Ballet in 3 tableaux by Élisabeth de Gramont

> MUSIC: Jacques Ibert, after sixteenth-century airs and dances
> SETS AND costumes: Alexandre Benois
> SCENE PAINTING: Nicolas Benois
> STAGE DIRECTION: Jacques Copeau
> CHOREOGRAPHY: Michel Fokine
> CONDUCTOR: Gustave Cloez
> FIRST PERFORMANCE: Paris, Théâtre National de l'Opéra, April 30, 1934
> PRINCIPAL DANCERS: Ida Rubinstein (Diane), Anatole Vilzak (King)
> SINGERS: (?) Mahe, Jemmy Bachillat (Musiciennes), Edmond Chastenet, and Pierre Froumenty (Musicians)
> NOTE: Rubinstein's costumes were designed by Dimitri Bouchène. Copeau's name does not appear on the program, as he had resigned prior to the opening of the season.

Perséphone (Persephone): Poem by Andre Gide

> MUSIC: Igor Stravinsky
> SETS AND COSTUMES: André Barsacq

SCENE PAINTING: Georges Mouveau
STAGE DIRECTION: Jacques Copeau
CHOREOGRAPHY: Kurt Jooss
CONDUCTOR: Igor Stravinsky
FIRST PERFORMANCE: Paris, Théâtre National de l'Opéra, April 30, 1934
PRINCIPAL DANCERS: Ida Rubinstein (Persephone), Anatole Vilzak (Mercury), and Nathalie Krassovska (Demeter)
SINGERS: René Maison (Eumolpus), Zanglust (children's) Choir of Amsterdam
NOTE: Copeau's name does not appear on the program; he had resigned prior to the opening of the season.

Sémiramis: Danced poem by Paul Valéry

MUSIC: Arthur Honegger
SETS, COSTUMES, AND CURTAIN: Alexandre Jacovleff
CHOREOGRAPHY: Michel Fokine
CONDUCTOR: Gustave Cloez
FIRST PERFORMANCE: Paris, Théâtre National de l'Opéra, May 11, 1934
PRINCIPAL DANCERS: Ida Rubinstein (Sémiramis), Keith Lester (the Handsome Captive)
SINGERS: Henri le Clezio, Edmond Chastenet Pierre Froumenty, and Henri Medus (Astrologers)
NOTE: Rubinstein's costumes were designed by André Barsacq (first tableau), Léon Bakst (second tableau), and Dimitri Bouchène (third tableau).

Jeanne d'Arc au Bûcher (Joan of Arc at the Stake):
Lyric mystery play in a prologue and ten tableaux by Paul Claudel

MUSIC: Arthur Honegger
TEXT: Paul Claudel
FIRST PERFORMANCE: Basel, Kunstmuseum, May 12, 1938 (as a concert-oratorio in a German translation by Hans Reinhardt)
CONDUCTOR: Paul Sacher (Kammerorchester)
PRINCIPAL PERFORMER: Ida Rubinstein (Joan)
SINGERS: (?) Vivante (the Virgin), Jean Perier (Frère Dominique), and the Kammerchor of Basle
FIRST PERFORMANCE IN FRANCE: Orléans, Théâtre Municipal, May 6, 1939 (as a concertoratorio)
CONDUCTOR: Louis Fourestier
PRINCIPAL PERFORMER: Ida Rubinstein (Joan)
SINGERS: Solange Delmas (the Virgin), Jean Hervé (Frère Dominique), José de Trevi (Cauchon), and Henri Fabert (Heurtebise)
FIRST PERFORMANCE IN PARIS: Palais de Chaillot, June 13, 1939

SETS AND COSTUMES: Alexandre Benois
SCENE PAINTING: Helene (Benois) Braslawsky
CONDUCTOR: Louis Fourestier (Orchestre Philharmonique)
PRINCIPAL PERFORMER: Ida Rubinstein (Joan)
SINGERS: Andrée Chauveron, Jean Hervé (Frère Dominique), (?) Peyron, (?) Cauchemont, and the Chorale Raugel
NOTE: As *Jeanne au bûcher,* the work was first performed at the Paris Opéra on December 18, 1950, with "movements" choreographed by Serge Lifar and sets and costumes by Yves Bonnat.

UNPRODUCED WORKS

Oriane, la sans égale (Oriane, Unequaled)

LIBRETTO: Claude Seran (Mme A. Fauchier-Magnan)
MUSIC: Florent Schmitt
SETS AND COSTUMES: Alexandre Benois
NOTE: The premiere of this work, scheduled for May 11, 1934, did not take place. As *Oriane et le Prince d'Amour,* it was produced at the Paris Opéra on January 7, 1938, with choreography by Serge Lifar and sets and costumes by Pedro Pruna.

La Sagesse (The Wise One)

MUSIC: Darius Milhaud
TEXT: Paul Claudel, after the parable of the Wedding Feast or that of the Wise and Foolish Virgins
SETS AND COSTUMES: Alexandre Benois
NOTE: First conceived by Rubinstein in 1934, after attending a performance by the Ohel players from Palestine, the work was scheduled for performance on November 29, 1938 at the Paris Opéra. The premiere was canceled, although Claudel's text was subsequently published in the *Nouvelle Revue Francaise.* The work was first performed on a French radio broadcast in 1946; the first stage production took place at the Venice Festival in 1949. Another production, with designs by Benois, took place that year at the Festival of Sacred Art in Perugia.

Le Chevalier Errant (The Knight Errant): Choreographic epic in four tableaux by Élisabeth de Gramont, after the novel by Miguel de Cervantes

MUSIC: Jacques lbert
TEXT: Alexandre Arnoux
SETS: Hélène (Benois) Braslawsky

COSTUMES: Alexandre Benois

NOTE: As Benois's surviving costume designs are dated 1938, it seems likely that Rubinstein intended to mount the work for the Paris Opéra season scheduled for November of that year, which never took place. The ballet was first produced on April 26, 1950 at the Paris Opéra, with choreography by Serge Lifar and sets and costumes by Pedro Flores. Lifar danced the title role.

Lucifer, ou Le Mystère de Caïn (Lucifer, or the Mystery of Cain):
Mystery play in three episodes and a prologue, after the poem by Byron

TEXT: Rene Dumesnil

MUSIC: Claude Delvincourt

NOTE: According to Michael de Cossart, the work was completed in 1941, and accepted by Jacques Rouché for production at the Paris Opéra. The libretto was published by Durand in 1944, with a note stating that the work was performed that year at the Opéra. In fact, the first performance (with the title *Lucifer*) did not take place at the Opéra until December 15, 1948. The choreography was by Serge Lifar, the sets and costumes by Yves Brayer.

NOTES

NOTES TO THE PREFACE

1 Alison Smale, "The Ghosts of Ballets Russes Return to Paris," *New York Times*, July 6, 2012.

NOTES TO CHAPTER ONE

1 Annie Cohen-Solal, *Mark Rothko: Toward the Light in the Chapel* (Jewish Lives) (New Haven, CT and London: Yale University Press, 2005), 1.
2 J. C. Flugel, *The Psychology of Clothes* (New York, International Universities Press, 1930).
3 Vicki Woolf, *Dancing in the Vortex: The Story of Ida Rubinstein* (London: Routledge, 2000), 3.
4 Woolf, *Dancing in the Vortex*, 3.
5 When we visited St. Petersburg in 2017, we discovered a building on the site of 2 Angliskaya that now houses a huge corporation.
6 Woolf, *Dancing in the Vortex*, 5.
7 "Mystery Woman," posted at Hello, a Russian language text, Jewish-Observer.com.
8 "Mystery Woman," Jewish-Observer.com.

9   Cassandra Langer, *Romaine Brooks: A Life* (Madison: University of Wisconsin Press, 2015), 54.
10 Nathalie Stronhina, "Les racines russes d'Ida Rubinstein," in *Une utopie de la synthèse des arts á l'épreuve de la scène,* Pascal Lécroart, ed. (Paris: Presses Universitaires de Franche-Comté, 2008), 166.
11 Stronhina, "Les racines," 171.
12 Stronhina, "Les racines," 169.
13 Jacques DePaulis, *Ida Rubinstein: Une Inconue Jadis célèbre* (Paris: Honoré Champion, 1995), 525.
14 DePaulis, *Ida Rubinstein,* 218.
15 Langer, *Romaine Brooks: A Life,* 78.
16 DePaulis, *Ida Rubinstein,* 303.
17 Pascal Lécroart, editor, *Une utopie de la synthèse des arts á l'épreuve de la scène,* 265.
18 Jacques DePaulis, "Un Mécène atypique," in *Une utopie de la synthèse des arts á l'épreuve de la scène,* ed., Pascal Lécroart (Paris: Presses Universitaires de Franche-Comté, 2008), 155. All translations from French to English are mine. The original French text will be included in these end notes. "Ce qu'il faut en retenir ici, c'est que Walter Guinness a consacré une grande partie de sa fortune à soutenir sans défaillir tous les spectacles de Rubinstein et cela pendant 34 ans."
19 Paul Claudel, *Journal* (Paris: Gallimard, 1969), 516.
20 Claudel, *Journal,* 516.
21 Rubinstein letter to Bakst. Bib. De l'Opéra 1.a, numero 1.
22 Daniel Flannell Friedman, *Ida Rubinstein: Le Roman d'une vie d'artiste,* Monique Briend-Walker, trans. (Paris: Salvator, 2011), 31.
23 Friedman, *Ida Rubinstein,* 15. "J'ai eu la vie que je voulais. Je ne l'ai pas eue facilement. Née en russie dans une famille à qui le théâtre semblait une déchéance (disgrace), il m'a fallu rompre durement avec mon milieu."
24 Friedman, *Ida Rubinstein,* 30.
25 Louis Greenberg, *The Jews in Russia Volume 1: The Struggle for Emancipation* (New Haven, CT: Yale University Press, 1944), 4.
26 Benjamin Nathans, *Beyond the Pale. The Jewish Encounter with Late Imperial Russia* (Berkeley, Los Angeles, London: University of California, 2002), 3.
27 Nathans, *Beyond the Pale,* 100.
28 Steven J. Zipperstein, *Pogrom: Kishinev and the Tilt of History* (New York and London: Liveright, 2018), 5.
29 Greenburg, *The Jews in Russia,* 178.
30 Nathans, *Beyond the Pale,* 187.
31 Nathans, *Beyond the Pale,* 189.
32 Nathans, *Beyond the Pale,* 3.
33 Nathans, *Beyond the Pale,* 224.

34 Rubinstein letter to Iuvitskaiia. December 1904, N. N. Gorich and EAI. op., ed. khr. 104, 1, 1-2.
35 Karina Dobrotvorskaya, "The Lioness," *St. Petersburg Theater Journal1* (1993): 4.
36 Lynn Garafola, *Legacies of Twentieth-Century Dance* (Middletown, CT: Wesleyan University Press, 2005), 167n50.
37 Autumn, 1906, TsGALI Fond 1958, op. 1, ed. khr. 104, 1.18.
38 Akim Volynsky, *Ballet's Magic Kingdom* (New Haven, CT and London: Yale University Press, 2008), XXVI.
39 Volynsky, *Magic Kingdom*, 135.
40 Volynsky archives, RGALI, Moscow. (TsGALI.f.95, Volynsky, op 1., ed. khr. 761, 1, 154-55.)
41 Deidre Pridden, *The Art of Dance in French Literature* (London: A & C Black, 1952), 60.
42 n.d. (spring 1906), TsGALI, fond 95, (Volynsky), op. 1, ed. khr. 764, 1, 1-2.
43 Lynn Garafola, "Circles of Meaning: The Cultural Contexts of Ida Rubinstein's Le Martyre de Saint Sébastien," in *Proceedings of the Society of Dance History Scholars* (Provo, UT: Brigham Young University, 1994), 32.
44 Rubinstein letter to Volynsky. 1907, TsGALI, fond 95 (Volynsky), op. 1, ed. khr. 764, 1, 1-2.
45 Volynsky letter to Rubinstein. 1907 TsGALI, f. 95 (Volynsky), op. 1, ed. khr. 217, 1, 10.
46 "Mon mari arrive subitement. Excuse dérangement. Perds pas l'espoir vous rencontrer."
47 Rubinstein letter to Volynsky. n.d. (1907), TsGALI, fond 95, (Volynsky), op. 1, ed. khr. 764, 1, 1-2.
48 Stanley J. Rabinowitz, *And Then Came Dance: The Women Who Led Volynsky to Ballet's Magic Kingdom* (New York: Oxford University Press, 2019), 20.
49 Rabinowitz, *And Then Came Dance*, 39.
50 Rabinowitz, *And Then Came Dance*, 39.
51 Rabinowitz, *And Then Came Dance*, 55.
52 Rabinowitz, *And Then Came Dance*, 57.
53 Rabinowitz, *And Then Came Dance*, 57.
54 Rabinowitz, *And Then Came Dance*, 58.
55 Robert Leach, *Vsevolod Meyerhold* (Cambridge, UK: Cambridge University Press, 1989), 6.
56 Leach, *Vsevolod Meyerhold*, 84.
57 Garafola, "Circles of Meaning," 32.
58 C. Moody, "Commedia dell'arte," in *Modern Language Review* 73 (1978): 59-869, 859.
59 Selma L. Odom, "Delsartean Traces in Dalcroze Eurythmics," *Mime Journal* 23 (April 30, 2005).
60 Leach, *Vsevolod Meyerhold*, 63.

61 Leach, *Vsevolod Meyerhold*, 63.
62 Leach, *Vsevolod Meyerhold*, 114.
63 Leach, *Vsevolod Meyerhold*, 112.
64 John E. Bowlt, "Bold and Dazzling: Léon Bakst and Antiquity," in *Hymn to Apollo: The Ancient World and the Ballets Russes*, Clare Fitzgerald, ed., Institute for the Study of the Ancient World at New York (Princeton, NJ and Oxford, UK: University Princeton University Press, 2019), 67.
65 André Levinson, *Bakst: Story of an Artist's Life* (New York: B. Blom, 1971), 170.
66 Bowlt, "Bold and Dazzling," 67.
67 DePaulis, *Ida Rubinstein*, 49.
68 Irina Pruzhan, *Léon Bakst, Set and Designs, Book Illustrations, Paintings and Graphic Works*, Sergei Dyachenko, designer and from the Russian by Arthur Shkarovski-Raffé, trans. (Middlesex, UK: Penguin Books, 1986), 217. Original text from Russian publication *Solntse Rossii* or *Sun of Russia* 25 (1913): 12.
69 Konstantin Rudinsky, *Vsevolod Meyerhold, Meyerhold the Director*, Sydney Schultze, ed., and George Petrov, trans. (Ann Arbor, MI: Ardis, 1981), 196.
70 Rubinstein letter to Kommisarzhevskaia. 1908, TsGALI, f. 778, op 2, ed. Khr. 38, 1. 3.
71 Rubinstein letter to Kommisarzhevskaia. 1908, TsGALI, f. 778, op 2, ed. Khr. 38, 1, 3.
72 Rubinstein letter to Meyerhold. 1908, TsGALI, f. 998), op. 1, ed., khr. 2332, letter 5.
73 Rubinstein letter to Meyerhold. August 1908, TsGALI, f. 998 op. 1, ed., khr. 2332, letter 6.
74 Bakst letter to his wife. *Sergei Diagilev I russkoe iskusstvo*, vol. 2, ed. I. S. Zil'bershtein and V. A. Samkov (Moscow: Izobrazitel'noe iskusstvo, 1982), 477n2.
75 Sjeng Scheijen, *Diaghilev a Life* (Oxford, UK and New York: Oxford University Press, 2009), 179.
76 Woolf, *Dancing in the Vortex*, 18-19.
77 Scheijen, *Diaghilev .A Life*, 177.
78 Davina Caddy, "Variations of the Dance of the Seven Veils," in *Cambridge Opera Journal* 17, no. 1, (March 2005): 37.
79 Caddy, "Variations of the Dance of the Seven Veils," 37-58.
80 Gabriele Brandstetter, *Poetics of Dance: Body, Image, and Space in the Historical Avant-Gardes* (New York: Oxford University Press, 2015), 188.
81 Julian Barnes, *The Man in the Red Coat* (New York: Alfred A. Knopf, 2020), 146.

NOTES TO CHAPTER TWO

1 From the Garafola collection.
2 Fokine letter to Benois, June 1908, found in his *Protiv Techeniia: Vospominaniia baletmeistera, stat'I, pis'ma*, ed. Yuri Slonimskii, introduction by Yuri Slonimskii. (Leningrad: Izdatel'stvo iskusstvo, 1962), 479-80.

3   Fokine letter to Benois, June 1908.
4   Fokine letter to Benois, June 1908, from Fokine's archives, 11. 9, 10. 28, letter 4.
5   Solomon Volkov, *St. Petersburg: A Cultural History* (New York, London: Free Press, 1995), 145.
6   Judith Mackrell, *Bloomsbury Ballerina* (London: Orion Books, 2009), 42.
7   Marcel Schneider, *Danser* 164 (1998): 40.
8   Charles Mayer, "Rubinstein: A Twentieth-Century Cleopatra," *Dance Research Journal* 20, no. 2 (Winter 1989): 33.
9   Mackrell, *Bloomsbury Ballerina*, 36.
10 Arnold Haskell and Walter Nouvel, *Diaghileff His Artistic and Private Life* (New York: Simon and Schuster, 1935), 179.
11 Bowlt, "Bold and Dazzling," 72.
12 Vincent Cronin, *Paris on the Eve: 1900–1914* (New York: St. Martin's Press: 1990), 247.
13 Bronislava Nijinska, *Early Memoirs* (New York: Holt Rinehart and Winston, 1981), 276.
14 Benois letter to V. N. Argutinsky-Dologorukov, July 1909, the Garafola Collection, St. Petersburg, vol. 2. Moscow: Izobrazitel'noe iskusstvo, 1982), 185.
15 Benois letter to Argutinsky-Dologorukov, July 1909.
16 Marcel Billot, editor, *Journal of the Abbé Arthur Musnier (1879–1939)*, (Paris: Mercure de France, 1985), 185.
17 DePaulis, *Ida Rubinstein*, 74. "Elle l'a exécuté avec une technique prestigieuse. On dirait une idole Égyptienne subitement ressuscitée. Des lignes pures et aristocratiques, d'une beauté étrange et harmonieuse, elle est tout un poème de grâce antique et langoureuse."
18 DePaulis, *Ida Rubinstein*, 79.
19 DePaulis, *Ida Rubinstein*, 84.
20 DePaulis, *Ida Rubinstein*, 85.
21 Lynn Garafola, *Diaghilev's Ballets Russes* (New York and London: Oxford University Press, 1989), 199.
22 Garafola, *Diaghilev's Ballets Russes*, 33.
23 Michel Fokine, *Fokine: Memoirs of a Ballet Master*, Vitale Fokine, trans. (Boston: Little Brown, 1961), 155.
24 Fokine, *Memoirs*, 155.
25 Fernand Nozière, ed. R. Chibirre, Editions Sansot, 1926, microfilm.
26 Boris Kochno, *Le Ballet* (Paris, Hachette, 1954), 162. "Entre le mur vert et le sol rouge, 'une serre â passion,' [a hot house of passion] l'atmosphère confuse faisait sourdre la cruauté, la chaleur, le désir, la luxure, même si Nijinski n'avait pas été là, tapi dans les coussins [ensconced in the cushions], ou agité de soubresauts de fauve captif."
27 Woolf, *Dancing in the Vortex*, 66.
28 Woolf, *Dancing in the Vortex*, 67.
29 Scheijen, *Diaghilev a Life*, 221.

30 Susan Jones, *Literature, Modernism and Dance* (Oxford Scholarship online, 2013), 4.
31 Sylvia Kahan, *Music's Modern Muse: A Life of Winnaretta Singer, Princesse de Polignac* (Rochester, NY: University of Rochester Press, 2003), 148.
32 DePaulis, *Ida Rubinstein*, 90-91.
33 Meryle Secrest, *Between Me and Life: A Biography of Romaine Brooks* (Garden City, NY: Doubleday, 1974), 204.
34 Langer, *Romaine Brooks: A Life*, 52.
35 Diana Souhami, *Wild Girls: Paris, Sappho and Art* (New York: St. Martin's Press, 2004), 132.
36 Langer, *Romaine Brooks: A Life*, 72.
37 Secrest, *Between Me and Life*, 247.
38 DePaulis, *Ida Rubinstein*, 256.
39 Kahan, *Music's Modern Muse*, 195.
40 Kahan, *Music's Modern Muse*, 226.
41 Kahan, *Music's Modern Muse*, 226.
42 Secrest, *Between Me and Life*, 267.
43 Souhami, *Wild Girls*, 10.
44 Souhami, *Wild Girls*, 17.
45 Tirza True Latimer, *Women Together/Women Apart: Portraits of Lesbian Paris* (New Brunswick, NJ: Rutgers University Press, 2005), 9.
46 Secrest, *Between Me and Life*, 272.
47 Souhami, *Wild Girls*, 74.
48 Souhami, *Wild Girls*, 74.
49 DePaulis, *Ida Rubinstein*, 229.
50 DePaulis, *Ida Rubinstein*, 254.
51 DePaulis, *Ida Rubinstein*, 254.
52 Kahan, *Music's Modern Muse*, 290.
53 Langer, *Romaine Brooks: A Life*, 82.
54 DePaulis, *Ida Rubinstein*, 256.
55 True Latimer, *Women Together/Women Apart*, 38.
56 DePaulis, *Ida Rubinstein*, 377. "Nous avons toutes obtenu ce que nous voulions: Moi, J'ai eu mon salon, Romaine est devenue un grand peintre et Ida une danseuse renommée."
57 Guy Tosi, *Debussy et d'Annunzio, Correspondance inédite* (Paris 7e: Les Éditions Denoel, 1948), 18. "En écrivant, le poète ne cesse de penser à Rubinstein. Belle? Elle est, à ses yeux, plus que belle. Il la vit, perdue au milieu des frivoles actrices de Paris, comme une icone russe au milieu des bibelots de la rue de la Paix. C'est un être fabuleux."
58 Tosi, *Debussy et d'Annunzio*, 19. "Je suis encore tout émue de cette beauté inouie que vous m'avez apportée. Il faut que cela soit ce printemps s'il faillait pour cela remue ciel et terre."

59 Tosi, *Debussy et d'Annunzio*, 19. "Il y a en elle je ne sais quel comble de jeunesse, comme par un effet à rebours du courant des années.... Avant de danser, elle est assise en silence; assise comme la sibylle qui attend le dieu au-dedans d'elle même ou qui l'écoute en elle. Quel destin plastique et spirituel la sublime ainsi? Quand elle me regarde sans sourire, il y en elle quelle que chose de plus humaine et d'une plus dolente douceur. Par quel mystère m'apparaissez-vous plus humaine tout en étant plus divine? Elle baisse son regard sur ces genoux."

60 Tosi, *Debussy et d'Annunzio*, 21. "Vous souvient-il? Vous souvient-il? Toutes les flammes d'autrefois brûlent de nouveau pour ma punition. Je ne sais.... Elle se dresse hors du rêve dans le rêve, et elle danse dans la salle émaillée comme la très riche reliure d'un Coran ou de quelque livre sacré d'Iran. Elle danse, présente, absente, au delà de la nature, au delà de la magie, au delà de la musique."

61 Tosi, *Debussy et d'Annunzio*, 22.

62 Souhami, *Wild Girls*, 126.

63 Souhami, *Wild Girls*, 127.

64 Bakst letter to d'Annunzio, Lo Gatto, Anjuta Maver. "Otto Lettere inedited, di Léon Bakst à d'Annunzio" *Quadernni del Vittoriale* 7 (January-February 1978): 54-55.

65 Firuza Melville, "Les Ballets Russes to Les Ballets Persans, or Schéhérazade without Schéhérazade in Orientality," *Cultural Orientalism and Mentality*, vol. 1, Orientalist Museum Exhibition Catalogue (Milan: Silvana Editoriale, 2015), 55. "After the assassination of Russian Prime Minister Peter Stolypin in 1911, Bakst and other Jews were denied the right to reside in Metropolitan areas of St. Petersburg."

66 "Je suis poussé par un désir ardent de rassembler les plus violents contrastes pour obtenir l'impression d'une richesse et d'une passion affolante!"

67 "Voilà les éléments que j'adore: la couleur impérial, la belle et sensuelle forme, le sang, l'odeur de la transpiration, la voix etranglée par l'émotion, les spectacles d'émotions profondes, angoissantes et l'orgueil de la belle chaire saine et splendide."

68 "J'ai un si grand désir de vous voir pour vous entendre parler de St. Sébastien, pour que vous me disiez tout ce que je puis lire pour 'tout savoir' et me préparer au prochain travail pour entrer dans un état de grâce."

69 Rubinstein letter to d'Annunzio, n.d., folder XXIV/4, Il Vittoriale. "Je suis à Paris. C'est l'idée du jeune Saint qui m'y a ramenée. Je n'ai qu'un seul désir. C'est de jouer votre Saint Sébastien.... C'est là ma vie. Ai vu Rigaud. Tout s'arrange très bien. Votre frère qui est heureux."

70 Garafola, "Circles of Meaning," 33.

71 December 26, 1910, in Astruc papers Dossier 17, Archives Nationales. "Vous savez que je suis incognito et dans des conditions dangereuses."

72 "Tu vois luire l'aube, comme sa lueur rosée, fraîche soeur de la larme chaude. Au revoir, au revoir. Je pense à vous sans trêve, et je vous aime à travers la flamme de mon esprit."

73 "Sa compréhension est merveilleuse, c'est une joie rare de travailler avec un tel artiste."

74 Souhami, *Wild Girls*, 130.

75 Cronin, *Paris on the Eve*, 234.

76 Marcel Proust, *Correspondance 1914-1922*, 21 vols., edited and annotated by Philip Kolb (Paris: Editions Plon, 1970-1993). "Tout ce qu'il y a d'étranger chez d'Annunzio s'est réfugié dans l'accent de Madame Rubinstein. Mais pour le style comment croire que c'est un étranger. Combien de français écrivent avec tant de précision. Comme je finis toujours par venir à vos opinions j'ai trouvé les jambes de Madame Rubinstein qui ressemble moitié à Cloménil [célèbre courtesan] moitié à Maurice de Rothschild sublimes. Cela été pour moi, tout. Mais j'ai trouvé la pièce bien ennuyeuse malgré des moments, et la musique agréable mais bien mince, bien insuffisante, bien écrasée par le sujet, la réclame, et l'orchestre bien immense pour les quelques pets [farts]. Dans le temple du troisième acte, j'étais persuadé que c'était la marche des petits joyeux qu'on jouait. Mais tout à la fin, sous le soleil aux rayons raides, après la mort de Saint Sébastien, il y a un bel instrument joyeux."

77 Garafola, "Circles of Meaning," 37.

78 Michael de Cossart, *Rubinstein: A Theatrical Life (1885-1960)* (Liverpool, UK: Liverpool University Press, 1987), 42.

79 Kenneth Lapatin, Rachel Herschman, and Clare Fitzgerald, "Works in Focus," in *Hymn to Apollo*, 105.

80 Émile Verhaeren, "Hélène de Sparte, Tragédie en quatre actes" in *Éditions de la Nouvelle Revue Française* (Paris: Marcel Rivière, 1912), 8.

81 André Levinson, *Bakst: Story of an Artist's Life* (New York, B. Blom, 1971), 171.

82 Charles Spencer, *Léon Bakst and the Ballets Russes* (rev. ed.) (London: Academy Editions1995), 145.

83 Garafola, *Legacies of Twentieth-Century Dance*, 157.

84 Caddy, "Variations of the Dance of the Seven Veils," 37.

85 Robert Flers, *Le Figaro*, June 12, 1912. "Elle a dansé la danse des Sept Voiles avec une audace et une impudeur qui savent, parce qu'elles sont les siennes, garder de la noblesse et de la distinction."

86 Mary Fleischer, "D'Annunzio et Rubinstein: La Pisannelle, ou La Mort Perfumée," in *Ida Rubinstein, Une Utopie de la synthèse des arts à l'épreuve de la scène,* Pascal Lécroart, ed. (Paris: Presses Universitaires de Franche-Comté, 2008), 182.

87 Mayer, "Rubinstein: A Twentieth-Century Cleopatra," 39.

88 DePaulis, *Ida Rubinstein*, 178.

89 Konstantin, Rudnitsky, *Vsevolod Meyerhold, Meyerhold the Director,* Sydney Schultze, ed., George Petrov, trans. (Ann Arbor, MI: Ardis, 1981), 196.

90 Rudnitsky, *Vsevolod Meyerhold*, 197.
91 Rudnitsky, *Vsevolod Meyerhold*, 197.
92 Mary Fleischer, *Embodied Texts: Symbolist Playwright-Dancer Collaborations* (New York, Amsterdam: Rodopi, 2007), 21.

NOTES TO CHAPTER THREE

1 Woolf, *Dancing in the Vortex*, 79.
2 Joe Lucchesi, *The Modern Woman Revisited: Paris between the Wars*, Whitney Chadwick and Tirza True Latimer, eds. (New Brunswick, NJ: Rutgers University Press, 2003), 169.
3 Lucchesi, *The Modern Woman Revisited*, 169.
4 Woolf, *Dancing in the Vortex*, 78.
5 Woolf, *Dancing in the Vortex*, 78.
6 Mayer, "Rubinstein: A Twentieth-Century Cleopatra," 40.
7 Friedman, *Ida Rubinstein*, 198.
8 Elizabeth De Clermont-Tonnerre, *Robert de Montesquiou et Marcel Proust*, Ernest Flammarion, ed. (Paris: 26 rue Racine, 1925), 182.
9 De Clermont-Tonnerre, *Robert de Montesquiou et Marcel Proust*, 201.
10 Marcel Proust, *La Corréspondance de Marcel Proust*, vol. XVI, Philip Kolb, ed. (Urbana: University of Illinois Press, 1949), 276. "Mais il y aura une autre artiste, Madame Rubinstein, qui dit mes vers de la façon la plus émouvante."
11 Jullian, *Prince of Aesthetes*, 184.
12 Philippe Jullian, *Prince of Aesthetes: Count Robert de Montesquiou, 1855–1921* (New York: Viking Press, 1968), 257.
13 Mary Louise Roberts, *Disruptive Acts: The New Woman in Fin-de Siècle France* (Chicago: University of Chicago Press, 2002), 225.
14 DePaulis, *Ida Rubinstein*, 144.
15 Dobrotvorskaya, "The Lioness," 8.
16 Woolf, *Dancing in the Vortex*, 77.
17 Cronin, *Paris on the Eve*, 448.
18 De Clermont-Tonnerre, *Robert de Montesquiou et Marcel Proust*, 181.
19 Mayer, "Rubinstein: A Twentieth-Century Cleopatra," 40.
20 Woolf, *Dancing in the Vortex*, 75.

NOTES TO CHAPTER FOUR

1 Philippe Jullian, *Prince of Aesthetes* (New York: Viking Press, 1968), 258.
2 Jullian, *Prince of Aesthetes*, 271.
3 Jullian, *Prince of Aesthetes*, 271.
4 Souhami, *Wild Girls*, 131.
5 Kenneth Lapatin, Rachel Herschman, and Clare Fitzgerald, "Works in Focus," in *Hymn to Apollo*, 103.

6 Kenneth Lapatin, Rachel Herschman, and Clare Fitzgerald, "Works in Focus," in *Hymn to Apollo*, 103.
7 Pridden, *The Art of Dance in French Literature*, 147.
8 Pridden, *The Art of Dance in French Literature*, 147.
9 Paul Valéry, *Dance and the Soul*, edited and translated by William McCausland Stewart (Princeton, NJ: Princeton University Press, 1956, 1989), 47.
10 Walter Putnam, *Valéry Revisited* (New York: Twayne Publishers, 1995), 96.
11 Pridden, *The Art of Dance in French Literature*, 129. "Nos membres exécutant une suite de figures, dont la fréquence produit une sorte d'ivresse qui va de la langeur au délire ... L'état de la danse est crée."
12 Pridden, *The Art of Dance in French Literature*, 130.
13 Ida Rubinstein, *Conferencia: Journal de l'Université des Annales, Les Aspects de la Vie Moderne: L'Art aux trois visages* (December 5, 1924). Again, these quotes are from archival material from her lecture in the Bibliothèque Nationale and many of them did not have page numbers. Page numbers will be provided when possible. "La nature est un temple de vivants piliers, / laissent parfois sortir de confuses paroles."
14 Pridden, *The Art of Dance in French Literature*, 59.
15 Rubinstein, *L'Art aux trois visages*, 228.
16 Rubinstein, *L'Art aux trois visages*, 229.
17 Rubinstein, *L'Art aux trois visages*, 229.
18 Rubinstein, *L'Art aux trois visages*, 330.
19 Rubinstein, *L'Art aux trois visages*, 331.
20 Rubinstein, *L'Art aux trois visages*, 331.
21 Rubinstein, *L'Art aux trois visages*, 333.
22 Bowlt, "Bold and Dazzling," 71.
23 Émile Vuillermoz, *L'Excelsior* (May 3, 1922).
24 DePaulis, *Ida Rubinstein*, 269.
25 André Levinson, *Comoedia*, May 3, 1922.
26 DePaulis, *Ida Rubinstein*, 292.
27 Roger Ducasse, *Le Figaro*, June 13, 1926. "Orphée ce sera vous ... Par vous il vit: il revit en vous ... Oui, vous l'avez créé, Madame ... En l'écrivant cette oeuvre, j'avais présenté à mon esprit et à mon coeur vos gestes, vos attitudes, vos regards, vos silences mêmes."
28 DePaulis, *Ida Rubinstein*, 346.
29 Louis K. Epstein, "Toward a Theory of Patronage: Funding for Music Composition in France, 1918-1939" (Ph.D. diss., Harvard University, 2013), 238.
30 Epstein, *Toward a Theory of Patronage*, 242. In truth, Fokine was not one of the choreographers for the company that year. Epstein is mistaken.
31 Epstein, *Toward a Theory of Patronage*, 243.
32 For a full description of the dancers, artists, composers, designers, and so on, please see the Appendix.

33 Léonide Massine, *My Life in Ballet*, Phyllis Hartnoll and Robert Rubens, eds. (London: Macmillan, 1968).
34 Epstein, *Toward a Theory of Patronage*, 245.
35 Nina Tikanova, *La Jeune Fille en bleu* (Petersburg-Berlin-Paris-Lausanne: L'Âge d'Homme, 1991), 97.
36 Tikanova, *La Jeune Fille en bleu*, 97.
37 DePaulis, *Ida Rubinstein*, 362.
38 David Vaughan, "A Peruvian in Paris," *Dancing Times* (London) (October, 1974), 16.
39 Vaughan, "A Peruvian in Paris," 17.
40 Epstein, *Toward a Theory of Patronage*, 246.
41 Henri Prunières, "Paris Sees Ballet Novelties," *New York Times*, December 23, 1928.
42 Charles Greenwell, *New Mexico Philharmonic Program Book, 2017/18 Season* 7, no. 1:.22.
43 Greenwell, *New Mexico Philharmonic Program Book*, 2017/88 Season.
44 André Levinson, *Les Visages de la Danse* (Paris: Grasset, 1933), 101. "Vingt mâles fascinés par l'incantation charnelle (sensual) d'une seule femme [...] Par l'ondulation des bras et la torsion de la taille, par l'envoi contourné (twisting) de sa bassquine, par le pied, aussi qui trace des cercles á terre, la danseuse dessine les contours de la mélodie [...] Les vingt hommes qui, par leur trépignements et leurs battements de paumes, marquent les accents, forment une batterie aux timbres divers [...] Chaque da capo fait croître l'intensité de l'effet: le premier danseur, M. Vilzac, rampe et se tord, martyrise par le rut (sexual excitement) et le rythme."
45 Deborah Mawer, *The Ballets of Maurice Ravel: Creation and Interpretation* (New York: Routledge Press, 2006), 228.
46 Mawer, *The Ballets of Maurice Ravel*, 228.
47 Prunières, "Paris Sees Ballet Novelties" (December 23, 1928).
48 Henri Malherbe, "À l'Opéra: Les Ballets de Mme Ida Rubinstein," *Le Temps* (November 24, 1928). "Il est impossible de temoigner plus de somptuosité, et de goût dans l'ordonnance d'un divertissement chorégraphique. Épurée, flexible, Madame Rubinstein paraît avec recherché et manière dans trois ballets. Elle est entouré d'une troupe de danseurs d'une virtuosité accomplice. Elle mérite toutes les louanges pour son effort suprême, son choix, son exemple."
49 André Levinson, *Comoedia* (December 8, 1928). "C'est le principe décorative qui domine dans ce ballet et non la donnée chorégraphique. On hésite de mettre en valeur le décor."
50 Levinson, *Comoedia* (December 8, 1928).
51 Jane Catulle Mendès in *La Presse* (December 5, 1928). "Madame Rubinstein reste admirable dans tout ce qui est art plastique, mélodie lente et continue des poses et du hiératisme. Elle ne vaut rien dans la danse classique, quelles que soient son effort et son application, car sa longue structure linéaire y est

contradictoire ... En resumé, ces ballets n'ont rien apporté de nouveau à l'art qu'ils veulent server."
52 Émile Vuillermoz, in *Excelsior* (December 3, 1928). "Après l'avoir discrètement invitée à faire son examen de conscience professionnelle, la critique sera t-elle donc obligé de dire lourdement à Madame Rubinstein, que son obstination se réserver le plus beau rôle dans chacun des ses ballets et son impertinent dédain de la technique élémentaire qu'elle devrait posséder pour justifier cette diabolique persévérance, enlèvent à sa saison de ballets une grande partie de sa signification artistique?"
53 Scheijen, *Diaghilev .A Life,* 427.
54 Scheijen, *Diaghilev .A Life,* 428.
55 Scheijen, *Diaghilev .A Life,* 428.
56 Agnes De Mille, *Dance to the Piper* (Boston: Little Brown, 1952), 249.
57 DePaulis, *Ida Rubinstein,* 377.
58 Greenwell, *New Mexico Philharmonic Program Book,* 2017/88 Season.
59 Marcel Schneider, *Danser* 164 (March 1998). "C'était une espèce d'apothéose de la valse viennoise à laquelle se mèle dans mon esprit l'impression d'un tournoiement fantastique et fatal."
60 Millicent Hodson and Kenneth Archer, *Dance Now* 8, no. 2 (Summer 1999): 17-23.
61 Paul Valéry, *Amphion, Mélodrame or Lyric Play,* David Paul and Robert Fitzgerald, trans., dedicated to Rubinstein. (New York: Pantheon Books, 1960).
62 Véronique Fabbri, *Paul Valéry, Le Poème et la Danse* (Paris: Hermann Éditeurs, 2009), 102.
63 Sylvie David-Guignard, "Amphion: du mythe grec au mélodrama valéreyen," in *Rubinstein: une utopie de la synthèse des arts à l'épreuve de la scène,* 211. "Le mélodrame d'*Amphion* baigne dans la lumière apollonienne; le personage, éloigné de l'humanité ordinaire, incarne l'esprit créateur; ... Tout est symbole, abstraction, hiératisme."
64 Epstein, *Toward a Theory of Patronage,* 248.
65 Fabbri, *Paul Valéry,* 107.
66 Henri Malherbe, "Chronique musicale: À l'Opéra: les Ballets de Mme Ida Rubinstein: la nouvelle chorégraphie de *La Valse,* de Maurice Ravel," *Temps* (July 1, 1931).
67 Vicente Garcia-Márquez, *Massine: A Biography* (New York: Alfred Knopf, 1995), 214.
68 Levinson, *Les Visages de la Danse,* 111.
69 Garcia-Márquez, *Massine: A Biography,* 214. Quote from *Candide,* July 2, 1931.
70 Garcia-Márquez, *Massine: A Biography,* 214. Quote from *L'Excelsior* June 29, 1931.
71 Fabbri, *Paul Valéry,* 108. "La chorégraphie semble avoir été appréciée. Elle fut sans doute conçue dans le prolongement de son travail aux Ballets Russes, et

probablement poussée dans d'une plus grande rhithmicité. Elle semble aussi avoir laissé une grande place aux acrobats, en quoi il y eut entente au moins partielle entre le poète et le chorégraphe."

72 Hermann Fähnrich, "Music in the Letters of Paul Valéry," *Music and Letters* 55, no. 1 (January 1974): 60. "Vous avez lu un libretto avec des yeux qui cherchaient un poème. J'ai publié ce texte, à tort peut-être. Mais l'exécution de l'ouvrage fut telle que j'ai pensé par là établir pour quelques-uns mon intention. Je n'ai pu malheureusement imposer mes vues, qui étaient les plus simples du monde, et j'ai eu l'ennui d'assister à un ballet russe quand j'avais conçu une sorte de cérémonie religieuse."
73 Whitney Chadwick and Tirza True Latimer, eds., *The Modern Woman Revisited: Paris between the Wars* (New Brunswick, NJ: Rutgers University Press, 2003), 7.
74 Fernand Nozière, ed., R. Chibirre, (Editions Sansot, 1926), microfilm, 28.
75 Nozière microfilm, 29.
76 Mayer, "Ida Rubinstein: A Twentieth-Century Cleopatra," 36.
77 Keith Lester and Clement Crisp, "Rubinstein Revisited," *Dance Research* 1, no. 2 (Autumn 1983): 29.
78 Pierre Van Taassen, "Something Sacred Is Being Born in America Is Belief of Mme. Rubinstein, French Actress," *New York Evening World*, June 23, 1926.
79 Valerian Svetlov, *Le Ballet contemporain* (Paris: M. de Brunoff, 1912), 98–99.
80 Patricia Vertinsky, "Ida Rubinstein: Dancing Decadence and the 'Art of the Beautiful Pose.'" in *Nashim: A Journal of Jewish Women's Studies and Gender Issues* 26 (April 2014): 123.
81 Charles Batson, *Dance, Desire and Anxiety in Early Twentieth-Century French Theater, Playing Identities* (Burlington, VT: Ashgate Publishing, 2005), 21.
82 Batson, *Dance, Desire and Anxiety*, 22.
83 Eugen Weber, *France fin de Siècle* (Cambridge, MA: Harvard University Press, 1986), 32.
84 Karl Toepfer, *Empire of Ecstasy: Nudity and Movement in German Body Culture 1910–1935* (Berkeley: University of California Press, 1997), 1.
85 Colette, "Paysages et Portraits" in *Candide,* December 13, 1928. Microfilm at Bibliothèque Nationale (Paris: Flammarion, 1958), 154.
86 Colette, "Paysages et Portraits," 154.
87 Garafola, "Circles of Meaning," 33.
88 Colette, "Paysages et Portraits," 155.
89 Colette, "Paysages et Portraits," 157.
90 Colette, "Paysages et Portraits," 157.
91 Mayer, "A Twentieth-Century Cleopatra," 40.
92 There are three versions of Rubinstein in *La Nave* available for viewing on YouTube. First is the full-length film from 1921 that was based on the play by Gabriele d'Annunzio, written in 1908 and also informed by the opera, *La Nave*, which premiered in 1918. The feature film released on YouTube as

recently as October 18, 2016, was originally directed by Gabriellino d'Annunzio, the son of the author. Its screen text was by Mario Roncoroni and cinematography by Narciso Maffel to music by Ildebrando Pizzetti.
93. Lester and Crisp, "Rubinstein Revisited," 28.
94. Charles Joseph, *Stravinsky's Ballets* (New Haven, CN: Yale University Press, 2011).
95. Tamara Levitz, *Modernist Mysteries: Perséphone* (New York: Oxford University Press, 2012), 21.
96. Levitz, *Modernist Mysteries*, 145.
97. Levitz, *Modernist Mysteries*, 223.
98. "L'énorme succès de *Diane de Poitiers* vient donner quelques couleurs agréables à cette saison 1934," *Le Figaro*, May 2, 1934, 122.
99. Epstein, *Toward a Theory of Patronage*, 250.
100. Epstein, *Toward a Theory of Patronage*, 250.
101. Suzanne Demarquez, *La Revue Musicale* 147 (1934): 145. "Mme Rubinstein a trouvé, dans Sémiramis, un rôle qui convient parfaitement à sa plastique. Son apparition sur le char de guerre, le movement triumphant de la montée vers le trône, le geste de mort qui s'achève en tendre imploration, sont des visions dont on gardera longtemps le souvenir."
102. Mayer, "Ida Rubinstein: A Twentieth-Century Cleopatra," 46.
103. José Bruyr, *Honegger et son oeuvre* (Paris: Correa, 1947), 186.
104. Pierre Hébey, *La Nouvelle Revue Française des années sombres*, 1940-1941 (Paris: Gallimard, 1992), 354. "Presque tous les chefs d'orchestre de Paris sont juifs; on ne joue que de la musique juive. MM. Honegger et Darius Milhaud, etc., pourrait avoir beau jeu, ils ont tout le jeu."
105. Secrest, *Between Me and Life*, 326.
106. Epstein, *Toward a Theory of Patronage*, 253.

NOTES TO CHAPTER FIVE

1. Nick Stanley, "'Some Friends Came to See Us': Lord Moyne's 1936 Expedition to the Asmat" (London: British Museum Publications, 2016), Introduction, 1.
2. Robert D. McFadden, "David Stoliar, 91, Survivor of 1942 Disaster, Is Dead," *New York Times*, Sunday, January 24, 2016, 19.
3. Vladimir Jankélévitch, *Modern French Jewish Thought*, Sarah Hammerschlager, ed. (Waltham, MA: Brandeis University Press, 2018), 107.
4. Dobrotvorskaya, "The Lioness," 1.
5. Dobrotvorskaya, "The Lioness," 3.
6. Maurice Blanchot, "Intellectuals under Scrutiny," in *The Blanchot Reader*, Michael Holland, ed. (Oxford and Cambridge: Blackwell Publishers, 1995), 211.
7. Blanchot, "Intellectuals under Scrutiny," 211.

8 James Loeffler, *The Most Musical Nation: Jews and Culture in the Late Russian Empire* (New Haven, CT and London: Yale University Press, 2010), 116.
9 Mary Louise Roberts, *Disruptive Acts: The New Woman in Fin-de Siècle France* (Chicago: University of Chicago Press, 2002), 210.
10 Pierre Birnbaum, *Leon Blum, Prime Minister, Socialist, Zionist* in the *Jewish Lives* series (New Haven, CT and London: Yale University Press, 2015), 18-31.
11 Rebecca Rossen, *Dancing Jewish, Jewish Identity in American Modern and Post-Modern American Dance* (Oxford, UK and New York, Oxford University Press, 2014), 30-31.
12 Cassandra Langer, *Romaine Brooks: A Life* (Madison: University of Wisconsin Press, 2015), 70.
13 Garafola, "Circles of Meaning," 39. "On va essayer de faire de vous un sacrilège, et on aura vite prouvé que, pour la seconde fois, j'ai crucifié Dieu!"
14 Barbara Jepson, "This Music Befits a Saintly Legend," *New York Times*, March 30, 1997.
15 Garafola, "Circles of Meaning," 39.
16 Garafola, "Circles of Meaning," 40. These were quotes from a gossipy 1911 *New York Times* article.
17 Friedman, *Rubinstein*, 168.
18 Friedman, *Rubinstein*, 168.
19 Epstein, *Toward a Theory of Patronage*, 254.
20 Pascal Lécroart, Introduction to *Rubinstein, une utopie de la synthèse des arts à l'épreuve de la scène* (Paris: Presses universitaires de Franche-Comté, 2008), 8.
21 André Levinson, "La Danse au Théâtre en 1931," *Le Temps*, July 20, 1931.
22 Serge Lifar, *Histoire du Ballet Russe depuis les Origines jusqu'à nos jours* (Paris: Nagel, 1950), 240.
23 Mayer, "A Twentieth-Century Cleopatra," 46.
24 DePaulis, *Ida Rubinstein*, 555. "Tous les jours, et plus encore vers la fin de sa vie, elle s'imprègne des pages sacrées."
25 Fabbri, *Paul Valéry*, 132. "À la différence de beaucoup de ses contemporains, Rubinstein possède à la fois une solide formation musicale, une pratique non moins solide de la danse, même si elle ne fut pas 'accomplie,' et surtout une connaissance de la poésie et de sa prosodie, à la quelle Valéry comme Claudel furent sensibles. La capacité de pratiquer ces différents arts ne pouvait que la rendre apte à saisir leur spécificité et à la maintenir."
26 Fabbri, *Paul Valéry*, 132. "Le professionnalisme d'Rubinstein, sa volonté d'être une artiste la plus complète possible anticipent sur la formation des artistes de théâtre de l'après la guerre; elle offre surtout aux poètes comme Valéry des possibilities rares de poursuivre son étude des relations entre la danse et le poème."
27 Epstein, *Toward a Theory of Patronage*, 256.

28 Andrew Sheppard, *Revealing Masks, Exotic Influences and Ritualized Performance in Modernist Theatre, Berkeley* (Los Angeles: University of California Press, 2001), 100.
29 Epstein, *Toward a Theory of Patronage*, 259.
30 DePaulis, *Ida Rubinstein*, 531.

BIBLIOGRAPHY

Astruc, Gabriel. Papers of Gabriel Astruc, December 1910 in Archives Nationales, Paris
———. Papers of Gabriel Astruc. 1907-1914, the Jerome Robbins Dance Division of the New York Public Library.
Barnes, Julian. *The Man in the Red Coat*. New York: Alfred A. Knopf, 2020.
Batson, Charles. *Dance, Desire, and Anxiety in Early Twentieth-Century French Theater: Playing Identities*. Burlington, VT: Ashgate Publishing, 2005.
Beaunier, André. *L'Écho de Paris*. "Un Phaedre Inconnue de Gabriele d'Annunzio à l'Opéra." June 6, 1923.
———. *L'Écho de Paris*. November 29, 1923.
Benois, Alexandre. Letter 73, St. Petersburg, to V. N. Argutinsky-Dologorukov, July 1909. Vol. 2. Moscow: Izobrazitel'noe iskusstvo, 1982.
Billot, Marcel, ed. *Journal of the Abbé Arthur Musnier* (1879-1939), preface by Ghislain de Diesbach, with notes by Jean d'Hendecourt. Paris: Mercure de France, 1985.
Blanchot, Maurice. "Intellectuals under Scrutiny." *The Blanchot Reader*. Michael Holland, editor. Oxford and Cambridge: Blackwell Publishers, 1995.
Blum, Léon. *Comoedia* on May 23, 1911.
Birnbaum, Pierre. *Leon Blum, Prime Minister, Socialist, Zionist*. New Haven, CT and London: Yale University Press, 2015.
Boschot, Adolphe. "DePaulis." *L'Écho de Paris*.

Bowlt, John E. "Bold and Dazzling: Léon Bakst and Antiquity." In *Hymn to Apollo: The Ancient World and the Ballets Russes*. Edited by Clare Fitzgerald. Princeton, NJ and Oxford, UK: University Princeton University Press, 2019.

Brandstetter, Gabriele. *Poetics of Dance: Body, Image, and Space in the Historical Avant-Gardes*. New York: Oxford University Press, 2015.

Bruyr, José. *Honegger et son oeuvre*. Paris: Correa, 1947.

Caddy, Davina. "Variations of the Dance of the Seven Veils." *Cambridge Opera Journal* 17, no. 1 (March 2005): 37-58.

Catulle Mendès, Jane. *La Presse*. December 5, 1928.

Chadwick, Whitney, and Tirza True Latimer, Editors. *The Modern Woman Revisited: Paris between the Wars*. New Brunswick, NJ: Rutgers University Press, 2003.

Claudel, Paul. *Journal*. Vol. 1. Paris: Gallimard, 1969.

Cohen-Solal, Annie. *Mark Rothko: Toward the Light in the Chapel*. New Haven, London: Yale University Press, 2005.

Colette. "Paysages et Portraits." *Candide*. December 13, 1928. Microfilm. Bibliothèque Nationale. Paris: Flammarion, 1958.

Cronin, Vincent. *Paris on the Eve: 1900-1914*. New York: St. Martin's Press, 1990.

D'Annunzio, Gabriele. Archives, Il Vittoriale degli Italiani, Lago di Garda, Italy.

"D'Annunzio Jilted by Ida Rubinstein," *New York Times*, May 21, 1911, sect. 3, 1.

Debussy, Claude. Debussy letter to Jacques Durand, July 18, 1909. In *Lettres de Claude Debussy à son éditeur*. Paris: A. Durand et fils, Éditeurs, 1927.

De Clermont-Tonnerre, Elizabeth. *Robert de Montesquiou et Marcel Proust*. Ernest Flammarion, editor. Paris: 26 rue Racine, 1925.

De Cossart, Michael. *Ida Rubinstein (1885-1960): A Theatrical Life*. Liverpool, UK: Liverpool University Press, 1987.

———. "Ida Rubinstein and Diaghilev: A One-Sided Rivalry." *Journal of the Society for Dance Research* 1, no. 2 (Autumn 1983).

Demarquez, Suzanne. *La Revue Musicale* 147 (1934).

De Mille, Agnes. *Dance to the Piper*. Boston: Little Brown, 1952.

De Montesquiou, Robert. *Les Offrandes Blessées, élégies guerrières*. Paris: E. Sansot, 1915.

DePaulis, Jacques. *Paul Claudel et Ida Rubinstein: une collaboration difficile*. Paris: Diffusion les Belles Lettres, 1994.

DePaulis, Jacques. *Ida Rubinstein, Une Inconnue Jadis célèbre*. Paris: Honoré Champion, 1995.

Dobrotvorskaya, Karina. "The Lioness." *St. Petersburg Theater Journal* 1 (1993).

Ducasse, André. *Le Figaro*. June 13, 1926.

Epstein, Louis K. "Toward a Theory of Patronage: Funding for Music Composition in France, 1918-1939." Ph.D. diss., Harvard University, 2013.

Fabbri, Véronique. *Paul Valéry, le poème et la danse*. Paris: Hermann Éditeurs, 2009.

Fähnrich, Hermann. "Music in the Letters of Paul Valéry." *Music and Letters* 55, no. 1 (January 1974).
Fitzgerald, Clare, Editor. *Hymn to Apollo: The Ancient World and the Ballets Russes.* Princeton, NJ and Oxford, UK: Princeton University Press, 2019.
Fleischer, Mary. *Embodied Texts: Symbolist Playwright-Dancer Collaborations.* New York, Amsterdam: Rodopi, 2007.
Flers, Robert. *Le Figaro.* June 12, 1912.
Flugel, J. C. *The Psychology of Clothes.* New York: International Universities Press, 1930.
Fokine, Michel. *Fokine: Memoirs of a Ballet Master,* Translated by Vitale Fokine. Boston: Little Brown, 1961.
Friedman, Daniel Flannell. *Ida Rubinstein: Le Roman d'une vie d'artiste.* Paris: Salvator, 2011.
Garafola, Lynn. "Ida Rubinstein: A Theatrical Life." *Dance Research Journal* 21, no. 2 (Fall 1989).
———. *Diaghilev's Ballets Russes,* New York and London: Oxford University Press, 1989.
———. "Circles of Meaning: The Cultural Contexts of Ida Rubinstein's Le Martyre de Saint Sébastien." *Proceedings of the Society of Dance History Scholars* (February 10-13, 1994): 27-47.
———. *Legacies of Twentieth-Century Dance.* Middletown, CT: Wesleyan University Press, 2005.
Garcia-Márquez, Vicente. *Massine: A Biography.* New York: Alfred Knopf, 1995.
Greenberg, Louis. *The Jews in Russia.* Vol. 1. *The Struggle for Emancipation.* New Haven, CT: Yale University Press, 1944.
Greenwell, Charles. *New Mexico Philharmonic Program* 7, no. 1 (2017/18).
Haskell, Arnold, and Walter Nouvel. *Diaghileff His Artistic and Private Life.* New York: Simon and Schuster, 1935.
Hébey, Pierre. *La Nouvelle Revue Française des années sombres, 1940-1941.* Paris: Gallimard, 1992.
Henriot, Emile. "Ida Rubinstein 'La Pisanelle.'" *Comoedia Illustré,* June 8, 1913.
Heugel, Jacques. *Le Ménestrel,* June 15, 1923, 266.
Hodson, Millicent, and Kenneth Archer. *Dance Now* 8, no. 2 (Summer 1999): 17-23.
Jankélévitch, Vladimir. *Modern French Jewish Thought.* Edited by Sarah Hammerschlager. Waltham, MA: Brandeis University Press, 2018.
Jepson, Barbara. "This Music Befits a Saintly Legend." *New York Times,* March 30, 1997.
Jewish-Observer.com. "Mystery Woman."
Jones, Susan. *Literature, Modernism and Dance.* Oxford Scholarship Online, 2013.
Joseph, Charles. *Stravinsky's Ballets.* New Haven, CT: Yale University Press, 2011.
Jullian, Philippe. *D'Annunzio.* New York: Viking Press, 1971.

———. *Prince of Aesthetes: Count Robert de Montesquiou, 1855-1921.* New York: Viking Press, 1968.

Kahan, Sylvia. *Music's Modern Muse: A Life of Winnaretta Singer, Princesse de Polignac.* Rochester, NY: University of Rochester Press, 2003.

Kochno, Boris. *Le Ballet.* Paris: Hachette, 1954.

Langer, Cassandra. *Romaine Brooks: A Life.* Madison: University of Wisconsin Press, 2015.

Latimer, Tirza True. *Women Together/Women Apart: Portraits of Lesbian Paris.* New Brunswick, NJ: Rutgers University Press, 2005.

Leach, Robert. *Vsevolod Meyerhold.* Cambridge, UK: Cambridge University Press, 1989.

Lécroart, Pascal, ed. *Une utopie de la synthèse des arts á l'épreuve de la scène.* Besançon, France: Presses Universitaires de Franche-Comté, 2008.

Lester, Keith, and Clement Crisp. "Rubinstein Revisited." *Dance Research* 1, no. 2 (Autumn 1983).

Levinson, André. *Comoedia.* May 3, 1922.

———. *Comoedia,* December 8, 1928.

———. "La Danse au théâtre en 1931," *Le Temps,* July 20, 1931.

———. *Les Visages de la Danse.* Paris: Grasset, 1933.

———. *Bakst: Story of an Artist's Life.* New York: B. Blom, 1971.

Levitz, Tamara. *Modernist Mysteries: Perséphone.* New York: Oxford University Press, 2012.

Lifar, Serge. *Histoire du Ballet Russe depuis les Origines jusqu'à nos jours.* Paris: Nagel, 1950.

Loeffler, James. *The Most Musical Nation: Jews and Culture in the Late Russian Empire.* New Haven, CT and London: Yale, 2010.

Lo Gatto, Anjuta Maver. "Otto Lettere inedited, di Léon Bakst à d'Annunzio." *Quaderni del Vittoriale* 7 (January-February 1978): 54-55, 64.

Lucchesi, Joe. *The Modern Woman Revisited: Paris between the Wars.* Edited by Whitney Chadwick and Tirza True Latimer. New Brunswick, NJ: Rutgers University Press, 2003.

Mackrell, Judith. *Bloomsbury Ballerina.* London: Orion Books, 2009.

Malherbe, Henri. "À l'Opéra: Les Ballets de Mme Ida Rubinstein." *Le Temps.* November 24, 1928.

———. "Chronique musicale: À l'Opéra: les Ballets de Mme Ida Rubinstein: la nouvelle chorégraphie de *La Valse,* de Maurice Ravel." *Le Temps.* July 1, 1931.

Massine, Léonide. *My Life in Ballet.* Edited by Phyllis Hartnoll and Robert Rubens. London: Macmillan, 1968.

Mawer, Deborah. *The Ballets of Maurice Ravel: Creation and Interpretation.* New York: Routledge Press, 2006.

Mayer, Charles. "Ida Rubinstein: A Twentieth-Century Cleopatra." *Dance Research Journal* 20, no. 2 (Winter 1989): 33-51.

McFadden, Robert D. "David Stoliar, 91, Survivor of 1942 Disaster, Is Dead." *New York Times,* January 24, 2016.

Melville, Firuza. "Les Ballets Russes to Les Ballets Persans, or Schéhérazade without Schéhérazade in Orientality." *Cultural Orientalism and Mentality.* Vol. 1. Milan: Silvana Editoriale, 2015, 85-98n9.

Moody, C. "Commedia dell'arte." *Modern Language Review* 73 (1978): 59-869.

Nathans, Benjamin. *Beyond the Pale: The Jewish Encounter with Late Imperial Russia.* Berkeley, Los Angeles, and London: University of California Press, 2002.

Nijinska, Bronislava. *Early Memoirs.* New York: Holt Rinehart and Winston, 1981.

Nozière, Fernand, and R. Chibirre, eds. Editions Sansot, 1926. Microfilm.

Odom, Selma L. "Delsartean Traces in Dalcroze Eurythmics." *Mime Journal* 23 (April 30, 2005).

Pridden, Deidre. *The Art of Dance in French Literature.* London: A & C Black, 1952.

Proust, Marcel. *Correspondance 1914-1922,* 21 vols. Edited and annotated by Philip Kolb. Paris: Editions Plon, 1970-1993.

———. *La Corréspondance de Marcel Proust.* Vol. XVI. Edited by Philip Kolb. Urbana: University of Illinois Press, 1949.

Prunières, Henri. "Paris Sees Ballet Novelties." *New York Times.* December 23, 1928.

Pruzhan, Irina. *Léon Bakst, Set and Designs, Book Illustrations, Paintings and Graphic Works.* Translated by Arthur Shkarovski-Raffé. Middlesex, UK: Penguin Books, 1986.

Putnam, Walter. *Valéry Revisited.* New York: Twayne Publishers, 1995.

Rabinowitz, Stanley J. *And Then Came Dance: The Women Who led Volynsky to Ballet's Magic Kingdom.* New York: Oxford University Press, 2019.

Roberts, Mary Louise. *Disruptive Acts: The New Woman in Fin-de Siècle France.* Chicago: University of Chicago Press, 2002.

Rossen, Rebecca. *Dancing Jewish, Jewish Identity in American Modern and Post-Modern American Dance.* Oxford, UK and New York: Oxford University Press, 2014.

Rubinstein, Ida. *Solntse Rossii* or *Sun of Russia.* "Ida Rubinstein about Herself." *Solntse Rossii [Sun of Russia]* 25 (1913): 12.

———. *Conferencia: Journal de l'Université des Annales, Les Aspects de la Vie Moderne: L'Art aux trois visages* (December 5, 1924).

———. "Mes Rôles et mes chasses." *Lecture pour tous, Revue* (1913): 1-3.

———. *Conferencia, Vers l'Italie nouvelle, "Ma premiére rencontre avec d'Annunzio." Journal de l'Université des Annales* 21e, no. 19 (September 20, 1927).

Rudnitsky, Konstantin. *Vsevolod Meyerhold, Meyerhold the Director.* Edited by Sydney Schultze. Translated by George Petrov with an Introduction by Ellendea Proffer. Ann Arbor, MI: Ardis, 1981.

Schneider, Marcel. *Danser* 164 (March 1998).

Scheijen, Sjeng. *Diaghilev. A Life*. Oxford, UK and New York: Oxford University Press, 2009.

Secrest, Meryle. *Between Me and Life: A Biography of Romaine Brooks*. Garden City, NY: Doubleday, 1974.

Sheppard, Andrew. *Revealing Masks, Exotic Influences and Ritualized Performance in Modernist Theatre*. Berkeley and Los Angeles: University of California Press, 2001.

Smale, Alison. "The Ghosts of Ballets Russes Return to Paris." *New York Times*, July 6, 2012.

Souhami, Diana. *Wild Girls: Paris, Sappho and Art*. New York: St. Martin's Press, 2004.

Spencer, Charles. *Léon Bakst and the Ballets Russes*. Rev. ed. London: Academy Editions, 1995.

Stanley, Nick. "'Some Friends Came to See Us': Lord Moyne's 1936 Expedition to the Asmat." London: British Museum Publications, 2016, Introduction.

Stronhina, Nathalie. "Les racines russes d'Ida Rubinstein." In *Une utopie de la synthèse des arts á l'épreuve de la scène*. Edited by Pascal Lécroart. Paris: Presses Universitaires de Franche-Comté, 2008.

Svetlov, Valerian. *Le Ballet contemporain*. Paris: M. de Brunoff, 1912.

Tikanova, Nina. *La Jeune Fille en bleu*. Pétersburg-Berlin-Paris-Lausanne: L'Âge d'Homme, 1991.

Toepfer, Karl. *Empire of Ecstasy: Nudity and Movement in German Body Culture 1910-1935*. Berkeley: University of California Press, 1997

Tosi, Guy. *Debussy et d'Annunzio, Correspondance inédite*. Edited by Guy Tosi. Paris: Les Éditions Denoel 7e, 1948.

Valéry, Paul. *Amphion, Melodrame or Lyric Play*. Translated by David Paul and Robert Fitzgerald. New York: Pantheon Books, 1960.

———. *Dance and the Soul*. Princeton, NJ: Princeton University Press, 1956, 1989.

Van Taassen, Pierre. "Something Sacred Is Being Born in America Is Belief of Mme. Rubinstein, French Actress." *New York Evening World*, June 23, 1926.

Vaughan, David. "A Peruvian in Paris." *Dancing Times* London, October 1974.

Verhaeren, Émile. "Hélène de Sparte. Tragédie en quatre actes." *Éditions de la Nouvelle Revue Française*. Paris: Marcel Rivière, 1912.

Vertinsky, Patricia. "Ida Rubinstein: Dancing Decadence and the 'Art of the Beautiful Pose.'" *Nashim: A Journal of Jewish Women's Studies and Gender Issues* 26 (April 2014): 122-46.

Volkov, Solomon. *St. Petersburg: A Cultural History*. New York, London: The Free Press, 1995.

Volynsky, Akim. *Ballet's Magic Kingdom, Selected Writings on Dance in Russia: The Book of Exaltations, 1911-1925*. Translated, edited, and with an Introduction and notes by Stanley J. Rabinowitz. New Haven, CT and London: Yale University Press, 2008.

———. Volynsky archives. RGALI, Moscow. (TsGALI.f.95, Volynsky, op. 1. ed. khr. 761, 1, 154-55).
Vuillermoz, Émile. *L'Excelsior,* May 3, 1922.
———. *L'Excelsior.* December 3, 1928, 114.
———. *Candide.* July 2, 1931
Weber, Eugen. *France fin de Siècle.* Cambridge, MA: Harvard University Press, 1986.
Woolf, Vicki. *Dancing in the Vortex: The Story of Ida Rubinstein.* London: Routledge, 2000.
Zipperstein, Steven J. *Pogrom: Kishinev and the Tilt of History.* New York and London: Liveright, 2018.

LETTERS

December 1994, N. N. Gorich and EAI, op. ed. khr. 104, 1, 1-2.
Autumn 1906, to EAI, TsGALI Fond 1958, op. 1, ed. khr. 104, 1.18.
Spring 1906, TsGALI, fond 95 (Volynsky), op. ed. khr. 761, l, 98.
1907 TsGALI, fond 95 (Volynsky), op. 1, ed. khr. 764, 1, 1-2.
1907 TsGALI, f. 95 (Volynsky), op. 1, ed. khr. 217, 1, 10.
Fokine to Benois: From Caux, Switzerland, to Isola Bella, Italy, June 1908. In *Protiv Techeniia: Vospominaniia baletmeistera, stat'I, pis'ma.* Edited by Yuri Slonimskii. Introduction by Yuri Slonimskii. Leningrad: Izdatel'stvo iskusstvo, 1962, 479-80.
Ida writes Vera Kommisarzhevskaia in August 1908, TsGALI, f. 778, op. 2, ed. khr. 38, 1, 3.
Missive (TsGALI, f. 998 [Meyerhold], op. 1, ed., khr. 2332, letter 5), 33.
August 1908, TsGALI, f. 998 op. 1, ed., khr. 2332, letter 6.
Bakst writes his wife: *Sergei Diagilev I russkoe iskusstvo,* vol. 2. Edited by I. S. Zil'bershtein and V. A. Samkov. Moscow: Izobrazitel'noe iskusstvo, 1982, 477n2.
Bakst letter to d'Annunzio, Lo Gatto, Anjuta Maver. "Otto Lettere inedited, di Léon Bakst à d'Annunzio." *Quaderni del Vittoriale* 7 (January-February 1978): 54-55.
Letter to d'Annunzio, n.d., folder XXIV/4, Il Vittoriale.
Lettre non daté (November 17-18, 1910), Arch. Du Vittoriale.
Rubinstein's letter to Léon Bakst. September 11, 1921, Bib. De l'Opéra 1.a, numero.

INDEX

Page numbers in italics refer to images

Abbaye de Citeaux (Cistercian Abbey), 10
Abensour, Gérard, 79
Aleksandrovna Iuvitskaiia, Elizaveta (friend): correspondence with Ida Rubinstein, 13–17, 23
Alexander II, 12–13
Allan, Maud (actress), 36, 37
Amette, Léon-Adolphe (monsignor), 144
Amphion, 117–120, 163
And Then Came Dance: The Women Who Led Volynsky to Ballet's Magic Kingdom (Rabinowitz), 23–24
Antigone: about, 32
Antigone, 28, 29, 30, 32, 153
anti-Semitism, 3, 56, 114–115, 122, 125, 135, 142–145; Russia, 12–13. *See also* Jews
Antoine et Cléopâtre (*Antony and Cleopatra*), 117, 156
"A Peruvian in Paris" (Vaughan), 108–109
Apollonian (Greek tragedy), 18, 19, 101, 118

Archer, Kenneth: *Valse, La*, 117
Aristotle: Pity and Terror principles, 102
Artemis Troublée, 103, 156–157
Ashton, Fredrick, 108–109, *116*
Asmat people, 139
Astruc, Gabriel (theatre producer), 68–70, 144

Baiser de la Fée, Le (*The Fairy's Kiss*), 107, 113, 115, 130, 161
Bakst, Léon, *31*, *48*, 152; *Antigone*, 28, 29, 30, 32, 153; *Antoine et Cléopâtre*, 156; *Artemis Troublée*, 103, 156–157; Ballets Russes, 42; *Cléopâtre*, *43*, *44*; *Hélène de Sparte*, 72, 74, 154; *Istar*, 159; *Martyre de Saint (San) Sébastien, Le*, 66, 67, 154, 157; *Phaedre*, 98, 158; *Phèdre*, 90, 155; *Pisanelle ou la Mort parfumée, La*, 77, 80, 155; Rubinstein, Ida, 10; *Salomé*, 32–34, 36, 37, 153, 154; *Schéhérazade*, *47*, *48*, *49*; *Sémiramis*, 164

Bakst: Story of an Artist's Life (Levinson), 30, 74
ballet, the art of, 99–101
Ballets of Maurice Ravel, The (Mawer), 111
Ballets Russes, 41, 42, 44, 52
Barney, Natalie (Moonbeam), 58–61; Temple de l'Amitié (Temple of Friendship), 58, 61
Basiliola: about, 126–127
Batson, Charles, 122
Beaunier, André (critic), 98, 105
Benois, Alexandre, 6, 36, 44–45, 152; Amphion, 117, 118, 163; *Baiser de la Fée, Le*, 161; Ballets Russes, 39–40; *Bien-Aimée, La*, 160; *Boléro*, 107, 110, 161; *Chevalier Errant, Le* (unproduced work), 165–166; *Dame aux Camélias, La*, 158; *David*, 162; *Diane de Poitiers*, 163; *Enchantements de la Fée Alcine, Les*, 163; *Jeanne d'Arc au Bûcher*, 164–165; *L'Idiot*, 159; *L'Impératrice aux Rochers*, 160; *Noces de Psyché et de l'Amour*, 160; *Nocturne*, 107, 161; *Oriane, la sans égale* (unproduced work), 165; *Princesse Cygne, La*, 162; *Sagesse, La* (unproduced work), 165; Serge Diaghilev, 47; *Valse, La*, 108, 116, 162
Bernhardt, Sarah, 87, 92, 93, 104; anti-Semitism, 143; Rubinstein, Ida, 89, 91, 93
Bien-Aimée, La (The Beloved), 107, 109, 160–161
Birnbaum, Pierre, 143
Blanchot, Maurice: Dreyfus Affair, 142–143
Bloomsbury Ballerina, 42
Blum, Léon (critic, Prime Minister of France), 71–72
Blum, René, 68, 137–138
"Bold and Dazzling: Léon Bakst and Antiquity" (Bowlt), 30
Boléro, 107, 110–113, 115, 161
Book of Exaltations, The (Volynsky), 17, 18
Boschot, Adophe, 103–104
Bowlt, John E., 30, 103
Brooks. *See* Romaine Brooks, Beatrice

Caddy, Davinia (music and dance lecturer), 36, 37
Cahen d'Anvers, Julia (aunt), 4
Candide, 125
Carlton Hotel, 67, 87
Catulle Mendès, Jane, 114
censorship, 33, 36–37, 143–144
Chassaigne, Anne-Marie. *See* Pougy, Liane de
Chel Players (Biblical theatrical group), 146
Chevalier Errant, Le (The Knight Errant), 132–133, 165–166
Choéophores, Les, 146
Circles of Meaning (Garafola), 144, xiii–xiv
Claudel, Paul (poet), 9, 131, 133, 151; *Choéophores, Les*, 146; *Festin de Sagesse, Le*, 146, 165; *Jeanne d'Arc au Bûcher*, 134, 164
Clavel, Judith, 145
Cléopâtre, 41, 42, 43, 44, 47
Clermont-Tonnerre, Duchesse de. *See* Gramont, Élisabeth de
Cocteau, Jean, 42, 44, 71, 94, 143
Colette, 58, 125–126, 137
commedia dell'arte, 27
Copeau, Jacques, 131
"Correspondances" (Baudelaire), 100
Cossart, Michael de, 6, 36, 105, 143–144, xiv
Crimean War, 12
critics. *See* reviews; *individual critics*
Cronin, Vincent (writer), 44, 71, 94
cubism (art movement), 53, 80

Dalcroze, Jaques Emile: eurhythmics, 26, 132
Dame aux Camélias, La, 104–105, 117, 158
dance, the art of, 99–101
Dance of the Seven Veils, 32, 36, 37, 77, 122, 153
Dancing in the Vortex (Woolf), 3, xiv
Dancing Jewish (Rossen), 143
d'Annunzio, Gabriele, 47, 62, 64, 69, 152; *Martyre de Saint (San) Sébastien*, 57, 63–72, 99, 102, 144, 154, 157; *Nave, La*, 124, 126; *Phaedre*, 98, 158; *Pisanelle ou la Mort parfumée, La*, 77, 79, 155; Rubinstein, Ida, 53, 57–58, 91; World War I, 95

192   *index*

Danser (France), 42
d'Arbes, Guy (Gabriele d'Annunzio pseudonym), 64, 69
Daudet, Léon, 145
David, 107–108, 162
David-Guignard, Sylvie, 118
Debussy, Claude, 42, 63, 66–71, 144, 151, 154, 157
decadence, 71, 122, 124, 125, 142, 143
della Volpe (cardinal), 143–144
Delsartean Traces in Dalcroze Eurythmics (Odom), 26
Delsarte System (of movement), 25–26, 74, 125
Demarquez, Suzanne (critic), 133
DePaulis, Jacques, 6, 9, 30, 47, 61, 105–106, 146, 168n18, xiv
Diaghilev, Serge (Seriozha), 39–40, 77, 106, 114–115; Ballets Russes, 41–42, 44, 52; *L'Oiseau de feu*, 47; reviews of, 44–46; Rubinstein, Ida, 47, 50, 52, 72, 114–115, 145; *Salomé*, 33–34; *Schéhérazade*, 47; *Valse, La*, 117
Diaghilev .A Life. (Scheijen), 52
Diane de Poitiers, 60, 132, 163
Dionysian (Greek tragedy), 18, 101, 102, 103
Dobrotvorskaya, Karina (writer), 15, 142
Dreyfus Affair, 141, 142, 143
Ducasse, Roger, 64, 105, 152
Duncan, Isadora, 67, 94, 125
Dying Swan, The, 157–158

Early Memoirs (Nijinska), 44
Elektra, 22–23
Embodied Texts (Fleischer), 80
Emerson, Ralph Waldo, 102–103
Empire of Ecstasy: Nudity and Movement in German Body Culture 1910–1935 (Toepfer), 124
Enchantements de la Fée Alcine, Les (*The Enchantments of Fairy Alcine*), 163
Epstein, Louis K., 106, 118, 145, 148
eurythmics (movement system), 26

Fabbri, Véronique, 118, 119, 148
fascism, 61, 95, 140
Festin de Sagesse, 146

Final Act, xiii
Fleischer, Mary, 80
Flekser, Chaim. *See* Volynsky, Akim
Fokine, Michel (Mikhail), 48, 152; Ballets Russes, 42; *Boléro*, 161; *Cléopâtre*, 41, 44; *Diane de Poitiers*, 163; *Martyre de Saint (San) Sébastien, Le*, 64, 154, 157; *Pavillon D'Armide*, 39–40; *Pisanelle ou la Mort parfumée, La*, 79, 155; *Salomé*, 32, 33, 36, 37, 153, 154; *Schéhérazade*, 41, 48; *Sémiramis*, 164; Stravinsky, Igor, 131; *Valse, La*, 162
France: Dreyfus Affair, 141, 142, 143
France Chrétienne, La (anti-Semitic paper), 143
France Croisée, La (*the Cross of France*), 58, 84, 85, 117
Flanell Friedman, Donald, 10–11, 145

Garafola, Lynn, 1, 19, 33, 47–48, 69, 74, 125, 144, xiii–xiv
Garcia-Márquez, Vicente, 118–119
Gauthier, Marguerite (role of), 104–105
Geltser, Vasili: "plastique" movement system, 19, 125
Gide, André, 142–143, 151; *Antony and Cleopatra*, 97; *Perséphone*, 129–131
Glazunov, Alexander (composer), 40, 77; *Salomé*, 36, 37, 154
Gorvitz, Lydia (Ida Rubinstein pseudonym), 21
Gramont, Élisabeth (Lily) de (Duchesse de Clermont-Tonnerre), 59–60, 87; *Diane de Poitiers*, 60, 132
Greek classical theatre, 17–18, 25, 98, 102–103
Guerra, Nicola, 152, 156
Guinness, Evelyn (née Erskine), 9
Guinness, Walter (Lord Moyne), 7, 9, 87; explorer, 138–139; relationship with Ida Rubinstein, 6, 9, 87, 98, 109, 137–140, 148; *Struma*, 140
Guitry, Sacha, 94, 105

Hall. *See* Radclyffe Hall, Marguerite
Hautecombe Abbey, 141
Hélène de Sparte, 72, 74, 75, 77, 120–121, 154

Hélène of Troy: about, 74
Henriot, Emile (critic), 80
Heugel, Jacques (critic), 98
Hitler, 61
Hodson, Millicent: *Valse, La*, 117
Holy Synod (Russian Orthodox Church), 33, 36, 37
Honegger, Arthur (composer), 151; *Amphion*, 117, 163; *Jeanne d'Arc au Bûcher*, 134–135, 164; *L'Impératrice aux Rochers*, 105, 160; *Noces de Psyché et de l'Amour, Les*, 107, 109, 160; *Phaedre*, 158; *Sémiramis*, 133, 164
Horwitz (Aunt), 1, 3
Horwitz (Gorvitz), Vladimir (cousin/husband), 22, 34
House of Worth, 64, 91, 104, 106

Ibert, Jacques, 132, 152, 163
Ida Rubinstein (portraits of), 5, xii
Ida Rubinstein, Une Inconnue Jadis célèbre (DePaulis), xiv
Ida Rubinstein (1885–1960): A Theatrical Life (de Cossart), 143–144, xiv
Ida Rubinstein: A Twentieth-Century Cleopatra (Mayer), 79, xiv
Ida Rubinstein Ballet Company, 106–110, 110, 114, 116, 120
Idiot, The, 117
"Intellectuals Under Scrutiny" (Blanchot), 142–143
Isaacovna, Ernestina (mother), 4, 6, 11
Istar, 159

Jankélévitch, Vladimir, 141
Jeanne d'Arc au Bûcher, 134–135, 164–165
Jepson, Barbara, 144
Jeune Fille en bleu, La (Tikanova), 108
Jewish Observer, 4
Jews: anti-Semitism, 3, 12–13, 56, 114–115, 122, 125, 135; Dreyfus Affair, 142–143; pogroms, 2, 3, 12–13; rafle (round up), 137; Russian, 4–5, 11–13; *Struma*, 140
Joan of Arc, 23
Jones, Susan, 52
Jooss, Kurt (choreographer): *Perséphone*, 131–132, 152

Joseph, Charles, 129–130
Jouandeau, Marcel, 135
Jullian, Philippe, 89

Kahn, Marie (aunt), 4
Kharkov, 1, 4
Kishinev: pogrom, 2
Kommisarzhevskaia, Vera Fedorova (actress), 18, 25, 26, 33
Kugel, A. R. (critic), 80

L'Action Française (fascist right-wing journal), 143, 145
L'Âme et la danse (Valéry), 99
L'Après-midi d'un faune (*Afternoon of the Faun*), 42, 50, 72
L'Art aux trois visages (Rubinstein), 99–103, 128
Leblond, Roland (French pilot), 138
L'Écho de Paris, 98, 103, 105
Lécroart, Pascal, 145
Legion of Honor (awarded to Rubinstein), 94, 137
Lenski, Aleksandr, 15, 19
lesbianism. *See* Sapphism
Lester, Keith (leading dancer), 121, 129
Levinson, André (author), 30, 74, 103–104, 111, 113–114, 119, 145
Levitz, Tamara, 130–131
Lewisohn, Dr. (brother-in-law), 34
Lewisohn, Irene (sister), 6, 34
L'Excelsior, 103, 114, 133
L'Idiot, 159
Liepa, Andris (ballet dancer), xiii
Liepa, Ilse (ballet dancer), xiii
L'Impératrice aux Rochers, 105, 160
L'Imroulcaïs, le roi errant, 155
Literature, Modernism and Dance (Jones), 52
Loeffler, James, 143
L'Oiseau de feu, 47
Lucchesi, Joe, 84
Lucifer, ou Le Mystère de Caïn (*Lucifer, or the Mystery of Cain*), 166
Lunacharsky, Anatoly (critic), 80
Lvovska (Ida Rubinstein pseudonym), 30

Mackrell, Judith, 42

male roles, 53, 91, 105, 117, 120, 144
Malherbe, Henri (critic), 113, 118
Mallarmé, Stéphane (poet), 18, 99–101, 142–143
Martyre de Saint (San) Sébastien, Le, 10, 57, 63–72, 99, 102, 121, 143–144, 154, 157; images of, *65, 70, 73*
Massine, Léonide, 152; *Amphion*, 117, 118–119; *David*, 107–108
Mauri, Rosita (ballet dancer), 111
Mawer, Deborah (author), 111
Max, Édouard de (actor), 72, 154–157
Mayer, Charles S. (author), 79, 84, 121, 133–134, 146, xiv
"Mécène atypique, Un" ("A Rare Philanthropist") (DePaulis), 9, 168n18
Meyerhold, Vsevolod (actor/director), 151; *Antigone*, 28; murder of, 82; *Pisanelle ou la Mort parfumée, La*, 77, 79, 80, 155; *Salomé*, 32, 33, 37, 153; Sixteen Études (movement exercises), 27; Symbolist theatre, 25
"Meyerhold à Paris" (Abensour), 79
Milhaud, Darius (composer), 109–110, 146, 152, 160, 165
Mille, Agnes de, 115
Modern French Jewish Thought (Jankélévitch), 141
modernism, 52, 53, 93, 124, 144
Modernist Mysteries (Levitz), 130–131
Modern Woman Revisited: Paris between the Wars (Lucchesi), 84
Moment du Pleur Eternel, Un (de Montesquiou), 95
Montesquiou, Robert de (poet/friend), 68, *88*, 94, 97–98; *Moment du Pleur Eternel, Un*, 95; *Offrandes Blessées, Les (Wounded Offerings)*, 87, 89; Rubinstein, Ida, 46–47, 53, 56, 91
Moscow Art Theatre, 25, 26
Moscow Conservatory, 16
Moscow Theatrical School, 15, 19
Moss, Kenneth B., 2–3
Most Musical Nation: Jews and Culture in the Late Russian Empire, The (Loeffler), 143
Motte, père Antonin (priest), 146

movement expression: Delsarte System, 25–26, 74, 125; eurhythmics, 26; "plastique," 19, 125; Symbolism, 18, 25, 53, 101, 124–125
Moyne, Lord. *See* Guinness, Walter
My Life (Massine), 107–108
"Mystery Woman" (Jones), 4

Nave, La, 60, 124, 126–128, 179n92
New Guinea, 139
Nicolas II (czar), 2, 13, 34, 40–41
Nietzsche, Friedrich, 100–101; Apollonian/Dionysian, 18, 19, 101; *Birth of Tragedy*, 41, 102
Nijinska, Bronislava, 44, 106–107, 109, *116*, 152; *Boléro*, 110–112; *Valse, La*, 116–117
Nijinsky, Vaslav, 27, 41, 42; rejection by Ida Rubinstein, 50, 52
Noces de Psyché et de L'Amour, Les, 107, 109, 160
Nocturne, 107, 161
Nozière, Fernand, 50, 121, 155

Odom, Selma L., 26
Offrandes Blessées, Les (The Wounded Offerings) (de Montesquiou), 87, 89
Oriane, la sans égale (Oriane, Unequaled), 165
Orientalism, 36, 42, 66, 122, 143
Orphée, 105, 159–160
Ozarovsky, Yuri (acting coach/director), 11, 23, 30, 74, 77, 153

Paray, Paul (composer), 103, 156
Paris: Ida Rubinstein's move to, 41; Sapphic subculture ("Paris-Lesbos"), 54, 58–61, 84, 120; World War I, 94; World War II, 137, 141
Paul Valéry, le poème et la danse (Fabbri), 119
Pavillon D'Armide, 39–40
Peril Juif, Le (anti-Semitic publication), 135
Perséphone: about, 130
Perséphone, 129–131, 163–164
"Peruvian in Paris, A" (Vaughan), 108–109
Phaedre (d'Annunzio), 98, 158
Phèdre (Racine), 89, *90*, 98, 155

index 195

Pisanelle: about, 79
Pisanelle ou la Mort parfumée, La, 77, 78, 79, 81, 155
Pizzetti, Ildebrando (composer), 79, 126, 155, 158
"plastique" movement system (Geltser), 19, 125
pogroms, 2, 3, 12–13, 141
Poliakov, Daniel (uncle), 10
Pougy, Liane de, 58–59
Prince of Aesthetes (Jullian), 89
Princesse Cygne, La (The Swan Princess), 107, 113–114, 162
Princesse lointaine, La, 93
Proust, Marcel, 42, 71
Prunières, Henri (critic), 110, 111, 112–113
Putnam, Walter, 99–100

Rabinowitz, Stanley J., 17, 18
Racine, Jean, 89, 98, 103, 155
"racines russes d'Ida Rubinstein, Les" (Stronhina), xiv
Radclyffe Hall, Marguerite (John), 60
Ravel, Maurice (composer), 42, 46, 110, 152; Boléro, 107, 110, 111, 113, 115; Valse, La, 108, 116–117
reviews: Amphion, 118–119; Artemis Troublée, 103; Baiser de la Fée, Le, 113, 115; Bien Aimée, La, 110; Boléro, 111, 112–113, 115; Cléopâtre, 44, 47; Dame aux Camélias, La, 105; Diane de Poitiers, 132; of Ida Rubinstein, 24, 30, 36, 42, 50, 74, 93, 103–104, 114–115, 125–126, 142, 148; Jeanne d'Arc au Bûcher, 134–135, 143; L'Impératrice aux Rochers, 106; Martyre de Saint (San) Sébastien, 71; Orphée, 105; Perséphone, 129; Phaedre, 98–99; Pisanelle ou la Mort parfumée, La, 79–80; Princesse Cygne, La, 113–114; Salomé, 36, 77; Sémiramis, 133–134
Robert de Montesquiou et Marcel Proust (de Gramont), 87
Romaine Brooks, Beatrice, 55; about, 54–56, 60–61; France Croisée, La (The Cross of France), 58, 85, 117; Ida Rubinstein (portrait), xii; Rubinstein, Ida, 15, 56–58, 64, 83–84, 135–136; Trajet, Le (the Crossing), 56, 57; Venus Triste (Weeping Venus), 57, 57
Romanovitch Rubinstein, Daniel (uncle), 6
Romanovitch Rubinstein, Lian (Leon) (father), 4, 11
Rossen, Rebecca, 143
Rouché, Jacques, 64, 108
Rubinstein, Ida: Ancient Greece, love for, 11, 16, 102, 128; anti-Semitism, 114–115, 134–136, 142–145; Catholicism, 146, 148, xv; censorship, 33, 36–37, 143–144; childhood of, 1, 3, 10–11, 91; correspondence, 13–24; dance, the art of, 99–101, 121; education, 11, 14; family, 1–4, 6, 10–11, 34; final years, 10, 141; health, 15–16, 22; hunting, 9–10, 139–140; Ida Rubinstein Ballet Company, 106–110, 110, 114, 120; Judaism, 6, 136, 141; L'Art aux trois visages, 99–103, 128; male roles, 53, 91, 105, 107–108, 117, 120, 144; marriage, 21–22, 34, 56; mime, 36–37, 47, 50, 125; movement, 74, 79, 125; nursing, 58, 60, 84, 86, 87, 95, 137, 138; Paris, 41, 47, 61; photos and drawings of, 3, 57, 74–75; privacy, 6, 34; pseudonyms, 21–22, 30; relationships, 6, 17, 19–20, 56–58, 83–84; religion, 5, 11, 141; sensuality, 34, 36, 42, 44, 57, 122, 124; sexuality, 15, 120; travel, 16, 64, 98, 139–140; wealth, 4, 6, 64, 84, 138, 145; World War I, 83–84, 94, 117; World War II, 137–138. See also Bakst, Léon; Bernhardt, Sarah; d'Annunzio, Gabrièle; Fokine, Michel; Guinness, Walter; Meyerhold, Vsevolod; Montesquiou, Robert de; reviews; Romaine Brooks, Beatrice; Volynsky, Akim
Rubinstein, Ida, portraits of, 8, 48, 76, 86, 104, 147, ii; France Croisée, La (the Cross of France), 58, 84, 85, 117; Ida Rubinstein (Romaine Brooks), xii; Ida Rubinstein (Serov), 5, 5; from productions, 29, 35, 43, 45, 51, 65, 70, 73, 75; productions continued, 78, 81, 90, 123, 124; productions continued 2, 81, 90, 123, 124; Trajet, Le (the Crossing), 56, 57; Venus Triste (Weeping Venus), 57, 57, 84

Rubinstein, Ida, productions: *Amphion*, 117–120, 163; *Antigone*, 28, 30, 32, 153; *Antoine et Cléopâtre* (Antony and Cleopatra), 117, 156; *Artemis Troublée*, 103, 156–157; *Baiser de la Fée, Le*, 107, 113, 161; Ballets Russes, 41, 42, 44, 53; *Bien-Aimée, La* (The Beloved), 107, 109, 160–161; *Boléro*, 107, 110–113, 115, 161; *Choéophores, Les*, 146; *Cléopâtre*, 41, 42–44, 47, 69, 143; *Dame aux Camélias, La*, 104–105, 117, 158; *David*, 107–108, 162; *Diane de Poitiers*, 60, 132, 163; *Dying Swan, The*, 157–158; *Enchantements de la Fée Alcine, Les*, 163; *Hélène de Sparte*, 72, 74, 75, 77, 120–121, 154; *Idiot, The*, 117, 159; *Istar*, 159; *Jeanne D'Arc au Bûcher*, 134–135, 164–165; *L'Impératrice aux Rochers*, 105, 160; *L'Imroulcaïs, le roi errant*, 155; *Martyre de Saint Sébastien*, 57, 63–72, 99, 121, 143–144, 154, 157; *Nave, La*, 60, 124, 126–128; *Noces de Psyché et de L'Amour, Les*, 107, 109, 160; *Nocturne*, 107, 161; *Offrandes Blessées, Les* (Wounded Offerings), 89; *Orphée* (Orpheus), 105, 159–160; *Perséphone*, 129–131, 163–164; *Phaedre*, 98, 158; *Phèdre*, 90, 155; *Pisanelle ou la Mort parfumée, La*, 77, 78, 79, 155; *Princesse Cygne, La* (The Swan Princess), 107, 113–114, 162; *Salomé*, 32–37, 77, 122, 153, 154; *Secret du Sphinx, Le* (The Secret of the Sphinx), 158–159; *Sémiramis*, 133–134, 164; *Shéhérazade*, 41, 46, 47, 49, 49–50, 51, 56, 122, 143; *Spirit of Venice, The*, 157; *Tragédie de Salomé, La*, 156; *Valse, La*, 108, 116–117, 162. See also reviews

Rubinstein family: conversion to Russian Orthodoxy, 13; Judaism, 3, 6, 11; Russian Jewish connections, 10; wealth, 2, 4, 6, 13

Rubinstein: Le Roman d'une vie d'artiste (Friedman), 10

Rubinstein L'vovna (Ida Rubinstein, in correspondence with Volynsky), 22, 23

Rudnitsky, Konstantin (critic), 32, 79–80

Russia: anti-Semitism, 2, 3, 12–13; Nicolas II (czar), 2, 13, 34, 40; revolution, 40–41; Silver Age, 28; St. Petersburg, 1–2, 40–41

Russian Jews. See Jews

Russian Orthodox Church: Holy Synod, 33, 36, 37

Russo-Turkish War, 12

Sagesse, La (The Wise One), 165

Saint Cloud mental health clinic, 34

Salomé, 32–37, 77, 153, 154; reviews of, 36, 77

salons, 4, 10, 25, 55–56, 58, 61, 89

Sanin, Alexandre (director), 72, 77, 154, 160

Sapphism, 54, 58, 59, 120

Schéhérazade, 41, 46, 47, 48–49, 49, 51, 56, 122

Scheijen, Sjeng (author), 36, 114–115

Schiller, Friedrich, 102

Schmitt, Florent (composer), 67, 151, 156, 165

Schneider, Marcel, 42, 117

Sebastian, Saint: about, 64–65

Secret du Sphinx, Le, 158–159

Sémiramis, 133, 164

Serov, Valentin (painter), 5–6

Sert, Misia, 94

Séverac, Déodat de, 72, 152, 154

Sheppard, Andrew (scholar), 148

Silver Age (Russia), 28

Singer, Winnaretta, 55–56

Solntse Rossii (Sun of Russia), 32

Spirit of Venice, The, 157

Staats, Léo (choreographer), 152, 159, 160

Stael, Madame de, 103

Stanislavsky, 25, 129

St. Petersburg. See Russia

St. Petersburg Conservatory, 16, 20

St. Petersburg Theater Journal, 15, 142

Stravinsky, Igor (composer), 151; *Baiser de la Fée, Le*, 107, 113, 115, 130; Ballets Russes, 53; Fokine, Michel, 131; *Perséphone*, 129, 131; *Rite of Spring*, 42; Rubinstein, Ida, 145

Stravinsky's Ballets (Joseph), 129–130

Stronhina, Nathalie, 4–5, xiv
Struma (refugee ship), 140
Sun of Russia, 32
Symbolism (movement), 18, 25, 53, 101, 124–125

Tcherepnin, Nicolay (Nicolas Tcherepnine), 39, 107
Temple de l'Amitié (Temple of Friendship), 58, 61
Théâtre des Champs-Elysées, xiii
Théâtre du Châtelet, 42, 47, 69, 71, 72, 77
Théâtre National de l'Opéra, 107, 145
Théâtre Sarah-Bernhardt, 89, 104
Tikanova, Nina, 108, 113
Toepfer, Karl, 124
Torelli, Lina (Ida Rubinstein pseudonym), 21–22
Tragédie de Salomé, Le, 156
Trajet, Le (the Crossing), 56, 57
Tribout, Georges, 74
Trubridge, Una, 60

Ukraine, 1, 4, 5, 11; pogroms, 12

Valéry, Paul, 99–100, 142–143, 151; *Amphion*, 117–120; *Sémiramis*, 133
"Valéry et la musique" (Mayer), 133–134
Valse, La, 108, 116–117, 162

Vaughan, David, 108–109
Venus Triste (*Weeping Venus*), 57, 57, 84
Verhaeren, Émile (poet), 72, 74, 144
Vilzak, Anatole (dancer), 107, 108, 109, 130
Visages de la Danse, Les (Levinson), 111
Vittoria: about, 105
Vivien, Renée, 59
Volynsky, Akim (ballet critic), 101; *Book of Exaltations, The*, 17–18; Rubinstein, Ida, 18–23, 41; *And Then Came Dance*, 23–24
Vuillermoz, Émile (critic), 103, 114, 119, 133

Walkabout (Moyne), 139–140
Weber, Eugen, 122
Wilde, Oscar, 36, 37, 77
Woolf, Vicki, 3, xiv
World War I, 61, 83, 87, 93–95
World War II, 137–143
Wounded Offerings, The (*Les Offrandes Blessées*) (de Montesquiou), 87, 89

Yavorskaya (Yavorskaia), Lydia (actress), 11, 28

Zelinsky, Faddei, 28
Zobéide (*Schéhérazade*), 41, 46, 47, 48, 49, 56, 122

www.ingramcontent.com/pod-product-compliance
Lightning Source LLC
Chambersburg PA
CBHW030653230426
43665CB00011B/1066